BEYOND THE LETTER OF THE LAW

A Chassidic Companion
to the Talmud's *Ethics of the Fathers*

Sixty essays based on the teachings of the Lubavitcher Rebbe,
Rabbi Menachem M. Schneerson

By Yanki Tauber

Copyright © 2012 by Meaningful Life Center
All rights reserved.
Printed in the United States of America.
No part of this book may be used or reproduced in any manner whatsoever without written permission from the Meaningful Life Center, except for brief quotations for the purpose of review.

Published by:
MLC   Meaningful Life Center
788 Eastern Parkway, Suite 303
Brooklyn, NY 11213-3409
(718) 774-6448

MLC offers a wide array of published and online programming.
For more information, visit www.meaningfullife.com.

ISBN 978-1-886587-15-1

Publication of this Book
was Made Possible Through the Generosity
of
Mark and Andrea Stein
Johannesburg, South Africa

And
Is Lovingly Dedicated
In Memory
of
Our Dear Parents, Mentors and Teachers
Lazar and Leah Stein, and Norman Kramer

CONTENTS

Introduction vi

Ethics of the Fathers 2

Essays 34

The Essays: A General Index 336

Index 344

Glossary 361

INTRODUCTION

The *Ethics of the Fathers* is one of those books that are never read for the first time. Who is not already familiar with *"Do not judge your fellow until you have stood in his place"* (*Ethics* 2:4)? Who has not expressed on occasion, *"According to the pain is the gain"* (5:21)? So deeply ingrained are the sayings of the *Ethics* in Jewish thought and life, so widely and universally are they cited, that even one who has never held a copy of the Talmud's 39th tractate in his hands knows that *"The more possessions, the more worry"* (2:7), and that *"Every man has his hour, and every thing has its place"* (4:3).

Nor can the *Ethics* ever be studied for the final time. Beneath the apparent simplicity of its words lie layer upon layer of meaning and profundity. No one has ever attempted to count the volumes of commentary that have been written on the *Ethics* since its compilation almost eighteen centuries ago; they number in the many hundreds,[1] and the flow of exposition, analysis and interpretation shows no signs of abating. For such is the nature of Torah: "Greater than the land is its measure, and broader than the sea."[2] In the words of the *Ethics*: "*Delve and delve into it, for all is in it; see with it; grow old and worn in it; do not budge from it, for there is nothing better.*"[3]

It is in this spirit that we offer *Beyond the Letter of the Law*, a collection of essays based on the teachings of the Lubavitcher Rebbe, Rabbi Menachem M. Schneerson. Each of these sixty essays focuses on one or more of the *Ethics*' sayings, delving and delving into its words. To behold a *mishnah* of the *Ethics* through the Rebbe's eyes is to indeed "see with it"—to see that all is indeed in it, and to view every aspect of our existence through its illuminating perspective.

Ethics of the Fathers is one of the sixty-three tractates of the *Mishnah*, compiled in the Holy Land at the end of the second century C.E. by Rabbi Judah haNassi.

The *Mishnah* (the word means "study" and "review") is the first codification of Torah law to be set down in writing. For the thirty-five generations from Moses to Rabbi Judah, the entire body of Torah law, and the principles by which it is derived from the "Written Torah" (the Five Books of Moses), were handed down from master to disciple in the unbroken chain of tradition outlined in the first chapter of the *Ethics* and detailed in Maimonides' famed introduction to his *Mishneh Torah*.[4] Rabbi Judah, who witnessed the ever-widening dispersion of the Jewish people and foresaw their eventual breakup into communities with little or no contact between them, took the unprecedented step of committing this oral tradition to writing "lest the Torah be forgotten from Israel."

He did so in an extremely concise, even cryptic style, condensing myriads of laws and principles in the *Mishnah*'s every sentence. Everything in a section (a *mishnah*) of the *Mishnah* is significant: the specific case to illustrate a law is carefully chosen so that several other laws are parenthetically derived; a specific word, phrase or inflection, or even a variant spelling, is likewise employed to compact as much information in as few words as possible.[5] The compilation of the *Mishnah* was followed by close to 300 years of analysis, discussion and debate among the sages, for the most part in Babylonia where the epicenter of Torah scholarship had shifted. This exposition of the *Mishnah*, known as the *Gemara* ("learning"), was set down in writing in the fifth century by Rav Ashi and Ravina.[6] Together, the *Mishnah* and *Gemara* comprise the Talmud—the vast anthology of Jewish law and lore which embodies forty generations of the study, interpretation and application of Torah.

The *Mishnah* consists of sixty-three tractates,[7] thirty-seven of which are accompanied by the *Gemara's* analysis and commentary. The 39th tractate is *Avot* ("Fathers," also referred to as *Pirkei Avot*, "Chapters of the Fathers"), or, as its title is commonly rendered in English, *Ethics of the Fathers*.

"One who wishes to be a chassid," says the Talmud, "should study *Ethics of the Fathers*."[8]

Chessed, the etymological root of *chassid*, means "benevolence" or "loving-kindness"; a chassid, says the *Zohar*, is "one who conducts himself with benevolence toward his Creator and Source."[9]

The chassid, then, was not invented in 1734, when Rabbi Israel Baal Shem Tov founded the chassidic movement. Nor was he a new phenomenon when Rabbi Judah haNassi compiled the *Ethics* for the aspiring chassid fifteen centuries earlier. Indeed, Chassidism is as old as man's endeavor to serve his Creator.[10]

What does it mean to be benevolent toward G-d? If *Ethics of the Fathers* is the chassid's primer, then perhaps we may best understand his "benevolence" by examining the *Ethics* and its unique place among the Talmud's tractates.

Sixty-two of the Talmud's tractates address the dos and don'ts of life, instructing the Jew how to pray and how to study, how to eat and how to marry, how to set his calendar and observe Shabbat and the festivals, how to bury his dead, punish criminals, conduct his business, and so on. The single exception is the *Ethics of the Fathers*, which deals not with the law (*din*) but with the area defined as *lifnim mishurat ha-din*—"beyond the line of the law," or, in the more literal translation of the Hebrew word *lifnim*, "*within* the line of the law."

What does it mean to go beyond or "within" the line of the law? On the most basic level, it means going beyond the law's minimum requirements. Thus, the *Ethics* deals not with what is mandatory according to Torah law, but offers a wealth of ethical maxims for the individual who aspires to a higher standard of morality and piety. The Torah may forbid one from slandering, insulting[12] or cursing[13] one's fellow, but does not legislate smiles and "Good mornings"; the *Ethics*, however, enjoins, *"Receive every man with a pleasant countenance."*[14] Torah law obligates us to lend material support to the needy; the *Ethics* instructs that *"the poor should be members of your household."*[15] According to the strict letter of the law, "Even if a person studies but one chapter in the morning and one chapter in the evening, he has fulfilled the commandment, 'This[16] book of the Torah shall not depart from your mouth—you shall study it day and night'"[17]; but the *Ethics* recommends to "Engage minimally in business and occupy yourself with Torah." The strict letter of the law states that "One who says, 'I am giving this *sela* to charity so that my son shall live,' is a perfectly righteous individual"[19]; the *Ethics* admonishes, *"Do not be as slaves who serve their master for the sake of reward."*[20]

On a deeper level, *lifnim mishurat ha-din* means to go within the parameters of the law: to enter within the "body" of the deed and inculcate oneself with its essence and soul.

One who refrains from injuring his fellow man, studies a chapter of Torah every morning and evening, sends his charity check in the mail and observes G-d's commandments so that he should merit long life—fulfills the letter of Torah law. The practitioner of the *Ethics*, however, is one who does not suffice with making his behavior conform to the Torah's directives; he insists that all of him—his outlook, his desires, his feelings—indeed, the very essence of his character—be permeated with the vision contained in the divine blueprint for life. He demands of himself to not only aid but also care for the poor; to not only study Torah but make it the focus of his life; to not only act lovingly toward his fellow but to love him. And he strives to remake his self and character so that G-d's will is not something he does for some external reason—be it the fear of punishment, the promise of reward or a sense of duty—but what he desires to do with every fiber of his being.

This is the deeper significance of Rabbi Judah haNassi's statement, cited in the opening words of the *Ethics'* second chapter, "*Which is the right path for man to choose? Whatever is harmonious for the one who does it, and harmonious for mankind.*" Therein lies the very essence of the *Ethics*: the endeavor to translate the externalities of Torah-mandated conduct into a Torah-true self. To make the "right path" of Torah the path of one's choice, the path that is in harmony with one's inner drives and desires. In the words of Rabbi Judah's son Rabban Gamliel, quoted later in the chapter, "*Make that His will should be your will.*"[21]

These two definitions of *lifnim mishurat ha-din* are two sides of the same coin. The person to whom Torah is an obligatory or beneficial code of conduct, will do just that—whatever is obligatory or beneficial to him. But one who has "internalized" his observance of Torah will go beyond what is required of him—beyond even what is beneficial to him;[22] since this is what he *wants* to do, he will do it in the most optimal and integral manner.

Thus, the chassid is one who conducts himself with benevolence toward his Creator. "Abraham, who loved Me,"[23] says G-d of an earlier chassid, and the aspiring chassid strives to emulate the first Jew's example: to serve G-d because he loves Him and desires to implement His will. And because the chassid is motivated by love, he is also "benevolent" in the other sense of the word as well—he is generous in his service, giving of himself beyond the call of duty and beyond the realm of personal gain.

So the chassid's is an inward journey—a journey from the externalities of behavior to a nature and character molded by the maxims of the *Ethics*. It is also a journey into the interior of the *Ethics* itself, delving beneath its obvious applications to uncover a deeper, and deeper yet, significance within.

Nowhere is this journey more emphasized than in Chassidism, as the teachings of Rabbi Israel Baal Shem Tov (the "Besht") and his disciples have come to be known. As its name implies, Chassidism is a philosophical and behavioral system focused on the goal of achieving the inwardness and integrity (*p'nimiut*) of the chassid. "The entire point of Chassidism," said Rabbi Schneur Zalman of Liadi, disciple of the Besht's successor, Rabbi Dov Ber of Mezeritch, and the founder of the "Chabad"[24] branch of Chassidism, "is that a person transform the nature of his character."[25]

The works of the Lubavitcher Rebbe culminate nine generations of chassidic teaching, beginning with the Besht and Rabbi Dov Ber and continuing through seven generations of Chabad-Chassidic rebbes.[26]

Introduction

This volume is a humble attempt to convey something of the tremendous depth and scope of the Rebbe's writings and talks, particularly as they pertain to and derive from the quintessential chassidic work, the Talmud's *Ethics of the Fathers*.

To characterize the Rebbe teachings would be an ambitious undertaking for a full-scale volume, and certainly beyond the scope of this introduction. Much has been written on the subject,[27] and much more certainly will. But "characterizations" of this sort have a limited relevance: the Rebbe's teachings embrace all levels of Torah discourse, including the rudimentary, analytical, *halachic*, metaphorical, allusive, homiletical and mystical faces of Torah. Indeed, if there is any one principle that pervades the Rebbe's teachings it is that all of Torah is a unified whole, its many facets and levels of interpretation complementing and elucidating one another. So any one of them may serve as the starting point of the inward journey towards the soul of a Torah concept, law, statement or story; any one of them may serve as the avenue to its very core and thus illuminate and enrich its other faces and integrate them all as one.[28]

In any case, instead of studying one man's scholastic experience of the Rebbe, the reader is best advised to simply plunge into the fascinating world of the Rebbe's thought. This is the best way I know of gaining an appreciation of the Rebbe's unique contribution to 4,000 years of Jewish learning.

I will therefore suffice with a few words on the Rebbe's approach to the *Ethics of the Fathers*. Because of its homiletical, rather than legal-*halachic*, nature, the *Ethics* is often regarded as a rather "untalmudic" part of the Talmud. While the premise of the talmudist is that a *mishnah's* every phrase, word and letter is laden with "mounds upon mounds of laws,"[29] many are less demanding of the *Ethics*; the *Ethics*, after all, is not an encapsulation of the Torah law, only a collection of

Beyond the Letter of the Law

inspiring sayings and ethical maxims. However, when one sees the *Ethics*, as does the Rebbe, as the "chassidic" or inner dimension of the Talmud, the very opposite is true.

"Torah," the Rebbe constantly reminds us, means "instruction." So everything in Torah is instructive, bearing a message that is applicable to our lives. Also the realm of *lifnim mishurat ha-din*, the "beyond" and the "within" of Torah's legislation of life, has its *Shulchan Aruch*, its "Code of Law." *Ethics of the Fathers* is the *Shulchan Aruch* of Chassidism, the code which defines and instructs the Jew's interior life: his intellectual, emotional and spiritual development and his relationship with his Creator. So each phrase and word of the *Ethics* is no less instructive than those of the Talmud's other sixty-two tractates. Indeed, as the soul of Torah law, *Ethics'* every nuance is far more heavily—and far more subtly—laden with significance than the Talmud's external or "bodily" components.

So when the *Ethics* tells us, in the opening *mishnah* of its third chapter, to contemplate our origins and destiny so as not to lose sight of the true priorities of life, and does so with three wordy sentences when the basic idea could have been stated in a concise one, the Rebbe reads three distinct messages, all variations on the *mishnah's* basic theme but each directed to a another of three basic types of individuals.[30] When the *Ethics* speaks in the praise of altruism in one's service of the Almighty, but does so by employing a long, repetitious metaphor, the Rebbe uncovers a deeper layer of meaning: the *mishnah* is defining four degrees of self and selflessness in the human soul.[31] And when the *Ethics* summarizes the first twenty-three generations of Torah's transmission as five general phases, these also define the five prerequisite tools with which to approach the study of G-d's wisdom.[32]

Introduction

To the Rebbe, there is nothing insignificant or repetitive in a *mishnah* of the *Ethics*. Phrases such as "falling into the hands of transgression," "a man would swallow his fellow alive" or "making a fence around the Torah" are never merely figures of speech, but point to a deeper and broader understanding of the issues at hand.[33] The name and life-experience of the sage who is being quoted,[34] the inclusion of two seemingly unconnected sayings in a single *mishnah*,[35] or even the chapter number[36]—all yield insight into the interior world of the chassid, the benevolent lover of G-d.

It would be wrong to define this volume as a book of the Rebbe's commentary on the *Ethics*. It is both much less and much more than that.

Less, because these essays represent but a sampling of the Rebbe's expositions on the *Ethics*, which span five decades and number in the many hundreds.[37] More, because although each essay is anchored to a *mishnah*, phrase or concept of the *Ethics*, it soon soars into the vast, sublime skies of chassidic thought to accord us a bird's-eye view of life's terrain, of which our launch point is but a particular (though integral) part.

Here one finds the Rebbe's illumination of issues such as freedom of choice, divine providence, absolute and relative truth, good and evil, love, ego and the nature of the physical reality. Here one finds the Rebbe addressing the paradoxes of the human condition: the tensions engendered by the polar pulls upon our lives of communality and individuality, elitism and equality, growth and productivity, and selfhood and the yearning for transcendence. Here, one finds the Rebbe's torahic-chassidic perspective on education, marriage, language, business, property, food and crime. Here one finds the Rebbe's views on "religious" issues such as what defines a Jew, dogmatism and human creativity in Torah, religion and state, the function of the *mitzvah*, reward and retribution, Moshiach and the World to Come. In a word, these sixty essays present the reader with a broad (though by no means comprehensive) cross section of the Rebbe's unique vision of life through the lens of Torah.

The essays in this collection first appeared in *Synopsis* and *Week In Review*, two weekly English-language renditions of the Rebbe's talks that I have been privileged to write beginning in September of 1989.

Throughout the forty-four years of his leadership, the Rebbe's primary medium of teaching was the *farbrengen*—the "chassidic gathering," lasting as long as seven hours, in which he delivered his talks and discourses to thousands of chassidim and other participants from all walks of life. The *farbrengen* consisted of *sichot* (talks), each lasting an hour or more, interposed by several minutes of song, dance and *l'chayim* (sharing of vodka or other spirits, with the invoking of holy blessings). A *farbrengen* with the Rebbe is an experience that defies description: only one who has participated in a *farbrengen* can envision the hours and hours of flowing wisdom bracketed by soul-transporting wellings of chassidic joy.

At a typical *farbrengen*, the Rebbe might begin with a discussion on the nature of the day in context of the several cycles of the Jewish calendar (the day of the week, the weekly Torah reading, the day of the month, an approaching or receding festival), weaving a tapestry of significance out of the various currents of time that have converged to form the unique time-juncture occupied by the day of the *farbrengen*. In his next talk, the Rebbe might follow with a profound commentary on a discourse of chassidic teaching penned by one of his predecessors. In subsequent *sichot* he might examine a debate in the Talmud, exploring it first with the "conventional" tools of talmudic logic and moving on to uncover its inner "chassidic" dimension, and then do the same with a section of Rashi's commentary on the Bible, a saying of the *Ethics*, a *halachic* nuance in Maimonides' *Mishneh Torah* and a mystifying allegory in the *Zohar*. The *farbrengen* might also include an analysis of some historical event, a quirk of human nature, a scientific discovery and a recent news story. But no matter the topic of his talk, the Rebbe always returned to his trademark "bottom line": How is all of this to be concretely applied to our daily lives? And no *farbrengen* ended without the Rebbe issuing directives to his chassidim—directives regarding our personal development and our responsibilities toward our fellow man.

The Rebbe conducted *farbrengens* several times a month: on Shabbat afternoons, at the conclusion of the festivals and on special dates of the Jewish and chassidic calendar. After each *farbrengen*, a select group of chassidim, known as *chozrim* (reviewers), reviewed and transcribed the Rebbe's talks. This was an especially demanding task, since most of the *farbrengens* took place on Shabbat or a festival when Torah law prohibits the use of electronic recording devices; this means that the *chozrim* had to literally memorize the entire *farbrengen*.

In later years, the dissemination of the Rebbe's talks was much enhanced by the communications technology explosion of the '80s and '90s. Within twenty-four hours of the *farbrengen*, a transcript was prepared, faxed to dozens of cities, re-faxed and reproduced in thousands of copies and read by tens of thousands across the globe. Meanwhile, the senior *chozrim* were preparing a comprehensive treatment of the *farbrengen* for submission to the Rebbe, who devoted many hours to editing them. Within a week, an official, edited and annotated version was ready for publication and electronic media distribution. To date, forty-five volumes of edited *sichot*, and dozens more containing unedited transcripts (*hanochot*) of the *farbrengens*, have been published.

In the late 1970s, Sichos in English, headed by Rabbi Yonah Avtzon, began preparing English language transcripts and treatments of the *farbrengens*. But there remained a need for a more concise and speedier medium for the Rebbe's words, one that would offer the English-speaking public the immediate access to his timely insights and directives thus far available only to those proficient in Yiddish and Hebrew and equipped with a working knowledge of Torah, Chassidism and the Rebbe's methodology.

In 1988, three Yeshivah students, Rabbis Yehudah Shemtov, Mendel Herson, and Reuven New stepped in to fill this void, and the *Synopsis* was born. Working with the *chozer* Rabbi Simon Jacobson of *Vaad Hanochos Hatmimim* (Committee to Transcribe the Rebbe's Talks), they began preparing a weekly essay—the Rebbe was *farbrenging* every Shabbat at that time—which focused on the main points of the *farbrengen* and included the necessary contextual information. By Sunday evening, the phone lines radiating from the *VHH* office on Eastern Parkway were carrying the *Synopsis* to fax machines on every continent. The *Synopsis* was also published in booklet form and distributed worldwide.

My involvement with the *Synopsis* began more than a year later, when I was asked to join the trio of my fellow students in their labor of love. At that time—Rosh Hashanah 5750 (1989)—we also launched the *Synopsis*' sister publication, the *Week In Review*, a newsletter-style sheet which offered shorter "bite-size" renditions of the insights expounded at the Shabbat *farbrengen* and the shorter addresses delivered by the Rebbe during the week (in September of 1992, the two publications were merged as the expanded *Week In Review*). As Yudy, Mendy and Ruby went on to pursue their respective callings in life, the *Synopsis/Week In Review* went on to consume more of my days, nights and heart. I soon found myself a full-time staff member of *Vaad Hanochos Hatmimim*, responsible for their English language adaptations of the Rebbe's talks.[38]

The driving force and editorial authority behind the *Synopsis* and *Week In Review* was Rabbi Simon Jacobson, official *chozer* to the Rebbe and director of *VHH*. Simon began transcribing the Rebbe's talks in 1979, and was one of the privileged few who prepared *sichot* for the Rebbe's editing and approval. Simon gave himself, mind and soul, to the *Week In Review* project, inspiring, critiquing and encouraging my efforts to convey something of profundity and relevance of the Rebbe's teaching across the gulf of language and culture that separates them from the English-speaking, Western-thinking world. Simon's many years' experience in writing for the Rebbe—with his intimate knowledge of how the Rebbe envisioned his words on paper—has enabled me to offer an authoritative rendition of the Rebbe's teachings; although I obviously offer nothing more than my personal understanding of the Rebbe's words, I was able to do so with the confidence that I was not violating their substance and spirit.

I also owe a great debt of thanks to the other members of the *VHH* family, who have faithfully accompanied the *Synopsis/Week In Review* since its inception; without them, none of this would have been possible. Mr. Benzion Rader, who sits in London and exerts his literary authority over New York and Jerusalem, imparted English correctness (and correct English) to my errant pen. Rabbi Chaim Abrahams, administrative director of *VHH*, did wonders in making our fantasies work in the real world. Benny Forta helped a group of computer-illiterate young men make sense of the hard- and software of modern-day publishing and communications. And Baruch Gorkin's redesign of *Week In Review*, in December of 1993, did much to bolster its impact and reach. In the preparation of this volume, these essays have been greatly enriched by the editorial and annotative input of Mordechai Staiman, of blessed memory, Rochel Chana Riven, Phillip Namanworth, and Naomi Perlman.

No history, however brief, of the *Week In Review* can be sketched without the mention, fraught with pride and pain, of Daniel Namdar, of blessed memory. A dear friend and enthusiast of the *Week In Review* from its very first issues, Danny gave himself, heart and soul, to its goals and aspirations. His, and the entire Namdar family's, generous financial support made its publication possible, and their tireless efforts at its distribution earned it numerous readers across the globe, from Milan to Bangkok. After the tragedy that took him in the prime of life, the Daniel Foundation, established by the family in his memory, continues Danny's devotion to the *Week In Review*. In its weekly pages, Danny lives on.

On a personal note, I wish to express my gratitude to my parents, Berel and Esther Tauber, and my grandparents of fond and blessed memory, Rabbi Zvi Meir (Hebrew poet Zvi Yair) and Devorah Steinmetz. To my wife Riki, who has been sharing my life and dreams these past twenty years, and to our daughters Leah, Chany and Racheli. Though partners all to the efforts contained in this book, their true contribution to it lies in the love and joy with which they imbue the life of its author.

As the first edition of this book was being readied for publication, our world was plunged into darkness. In the pre-dawn hours of Tammuz 3, 5754 (Sunday, June 12, 1994), the soul of the Lubavitcher Rebbe, Rabbi Menachem Mendel Schneerson, departed its earthly embodiment and ascended on high, leaving us, stunned and anguished, in a suddenly cold and barren world.

The Rebbe was everything to us—more than a father, and more than a teacher. To us, the Rebbe embodied the core of truth and purity that holds life together, the essence that imbues our existence with purpose and meaning. To us, the Rebbe was the Torah of flesh and blood that made real the Torah of parchment and ink. Without the Rebbe we felt utterly lost—rationally confounded, emotionally devastated and bereft of vision and direction.

And yet, somehow, inexplicably, we were not paralyzed. Somehow, we did not succumb to despair. The Rebbe didn't let us. The Rebbe, who redefined for us virtually every aspect of the human experience, did the same with the very concept of death and bereavement. For forty-four years the Rebbe insisted, by teaching and example, that every event and experience of our lives is a move forward, an integral step in history's unceasing progression toward fulfillment and perfection. Even this. If we compel ourselves to transcend the surface darkness, we can recognize the positive potential in the most painful void.

Thirty-three centuries ago, the world experienced a tremendous, unprecedented revelation of divine truth: G-d descended upon Mount Sinai and communicated His wisdom and will to man. The Talmud interprets the first word of this communication, *anochi* ("I," the opening word of the Ten Commandments), as an acronym of the phrase *ana nafshi ketavit yehavit*—"My Soul I have written and given over."[39] *My moment of revelation to you will soon end*, G-d was saying, *but I am giving you My Torah, into which I have written My very essence. Study My writings and follow their directives and I shall remain a manifest presence in your minds and lives.*

Our sages tell us that "The righteous emulate their Creator."[40] The Rebbe's soul may have passed on to a state of unfettered spirituality, but he remains a very real part of our physical world. For he has left us his writings—over 300,000 pages of essays, letters and transcribed talks. In these, the Rebbe lives, and continues his life's work of bringing to light the divine harmony and perfection inherent in our world and in every human soul.

Yanki Tauber

---

(1) Including the Talmud's own Avot D'Rabbi Nathan *(3rd century); Rashi's commentary, by Rabbi Shlomo Yitzchaki (1040-1105);* Machzor Vitri, *by Rabbi Simcha ben Shmuel (1040-1105); a commentary by Maimonides (Rabbi Moshe ben Maimon, 1135-1204); a commentary by Rabbeinu Yonah (d. 1263);* Nachalat Avot, *by Rabbi Don Isaac Abarbanel (1437-1508); the Bartinoro commentary, by Rabbi Ovadia Bartinoro (1450-1510);* Zechut Avot, *by kabbalist Rabbi Abraham Galanti (d. 1560);* Midrash Shmuel, *by Rabbi Shmuel Uceda (1540-1600);* Tosafot Yomtov, *by Rabbi Yomtov Lippman Heller (1579-1654);* Me'am Lo'ez, *by Rabbi Yitzchak Magriso (circa 1730);* Biurei HaGra, *by Rabbi Elijah, the Gaon of Vilna (1720-1797);* Petach Ena'im, *by Rabbi Chaim Yosef David Azzulai ("The Chida," 1724-1806);* Tiferet Yisroel, *by Rabbi Israel Lifschitz (1782-1860); a German-language translation and commentary by Rabbi Samson Raphael Hirsh (1808-1888); the* Kahati *commentary, by Rabbi Pinchas Kahati (d. 1977);* Ethics From Sinai, *by Irving M. Bunim;* Chapters of the Sages: A Psychological Commentary on Pirkey Avoth, *by Reuven P. Bulka;* Mili D'chassidusah, *by Rabbi Yekutiel Green;* The Baal Shem Tov on Pirkey Avos, *by Isaiah Aryeh and Joshua Dvorkin;* The Hafetz Hayyim on Pirkei Avot, *by David Zaretzky; and many, many others. Two compilations of the Lubavitcher Rebbe's elucidations on the* Ethics *are* Biurim L'Pirkei Avot, *compiled by*

Rabbi A.A. Friedman *and* In the Paths of Our Fathers, *by Rabbi Eliyahu Touger.*
(2) Job *11:9.*
(3) Ethics of the Fathers *5:21.*
(4) See footnote 1 on pg. 45 and Written and Relayed: The Dynamics of a Partnership *on pg. 266.*
(5) Typical is the first mishnah *of the third chapter of* Bava Kama: If someone sets down a jug (*kad*) in a public domain, and another goes by, and stumbles on it, and breaks it, he is absolved from liability; and if he was injured by it, the owner of the cask (*chavit*) is liable. *Why, asks the Talmud, does the author of the* mishnah *begin speaking of a* kad *(jug) and, in conclusion, refer to the vessel in question as a* chavit *(cask)? The Talmud explains that these terms are interchangeable, and their usage varies from place to place. The* mishnah *uses them interchangeably in order to emphasize that, legally, they are synonymous. Thus, if Reuven contracts to purchase 100* chaviot *(casks) from Shimon, and Shimon delivers to him 100 jugs, Reuven cannot claim that the contract stipulates the larger "cask." From this the Talmud derives yet another principle: "Concerning monetary matters, we do not go by the majority" as we do in other areas of law. This is derived from the very fact that the* mishnah *finds it necessary to inform us that the words* kad *and* chavit *on a contract may both connote either "jug" or "cask." For if, in the locale of the contract, the majority of people use the terms interchangeably, the* mishnah *would have no need to emphasize this; obviously, then, the* mishnah *is telling us that even in a place where most people use* kad *for the smaller "jug" and* chavit *for the larger "cask," nevertheless, as long as there is a minority that does otherwise, the burden of proof lies with the claimant. The Talmud also makes an issue of the* mishnah's *interjecting the words "and stumbles on it"—why not simply say "and another goes by and breaks it"? Since the basis of the* mishnah's *ruling is that the owner of the jug is always in the wrong because he had no right placing a hazard in a public thoroughfare, what difference does it make if it was broken intentionally or unintentionally? Are we therefore to understand from the* mishnah *that it is forbidden to take the law into one's own hands, even when there is a clear and present danger involved? On the other hand, the* mishnah *may be telling us*

that although, in such a case, one may take the law into his hands, one does so at his own risk, so that the latter part of the mishnah, *"if he was injured by it, the owner of the cask is liable"* indeed applies only in the case that he *"stumbles on it."* The Talmud launches into lengthy discussion of these issues, citing similar inflections from other mishnayot to prove its point. And these are but some of the laws and principles that Rabbi Judah HaNassi compacted into the several lines of this mishnah!

(6) A *"Jerusalem Talmud,"* which summarizes the interpretation and exposition of the Mishnah by the Holy Land sages, was compiled a century earlier.

(7) *The actual number is sixty:* Bava Kama, Bava Metziah, and Bava Batra are three sections of the prodigious tractate Nezikin, and Makot is actually the final three chapters of Sanhedrin.

(8) Talmud, Bava Kama 30a.

(9) *Introduction to* Tikkunei Zohar.

(10) See Talmud, Eruvin *18a:* "Adam the First was a great chassid."

(11) Leviticus *19:16, as per* Talmud, Erchin *16 (see* Maimonides' Book of Mitzvot, *Prohibition 301).*

(12) Ibid., *19:17, as per* Talmud, Erchin *16b*

(13) Ibid., *19:14, as per* Talmud, Sanhedrin *36a.*

(14) Ethics *1:15.*

(15) Deuteronomy *15:7-8.*

(16) Joshua *1:8.*

(17) Talmud, Menachot *99b.*

(18) Ethics *4:10*

(19) Talmud, Pesachim *8a.*

(20) Ethics *1:3.*

(21) *See* On The Essence of the Ethics *and* Inside Work, *on pgs. 97 and 256 of this book.*

(22) Thus the Talmud *(Niddah 17a)* states: "Three things were said concerning the parings of one's nails: one who burns them is a chassid, *one who buries them is righteous, and one who throws them away is wicked."* Since nail parings are dangerous (the Talmud *says that if a pregnant woman steps on them, she may miscarry),* one who throws them about, without a thought to the injury his deed may cause, is obviously wicked. But what is the differ-

ence between burying them or burning them, to the extent that this is what distinguishes the chassid *from the merely righteous?* The Tosafot commentary explains that it is spiritually harmful to destroy what was once a part of one's body. But the chassid *is one who cannot tolerate the thought that something exists which may cause injury to another; true, it may be buried, but who knows, perhaps, somehow, his parings may come to be unearthed? So he prefers to do something that is detrimental to his own self rather than assume the slightest chance of injuring his fellow.*

(23) Isaiah 41:8.

(24) For the fundamentals of Chabad Chassidism, as they pertain to this objective, see The Long But Short of It *on pg. 111.*

(25) B'Sha'ah SheHikdimu 5672, *Vol. II, pg. 772.*

(26) The Rebbe's six predecessors are: Rabbi Schneur Zalman of Liadi (1745-1812), Rabbi DovBer Schneuri of Lubavitch (1773-1827), Rabbi Menachem Mendel Schneersohn of Lubavitch (the Rebbe's great-great-grandfather and namesake, 1789-1866), Rabbi Shmuel Schneersohn of Lubavitch (1834-1882), Rabbi Sholom DovBer Schneersohn of Lubavitch (1860-1920) and the Rebbe's father-in-law, Rabbi Yosef Yitzchak Schneersohn of Lubavitch (1880-1950).

(27) See Rabbi Tuvia Blau's lengthy introduction to Klalei Rashi *(Kehot);* The Rebbe: Thirty Years of Leadership, *a voluminous anthology edited by Rabbis Hanoch Glitzenstein and Adin Steinsaltz (Vol. I, 1980; Vol. II, 1983), includes essays and articles by Rabbi Y.S. Zevin, Dr. Hillel Zeidman, Elie Wiesel, Rabbi Adin Steinsaltz and many other scholars and writers.*

(28) See the Rebbe's essay, On the Essence of Chassidus, *Kehot 1986.*

(29) Talmud, Eruvin *21b.*

(30) Three Times Three *(pg. 137).*

(31) Love and Fear: A Four-Runged Ladder *(pg. 58).*

(32) Five Steps to Sinai *(pg. 42).*

(33) See Three Times Three *(pg. 137),* The Contemporary Cannibal *(pg. 145) and* Barrier and Gateway *(pg. 46).*

(34) E.g., the Rebbe's analysis of Rabbi Akiva's words in Expression, Connection and Union *(pg. 164) and of Samuel the Small's message in* The Humble Witness *(pg. 205).*

(35) E.g., The Contemporary Cannibal *(pg. 145).*

(36) E.g., On the Essence of the Ethics *(pg. 97).*

(37) During the half-year from Passover to Rosh Hashanah, when it is customary to study a chapter of the Ethics *each Shabbat afternoon, the Rebbe's* farbrengens *regularly include an exposition on one or more of the* mishnahs *studied that week. It is on these expositions that many of the essays in this volume are based.*

(38) Vaad Hanochos Hatmimim *has also produced adaptations of the* farbrengens *in French, Spanish, Portuguese, Italian, Russian and Farsi.*

(39) Talmud, Shabbat *105a.*

(40) Midrash Rabba, Bereishit *67:8.*

A NOTE TO THE READER

Each of the sixty essays in this book was written as a wholly self-contained entity. However, as component parts of a philosophy and approach to life, each will enrich the reader's understanding of the others. The essays follow no intrinsic order other than their relationship with the sayings of *Ethics of the Fathers*. So open this book at any point, or browse through the *General Index* on pages 336-343 for a topic that catches your interest. For your easy reference, we have prefaced these essays with the full text of the Talmud's *Ethics of the Fathers*.

Ethics of the Fathers

All Israel has a share in the World to Come, as it is stated: "And your people are all righteous; they shall inherit the land forever. They are the shoot of My planting, the work of My hands, in which I take pride."[1]

Sanhedrin 11:1[2]

One

1   Moses received the Torah from (G–d at) Sinai and gave it over to Joshua. Joshua gave it over to the Elders, the Elders to the Prophets, and the Prophets gave it over to the Men of the Great Assembly. They (the Men of the Great Assembly) would always say these three things: Be cautious in judgment. Establish many pupils. And make a safety fence around the Torah.

2   Shimon the Righteous was from the last surviving members of the Great Assembly. He would say: The world stands on three things: Torah, the service of G–d and deeds of kindness.

3   Antignos of Socho received the tradition from Shimon the Righteous. He would say: Do not be as slaves who serve their master for the sake of reward. Rather, be as slaves who serve their master not for the sake of reward. And the fear of Heaven should be upon you.

Yossei the son of Yoezer of Tzreidah and Yossei the son of Yochanan of Jerusalem received the tradition from them.[3] Yossei the son of Yoezer of Tzreidah would say: Let your home be a meeting place for the sages; dust yourself in the soil of their feet, and drink thirstily of their words.

Yossei the son of Yochanan of Jerusalem would say: Let your home be open wide, and let the poor be members of your household. And do not engage in excessive conversation with a woman. This is said even regarding one's own wife—how much more so regarding the wife of another. Hence, the sages said: One who excessively converses with a woman causes evil to himself, neglects the study of Torah and, ultimately, inherits purgatory.

Joshua the son of Perachia and Nitai the Arbelite received from them. Joshua the son of Perachia would say: Assume for yourself[4] a master, acquire for yourself a friend and judge every man to the side of merit.

Nitai the Arbelite would say: Distance yourself from a bad neighbor, do not cleave to a wicked person and do not abandon belief in retribution.[5]

Judah the son of Tabbai and Shimon the son of Shotach received from them. Judah the son of Tabbai would say: When sitting in judgment, do not act as a counselor-at-law. When the litigants stand before you, consider them both guilty; and when they leave your courtroom, having accepted the judgment, regard them as equally righteous.

9   Shimon the son of Shotach would say: Increasingly cross-examine the witnesses. Be careful with your words, lest they learn from them how to lie.

10 Shmaayah and Avtalyon received from them. Shmaayah would say: Love work, loathe mastery[6] and avoid intimacy with the government.

11 Avtalyon would say: Scholars, be careful with your words. For you may be exiled to a place inhabited by evil elements (who will distort your words to suit their negative purposes). The disciples who come after you will then drink of these evil waters and be destroyed, and the Name of Heaven will be desecrated.

12 Hillel and Shammai received from them. Hillel would say: Be of the disciples of Aaron—a lover of peace, a pursuer of peace, one who loves his fellow creatures and draws them close to Torah.

13 He would also say: One who advances his name, destroys his name. One who does not increase, diminishes. One who does not learn is deserving of death. And one who makes personal use of the crown of Torah shall perish.

14 He would also say: If I am not for myself, who is for me? And if I am only for myself, what am I? And if not now, when?

15 Shammai would say: Make your Torah study a permanent fixture of your life. Say little and do much. And receive every man with a pleasant countenance.

Rabban Gamliel would say: Assume for yourself[7] a master; stay away from doubt; and do not accustom yourself to tithe by estimation.   16

His son, Shimon, would say: All my life I have been raised among the wise, and I have found nothing better for the body than silence. The essential thing is not study, but deed. And one who speaks excessively brings on sin.   17

Rabbi Shimon the son of Gamliel would say: On three things the world endures: law, truth and peace. As is stated, "Truth, and a judgment of peace, you should administer at your (city) gates."[8]   18

Two

Rabbi (Judah HaNassi[9]) would say: Which is the right path for man to choose for himself? Whatever is harmonious for the one who does it, and harmonious for mankind. Be as careful with a minor *mitzvah* as with a major one, for you do not know the rewards of the *mitzvot*. Consider the cost of a *mitzvah* against its rewards, and the rewards of a transgression against its cost. Contemplate three things, and you will not come to the hands of transgression: Know what is above you: a seeing eye, a listening ear and all your deeds being inscribed in a book.   1

Rabban Gamliel the son of Rabbi Judah HaNassi would say: Beautiful is the study of Torah with the way of the world, for the toil of them both causes sin to be forgotten. Ultimately, all Torah study that is not accompanied with work is destined to cease and to cause sin. Those who work for the community should do so for the sake of Heaven; for the merit of their ancestors shall aid   2 them, and their righteousness shall endure forever. And you, (says G–d,) I shall credit you with great reward as if you had achieved it yourselves.

3 Be careful with the government, for they befriend a person only for their own needs. They appear to be friends when it is beneficial to them, but they do not stand by a person at the time of his distress.

4 He would also say: Make that His will should be your will, so that He should make your will to be as His will. Nullify your will before His will, so that He should nullify the will of others before your will. Hillel would say: Do not separate yourself from the community. Do not believe in yourself until the day you die. Do not judge your fellow until you have stood in his place. Do not say something that is not readily understood in the belief that it will ultimately be understood.[10] And do not say, "When I free myself of my concerns, I will study," for perhaps you will never free yourself.

5 He would also say: A boor cannot be sin-fearing, an ignoramus cannot be pious,[11] a bashful one cannot learn, a short-tempered person cannot teach nor does anyone who does much business grow wise. In a place where their are no men, strive to be a man.

6 He also saw a skull floating upon the water. Said he to it: Because you drowned others, you were drowned; and those who drowned you will themselves be drowned.

7 He would also say: One who increases flesh, increases worms; one who increases possessions, increases worry; one who increases wives, increases witchcraft; one who increases maidservants,

increases promiscuity; one who increases man-servants, increases thievery; one who increases Torah, increases life; one who increases study, increases wisdom; one who increases counsel, increases understanding; one who increases charity, increases peace. One who acquires a good name, acquires it for himself; one who acquires the words of Torah, has acquired life in the World to Come.

8 Rabban Yochanan the son of Zakkai received the tradition from Hillel and Shammai. He would say: If you have learned much Torah, do not take credit for yourself—it is for this that you have been formed.

9 Rabban Yochanan the son of Zakkai had five disciples: Rabbi Eliezer the son of Hurkenos, Rabbi Joshua the son of Chananya, Rabbi Yossei the Kohen, Rabbi Shimon the son of Nethanel, and Rabbi Elazar the son of Arach. He would recount their praises: Rabbi Eliezer the son of Hurkenos is a cemented cistern that loses not a drop; Rabbi Joshua the son of Chananya—fortunate is she who gave birth to him;[12] Rabbi Yossei the Kohen—a chassid; Rabbi Shimon the son of Nethanel fears sin; Rabbi Elazar ben Arach is as an ever-increasing wellspring. (Rabbi Yochanan) used to say: If all the sages of Israel were to be on one side of a balance-scale, and Eliezer the son of Hurkenos were on the other, he would outweigh them all. Abba Shaul said in his name: If all the sages of Israel were to be on one side of a balance-scale, Eliezer the son of Hurkenos included, and Elazar the son of Arach were on the other, he would outweigh them all.

10   (Rabbi Yochanan) said to them: Go and see which is the best trait for a person to acquire. Said Rabbi Eliezer: A good eye. Said Rabbi Joshua: A good friend. Said Rabbi Yossei: A good neighbor. Said Rabbi Shimon: To see what is born.[14] Said Rabbi Elazar: A good heart. Said he to them: I prefer the words of Elazar the son of Arach to yours, for his words include all of yours.

He said to them: Go and see which is the worst trait, the one from which a person should most distance himself. Said Rabbi Eliezer: An evil eye. Said Rabbi Joshua: An evil friend. Said Rabbi Yossei: An evil neighbor. Said Rabbi Shimon: To borrow and not to repay; for one who borrows from man is as one who borrows from the Almighty, as it is stated, "The wicked man borrows and does not repay; but the righteous one is benevolent and gives."[15] Said Rabbi Elazar: An evil heart. Said he to them: I prefer the word of Elazar the son of Arach to yours, for his words include all of yours. They would each say three things: Rabbi Eliezer would say: The honor of your fellow should be as precious to you as your own, and do not be easy to anger. Repent one day before your death.[16] Warm yourself by the fire of the sages, but be beware lest you be burned by its embers; for their bite is the bite of a fox, their sting is the sting of a scorpion, their hiss is the hiss of a serpent, and all their words are like fiery coals.

11   Rabbi Joshua would say: An evil eye, the evil inclination and the hatred of one's fellows, drive a person from the world.

12   Rabbi Yossei would say: The property of your fellow should be as precious to you as your own. Perfect yourself for the study of Torah, for it is not an inheritance to you. And all your deeds should be for the sake of Heaven.

Rabbi Shimon would say: Be meticulous with the reading of the *Shema* and with prayer. When you pray, do not make your prayers routine, but (an entreatment of) mercy and a supplication before the Almighty, as it is stated, "For He is benevolent and merciful, slow to anger and abundant in loving-kindness and relenting of the evil decree."[17] And do not be wicked in your own eyes.

Rabbi Elazar would say: Be diligent in the study of Torah. Know what to answer a heretic. And know before Whom you toil, and Who your Employer is, Who will repay you the reward of your labors.

Rabbi Tarfon would say: The day is short, the work is much, the workers are lazy, the reward is great, and the Master is pressing.

He would also say: It is not incumbent upon you to finish the task, but neither are you free to absolve yourself from it. If you have learned much Torah, you will be greatly rewarded, and your Employer is trustworthy to pay you the reward of your labors. And know that the reward of the righteous is in the World to Come.

Three

Rabbi Akavia the son of Mahalalel would say: Reflect upon three things and you will not come to the hands of transgression. Know from where you came, where you are going, and before Whom you are destined to give a judgment[18] and accounting. From where you came—from a putrid drop; where you are going—to a place of dust, maggots and worms; and before Whom you are destined to give a judgment and accounting—before the supreme King of kings, the Holy One, blessed be He.

2   Rabbi Chanina, deputy to the *kohanim*, would say: Pray for the integrity of the sovereignty; for were it not for the fear of its authority, a man would swallow his neighbor alive. Rabbi Chanina son of Tradyon would say: Two who sit and no words of Torah pass between them, this is a session of scorners, as it is stated, "And in a session of scorners he did not sit."[19] But two who sit and exchange words of Torah, the Divine Presence rests amongst them, as it is stated, "Then the G–d-fearing conversed with one another, and G–d listened and heard; and it was inscribed before Him in a book of remembrance for those who fear G–d and give thought to His name."[20] From this, I know only concerning two individuals; how do I know that even a single individual who sits and occupies himself with the Torah, G–d designates reward for him? From the verse, "He sits alone in meditative stillness; indeed, he receives (reward) for it."[21]

3   Rabbi Shimon would say: Three who eat at one table and do not speak words of Torah, it is as if they have eaten from the slaughter of the dead,[22] as it is stated, "Indeed, all tables are filled with vomit and filth, devoid of the Omnipresent."[23] But three who eat at one table and speak words of Torah, it is as if they have eaten at G–d's table, as it is stated, "And he said to me: 'This is the table that is before G–d.'"[24]

4   Rabbi Chanina the son of Chachina'i would say: One who stays awake at night, or travels alone on the road, and turns his heart to idleness, has forfeited his life.

5   Rabbi Nechunia the son of Hakanah would say: One who accepts upon himself the yoke of Torah is exempted from the yoke of government duties and the yoke of worldly cares;[25] but one who

casts off the yoke of Torah is saddled with the yoke of government duties and the yoke of worldly cares.

6 Rabbi Chalafta the son of Dosa of the village of Chanania would say: Ten who sit together and occupy themselves with Torah, the Divine Presence rests amongst them, as it is stated: "The Almighty stands in the community of G–d."[26] And from where do we know that such is also the case with five? From the verse, "He established His band on earth."[27] And three? From the verse, "He renders judgment in the midst of judges." And two? From the verse, "Then the G–d-fearing conversed with one another, and G–d listened and heard."[29] And from where do we know that such is the case even with a single individual? From the verse, "Every place where I have My name mentioned, I shall come to you and bless you."[30]

7 Rabbi Elazar of Bartosa would say: Give Him what is His, for you, and whatever is yours, are His. As (King) David says: "For everything comes from You, and from Your own hand we have given to You."[31] Rabbi Yaakov would say: One who walks along a road and studies, and interrupts his studying to say, "How beautiful is this tree!", "How beautiful is this plowed field!"—the Torah considers it as if he had forfeited his life.

8 Rabbi Dusta'i the son of Rabbi Yannai would say in the name of Rabbi Meir: Anyone who forgets even a single word of his learning, the Torah considers it as if he had forfeited his life. As it is stated, "Just be careful, and verily guard your soul, lest you forget the things that your eyes have seen."[32] One might think that this applies also to one who (has forgotten because) his studies proved

Ethics of the Fathers

too difficult for him; but the verse goes on to tell us "and lest they be removed from your heart, throughout the days of your life." Hence, one does not forfeit his life unless he deliberately removes them from his heart.

9   Rabbi Chanina the son of Dosa would say: One whose fear of sin takes precedence to his wisdom, his wisdom endures. But one whose wisdom takes precedence to his fear of sin, his wisdom does not endure.

10 He would also say: One whose deeds exceed his wisdom, his wisdom endures. But one whose wisdom exceeds his deeds, his wisdom does not endure. He would also say: One who is pleasing to his fellow men, is pleasing to G–d. But one who is not pleasing to his fellow men, is not pleasing to G–d. Rabbi Dosa the son of Harkinas would say: Morning sleep, noontime wine, children's talk and sitting at the meeting places of the ignorant, drive a person from the world.

11 Rabbi Elazar of Modi'in would say: One who profanes the *kodoshim*,[33] degrades the festivals, humiliates his friend in public, abrogates the covenant of our father Abraham or who interprets the Torah contrary to its true intent—although he may possess Torah knowledge and good deeds, he has no share in the World to Come.

12 Rabbi Ishmael would say: Be yielding to a leader, affable to the black-haired,[34] and receive every man with joy.

Rabbi Akiva would say: Jesting and frivolity accustom a person to promiscuity. Tradition is a safety fence to Torah, tithing a safety fence to wealth, vows a safety fence for abstinence; a safety fence for wisdom is silence.

13

He would also say: Beloved is man, for he was created in the image (of G–d); it is a sign of even greater love that it has been made known to him that he was created in the image, as it is stated, "For in the image of G–d, He made man."[35] Beloved are the people Israel, for they are called children of G–d; it is a sign of even greater love that it has been made known to them that they are called children of G–d, as it is stated: "You are children of the L–rd your G–d."[36] Beloved are the people Israel, for they were given a precious article; it is a sign of even greater love that it has been made known to them that they were given a precious article, as it is stated: "I have given you a good purchase; My Torah, do not forsake it."[37]

14

All is foreseen, and freedom of choice is granted. The world is judged with goodness,[38] but in accordance with the amount of man's positive deeds.

15

He would also say: Everything is placed in pledge, and a net is spread over all the living. The store is open, the storekeeper extends credit, the account book lies open, the hand writes, and all who wish to borrow may come and borrow. The collection officers make their rounds every day and exact payment from man, with his knowledge and without his knowledge. Their case is well founded, the judgment is a judgment of truth, and ultimately, all is prepared for the feast.

16

17 Rabbi Eliezer the son of Azariah would say: If there is no Torah, there is no common decency;³⁹ if there is no common decency, there is no Torah. If there is no wisdom, there is no fear of G–d; if there is no fear of G–d, there is no wisdom. If there is no applied knowledge, there is no analytical knowledge; if there is no analytical knowledge, there is no applied knowledge. If there is no flour, there is no Torah; if there is no Torah, there is no flour. He would also say: One whose wisdom is greater than his deeds, to what is he compared? To a tree with many branches and few roots; a storm comes and uproots it, and turns it on its face. As it is stated, "He shall be as a lone tree in a wasteland, and shall not see when good comes; he shall dwell parched in the desert, a salt-land, uninhabited."⁴⁰ But one whose deeds are greater than his wisdom, to what is he compared? To a tree with many roots and few branches, whom all the storms in the world cannot budge from its place. As it is stated: "He shall be as a tree planted upon water, who spreads his roots by the river; who fears not when comes heat, whose leaf is ever lush; who worries not in a year of drought, and ceases not to yield fruit."⁴¹

18 Rabbi Eliezer (the son of) Chisma would say: The laws of *kinin*⁴² and the laws of menstrual periods—these, these are the meat of *halacha*. The calculations of solar seasons and *gematria*⁴³ are the condiments of wisdom.

Four

1 Ben Zoma would say: Who is wise? One who learns from every man. As it is stated: "From all my teachers I have grown wise, for Your testimonials are my meditation."⁴⁴ Who is strong? One who

overpowers his inclinations. As it is stated, "Better one who is slow to anger than one with might, one who rules his spirit than the captor of a city."[45] Who is rich? One who is satisfied with his lot. As it is stated: "If you eat of the toil of your hands, fortunate are you, and good is to you!"[46] "Fortunate are you" in this world, "and good is to you" in the World to Come. Who is honorable? One who honors his fellows. As it is stated: "For to those who honor me, I accord honor; those who scorn me shall be demeaned."[47]

Ben Azzai would say: Run to pursue a minor *mitzvah*, and flee from a transgression. For a *mitzvah* brings another *mitzvah*, and a transgression brings another transgression. For the reward of a *mitzvah* is a *mitzvah*, and the reward of a transgression is a transgression. 2

He would also say: Do not scorn any man, and do not discount anything. For there is no man who has not his hour, and no thing that has not its place. 3

Rabbi Levitas of Yavneh would say: Be very, very humble, for the hope of mortal man is worms. Rabbi Yochanan the son of Berokah would say: Whoever desecrates the Divine Name covertly, is punished in public. Regarding the desecration of the Name, the malicious and the merely negligent are one and the same. 4

Rabbi Ishmael the son of Rabbi Yossei would say: One who learns Torah in order to teach, is given the opportunity to learn and teach. One who learns in order to do, is given the opportunity to learn, teach, observe and do. Rabbi Tzaddok would say: Do not 5 separate yourself from the community. Do not act as a counselor-at-law.[48] Do not make the Torah a crown to magnify yourself with, or a spade with which to dig. So would Hillel say: One who makes personal use of the crown of Torah shall perish. Hence, one who benefits himself from the words of Torah, removes his life from the world.

6   Rabbi Yossei would say: Whoever honors the Torah, is himself honored by the people; whoever degrades the Torah, is himself degraded by the people.

7   His son, Rabbi Ishmael, would say: One who refrains from serving as a judge avoids hatred, thievery and false oaths. One who frivolously hands down rulings is a fool, wicked and arrogant.

8   He would also say: Do not judge alone, for there is none qualified to judge alone, only the One. And do not say, "You must accept my view," for this is their (the majority's) right, not yours.

9   Rabbi Jonathan would say: Whoever fulfills the Torah in poverty, will ultimately fulfill it in wealth; and whoever neglects the Torah in wealth, will ultimately neglect it in poverty.

10 Rabbi Meir would say: Engage minimally in business, and occupy yourself with Torah. Be humble before every man. If you neglect the Torah, there will be many more causes for neglect before you;[49] if you toil much in Torah, there is much reward to give to you.

11 Rabbi Eliezer the son of Yaakov would say: He who fulfills one *mitzvah* acquires for himself one advocate; he who commits one

transgression, acquires against himself one accuser. Repentance and good deeds are as a shield against retribution. Rabbi Yochanan the Sandal-Maker would say: Every gathering that is for the sake of Heaven will endure; gatherings that are not for the sake of Heaven will not endure.

Rabbi Eliezer the son of Shamua would say: The dignity of your student should be as precious to you as your own; the dignity of your colleague, as your awe of your master; and your awe of your master, as your awe of Heaven. 12

Rabbi Judah would say: Be careful with your studies, for an error of learning[50] is tantamount to a willful transgression. Rabbi Shimon would say: There are three crowns—the crown of Torah, the crown of priesthood and the crown of sovereignty—but the crown of a good name surpasses them all. 13

Rabbi Nehora'i would say: Exile yourself to a place of Torah; do not say that it will come after you, that your colleagues will help you retain it.[51] Rely not on your own understanding.[52] 14

Rabbi Yannai would say: We have no comprehension of the tranquility of the wicked, nor of the suffering of the righteous. Rabbi Matya the son of Charash would say: Be first to greet every man. Be a tail to lions, rather than a head to foxes. 15

Rabbi Yaakov would say: This world is comparable to the antechamber before the World to Come. Prepare yourself in the antechamber, so that you may enter the banquet hall. 16

Ethics of the Fathers

17 He would also say: A single moment of repentance and good deeds in this world is greater than all of the World to Come. And a single moment of bliss in the World to Come is greater than all of the present world.

18 Rabbi Shimon the son of Elazar would say: Do not appease your friend at the height of his anger; do not comfort him while his dead still lies before him; do not question his vow immediately when he makes it;[53] and do not endeavor to see him at the time of his degradation.

19 Shmuel the Small would say: "When your enemy falls, do not rejoice; when he stumbles, let your heart not be gladdened. Lest G–d see, and it will be displeasing in His eyes, and He will turn His wrath from him (to you)."[54]

20 Elisha the son of Avuyah would say: One who learns Torah in his childhood, to what is this comparable? To ink inscribed on fresh paper. One who learns Torah in his old age, to what is this comparable? To ink inscribed on erased paper. Rabbi Yossei the son of Judah of Kfar HaBavli would say: One who learns Torah from youngsters, to whom is he comparable? To one who eats unripe grapes and drinks (unfermented) wine from the press. One who learns Torah from the old, to whom is he comparable? To one who eats ripened grapes and drinks aged wine. Said Rabbi Meir: Look not at the vessel, but at what it contains. There are new vessels that are filled with old wine, and old vessels that do not even contain new wine.

21 Rabbi Elazar HaKapor would say: Envy, lust and honor drive a man from the world.

22 He would also say: Those who are born will die, and the dead will live. The living will be judged, to learn, to teach and to comprehend that He is G‑d, He is the Former, He is the Creator, He is the Comprehender, He is the Judge, He is the Witness, He is the Plaintiff, and He will judge. Blessed is He, for before Him there is no wrong, no forgetting, no favoritism, and no taking of bribes; know, that everything is according to the reckoning. Let not your heart convince you that the grave is your escape; for against your will you are formed, against your will you are born, against your will you live, against your will you die, and against your will you are destined to give a judgment and accounting before the King, King of all kings, the Holy One, blessed be He.

Five

1 The world was created with ten utterances.[55] What does this come to teach us? Certainly, it could have been created with a single utterance. However, this is in order to make the wicked accountable for destroying a world which was created with ten utterances, and to reward the righteous for sustaining a world which was created with ten utterances.

2 There were ten generations from Adam to Noah. This is to teach us the extent of G‑d's tolerance; for all these generations angered Him, until He brought upon them the waters of the Flood. There were ten generations from Noah to Abraham. This is to teach us the extent of G‑d's tolerance; for all these generations angered Him, until Abraham came and reaped the reward for them all.

3 Our father Abraham was tested with ten tests, and he withstood them all—to indicate how great was his love for G‑d.

4   Ten miracles were performed for our forefathers in Egypt, and another ten at the Sea. Ten afflictions were wrought by G–d upon the Egyptians in Egypt, and another ten at the Sea. With ten tests our forefathers tested G–d in the desert, as it is stated, "They tested Me these ten times, and did not hearken to My voice."[56]

5   Ten miracles were performed for our forefathers in the Holy Temple: No woman ever miscarried because of the smell of the holy meat. The holy meat never spoiled. Never was a fly seen in the slaughterhouse. Never did the High Priest have an accidental seminal discharge on Yom Kippur. The rains did not extinguish the wood fire burning upon the altar. The wind did not prevail over the column of smoke (rising from the altar). No disqualifying problem was ever discovered in the *omer* offering, the "two loaves"[57] or the showbread.[58] They stood crowded but had ample space in which to prostrate themselves. Never did a snake or scorpion cause injury in Jerusalem. And no man ever said to his fellow, "My lodging in Jerusalem is too cramped for me."

6   Ten things were created at twilight of Shabbat eve. These are: the mouth of the earth,[59] the mouth of the well,[60] the mouth of the donkey,[61] the rainbow, the manna, the staff (of Moses), the *shamir*,[62] the writing, the inscription and the tablets (of the Ten Commandments). Some say also the burial place of Moses and the ram[63] of our father Abraham. And some say also the spirits of destruction as well as the original tongs, for tongs must be made with tongs.

7   There are seven things that characterize a boor, and seven that characterize a wise man. A wise man does not speak before one

who is greater than him in wisdom or age. He does not interrupt his fellow's words. He does not hasten to answer. His questions are on the subject and his answers to the point. He responds to first things first and to latter things later. Concerning what he did not hear, he says, "I did not hear." He concedes to the truth. With the boor, the reverse of all these is the case.

Seven types of retribution come to the world for seven types of sin. When some tithe and others do not, a hunger caused by turmoil ensues: some are hungry, others have their fill. When all are unanimous in their failure to tithe, a hunger by drought ensues. For not separating *challah*, an utter, annihilating hunger results. Plagues come to the world for those capital crimes mentioned in the Torah that have not been given over to the *beth-din*, and for desecrating the produce of the sabbatical year. The sword comes to the world for the procrastination of justice, the corruption of justice and because of those who misinterpret the Torah.

Carnage by wild beasts comes to the world for false oaths and the desecration of G–d's name. Exile comes to the world for idol-worship, sexual promiscuity, murder and the failure to leave the land fallow on the sabbatical year. There are four time periods when plagues increase: on the fourth and seventh years (of the sabbatical cycle), on the year following the seventh, and following the festivals of each year. On the fourth year, because of (the neglect of) the tithe to the poor that must be given on the third year; on the seventh, because of the tithe to the poor that must be given on the sixth; on the year after the seventh, because of the produce of the sabbatical year; and following each festival, because of the robbing of the poor of the gifts due to them.

10 There are four types of people. One who says, "What is mine is yours, and what is yours is mine," is a boor. One who says, "What is mine is mine, and what is yours is yours"—this is a median characteristic; others say that this is the character of a Sodomite. One who says, "What is mine is yours, and what is yours is yours," is a *chassid* (pious one[64]). And one who says, "What is mine is mine, and what is yours is mine," is wicked.

11 There are four types of temperaments. One who is easily angered and easily appeased—his virtue cancels his flaw. One who it is difficult to anger and difficult to appease—his flaw cancels his virtue. One who it is difficult to anger and is easily appeased, is a *chassid*. One who is easily angered and is difficult to appease, is wicked.

12 There are four types of students. One who is quick to understand and quick to forget—his flaw cancels his virtue. One who is slow to understand and slow to forget—his virtue cancels his flaw. One who is quick to understand and slow to forget—his is a good portion. One who is slow to understand and quick to forget—his is a bad portion.

13 There are four types of contributors to charity. One who wants to give but does not want others to give—is begrudging of others. One who wants that others should give but does not want to give—begrudges himself. One who wants that he as well as others should give, is a *chassid*. One who wants neither himself nor others to give, is wicked.

14 There are four types among those who attend the study hall. One who goes but does nothing—has gained the rewards of going. One

who does (study) but does not go to the study hall—has gained the rewards of doing. One who goes and does, is a *chassid*. One who neither goes nor does, is wicked.

There are four types among those who sit before the sages: the sponge, the funnel, the strainer and the sieve. The sponge absorbs all. The funnel takes in at one end and lets it out the other. The strainer rejects the wine and retains the sediment. The sieve rejects the coarse flour and retains the fine flour. 15

Any love that is dependent on a specific thing—when the thing ceases, the love also ceases. But a love that is not dependent on a specific thing never ceases. Which is a love that is dependent on a specific thing? The love of Amnon for Tamar. And one that is not dependent on a specific thing? The love of David and Jonathan. 16

Any dispute that is for the sake of Heaven is destined to endure; one that is not for the sake of Heaven is not destined to endure. Which is a dispute that is for the sake of Heaven? The dispute(s) between Hillel and Shammai. Which is a dispute that is not for the sake of Heaven? The dispute of Korach and all his company. 17

One who causes the community to be meritorious, no sin will come by his hand. One who causes the community to sin, is not given the opportunity to repent. Moses was meritorious and caused the community to be meritorious, so the community's merit is attributed to him, as it is stated, "He did G–d's righteousness, and His laws with Israel."[65] Jeroboam the son of Nebat sinned and caused the community to sin, so the community's sin 18 is attributed to him, as it is stated, "For the sins of Jeroboam, which he sinned and caused Israel to sin."[66]

19 Whoever possesses the following three traits is of the disciples of our father Abraham; and whoever possesses the opposite three traits is of the disciples of the wicked Bilaam. The disciples of our father Abraham have a good eye, a meek spirit and a humble soul.[67] The disciples of the wicked Bilaam have an evil eye, a haughty spirit and a gross soul. What is the difference between the disciples of our father Abraham and the disciples of the wicked Bilaam? The disciples of our father Abraham benefit in this world and inherit the World To Come, as it is stated, "To bequeath to those who love Me there is, and their treasures I shall fill."[68] The disciples of the wicked Bilaam inherit purgatory and descend into the pit of destruction, as it is stated, "And You, G–d, shall cast them into the pit of destruction; bloody and deceitful men, they shall not attain half their days. And I shall trust in you."[69]

20 Judah the son of Teima would say: Be bold as a leopard, light as an eagle, swift as a deer and mighty as a lion to do the will of your Father in Heaven. He would also say: The brazen—to purgatory; the bashful—to paradise. May it be Your will, L–rd our G–d and G–d of our fathers, that the Holy Temple be rebuilt speedily in our days; and grant us our portion in Your Torah.

21 Ben Bag Bag would say: Delve and delve into it, for all is in it; see with it; grow old and worn in it; do not budge from it, for there is nothing better. Ben Hei Hei would say: According to the pain is the gain.

22 He would also say: Five years is the age for the study of Scripture. Ten, for the study of *Mishnah*; thirteen, for the obligation to observe the *mitzvot*; fifteen, for the study of Gemara; eighteen, for marriage; twenty, to pursue (a livelihood); thirty, for strength; forty, for understanding; fifty, for counsel; sixty, for sageness; seventy, for elderness; eighty, for power; ninety, to stoop. A hundred-year-old is as one who has died and passed away and has been negated from the world.

Six

1 The sages expounded in the language of the *Mishnah* (blessed is He who chose them and their learning):[70] Rabbi Meir would say: Whoever studies Torah for Torah's sake alone merits many things; not only that, but (the creation of) the entire world is worthwhile for him alone. He is called friend, beloved, lover of G‑d, lover of humanity, rejoicer of G‑d and rejoicer of humanity. The Torah enclothes him with humility and awe; makes him fit to be righteous, a *chassid*,[71] correct and faithful; distances him from sin and brings him close to merit. From him, people enjoy counsel and wisdom, understanding and power, as it is stated, "Mine are counsel and wisdom, I am understanding, mine is power."[72] The Torah grants him sovereignty, dominion and jurisprudence. The Torah's secrets are revealed to him, and he becomes as an ever-increasing wellspring and as an unceasing river. He becomes modest, patient and forgiving of insults. The Torah uplifts him and makes him greater than all creations.

2 Said Rabbi Joshua the son of Levi: Every day, an echo resounds from Mount Horeb,[73] proclaiming and saying: "Woe is to the crea-

tures who insult the Torah." For one who does not occupy himself in Torah is considered an outcast, as it is stated, "A golden nose-ring in the snout of a swine, a beautiful woman bereft of reason."[74] And it says: "And the tablets are the work of G–d, and the writing is G–d's writing, engraved on the tablets;"[75] read not "engraved" (*charut*) but "liberty" (*chairut*)—for there is no free individual, except for he who occupies himself with the study of Torah. And whoever occupies himself with the study of Torah is elevated, as it is stated, "And from the gift[76] to Nahaliel,[77] and from Nahaliel to the Heights."[78]

3   One who learns from his fellow a single chapter, or a single law, or a single verse, or a single word, or even a single letter, he must treat him with respect. For so we find with David, king of Israel, who did not learn anything from Achitofel except for two things alone, yet he called him his "master," his "guide" and his "intimate," as it is stated, "And you are a man of my worth, my guide and intimate friend."[79] Surely we can infer *a fortiori*: if David, king of Israel—who learned nothing from Achitofel except for two things alone—nevertheless referred to him as his master, guide and intimate, it certainly goes without saying that one who learns from his fellow a single chapter, a law, a verse, a saying, or even a single letter, is obligated to revere him. And there is no reverence but Torah, as it is stated, "The sages shall inherit honor;"[80] "and the integral shall inherit good;"[81] and there is no good but Torah, as it is stated, "I have given you a good purchase; My Torah, do not forsake it."[82]

4   Such is the way of Torah: Bread with salt you shall eat, water in small measure you shall drink, and upon the ground you shall

sleep; live a life of deprivation and toil in Torah. If so you do, "fortunate are you, and good is to you!"[83] "Fortunate are you" in this world, and "good is to you" in the World To Come.

5 Do not seek greatness for yourself, and do not lust for honor. More than you study, do. Desire not the table of kings, for your table is greater than theirs, and your crown is greater than theirs, and faithful is your Employer to pay you the rewards of your work.

6 Torah is greater than the priesthood or sovereignty, for sovereignty is acquired with thirty virtues,[84] the priesthood with twenty-four,[85] and Torah is acquired with forty-eight qualities. These are: study, listening, verbalizing, comprehension of the heart, awe, fear, humility, joy, purity, serving the sages, companionship with one's contemporaries, debating with one's students, tranquility, study of the scriptures, study of the *Mishnah*, minimizing engagement in business, minimizing socialization, minimizing pleasure, minimizing sleep, minimizing talk, minimizing gaiety, slowness to anger, goodheartedness, faith in the sages, acceptance of suffering, knowing one's place, satisfaction with one's lot, qualifying one's words, not taking credit for oneself, likableness, love of G‑d, love of humanity, love of charity, love of justice, love of rebuke, fleeing from honor, lack of arrogance in learning, reluctance to hand down rulings, participation in the burden of one's fellow, judging him to the side of merit, correcting him, bringing him to a peaceful resolution (of his disputes), deliberation in study, asking and answering, listening and illuminating, learning in order to teach, learning in order to observe, increasing the wisdom of one's teacher, exactness in conveying a teaching, and saying something in the name of its speaker. Thus we have learned:

One who says something in the name of its speaker brings redemption to the world, as it is stated, "And Esther told the king in the name of Mordechai."[86]

7 Great is Torah, for it gives life to its observers in this world, and in the World To Come. As it is stated: "For they[87] are life to he who finds them,[88] and a healing to all his flesh."[89] And it says: "It shall be health to your navel, and marrow to your bones."[90] And it says: "It is a tree of life for those who hold fast to it, and happy are those who support it."[91] And it says: "For they shall be a garland of grace for your head, and necklaces about your neck."[92] And it says: "It shall give to your head a garland of grace, a crown of glory it shall grant you."[93] And it says: "With me, your days shall be increased, and years of life shall be added to you."[94] And it says: "Long days in its right hand; in its left, wealth and honor."[95] And it says: "For long days, years of life and peace, they shall add to you."[96]

8 Rabbi Shimon the son of Judah would say in the name of Rabbi Shimon the son of Yochai: Beauty, strength, wealth, honor, wisdom, sageness, old age and children are becoming to the righteous and becoming to the world. As it is stated: "Old age is a crown of beauty, to be found in the ways of righteousness."[97] And it says: "The beauty of youths is their strength, and the glory of sages is their age."[98] And it says: "The crown of sages are their grandchildren, and the beauty of children their fathers."[99] And it says: "And the moon shall be abashed and the sun shamed, for the L–rd of Hosts has reigned in Zion, and before his elders is glory."[100] Rabbi Shimon the son of Menasia would say: these seven qualities enumerated by the sages for the righteous were all realized in Rabbi (Judah HaNassi) and his sons.

9 Said Rabbi Yossei the son of Kisma: Once, I was traveling and I encountered a man. He greeted me and I returned his greetings. Said he to me: "Rabbi, where are you from?" Said I to him: "From a great city of sages and scholars." Said he to me: "Rabbi, would you like to dwell with us in our place? I will give you a million dinars of gold, precious stones and pearls." Said I to him: "If you were to give me all the silver, gold, precious stones and pearls in the world, I would not dwell anywhere but in a place of Torah. Indeed, so it is written in the Book of Psalms by David the king of Israel: 'I prefer the Torah of Your mouth over thousands in gold and silver.'[101] Furthermore, when a person passes from this world neither silver, nor gold, nor precious stones nor pearls accompany him, only Torah and good deeds, as it is stated, 'When you go it will direct you, when you lie down it will watch over you, and when you awaken it shall be your speech.'[102] 'When you go it will direct you'—in this world; 'when you lie down it will watch over you'—in the grave; 'and when you awaken it shall be your speech'—in the World To Come. Also it says: 'Mine is the silver and Mine is the gold, so says the L–rd of Hosts.'[103]"

10 G–d acquired five acquisitions in his world. These are: one acquisition is the Torah, one acquisition is the heavens and the earth, one acquisition is Abraham, one acquisition is the people of Israel, and one acquisition is the Holy Temple. The Torah, as it is written, "G–d acquired me as the beginning of His way, before His works of yore."[104] The heavens and the earth, as it is written, "So says G–d: The heavens are My throne and the earth is My footstool; what house, then, can you build for Me, and where is My place of rest?"[105]; and it says, "How many are Your works, O G–d, You have made them all with wisdom; the earth is filled with

Ethics of the Fathers

Your acquisitions."[106] Abraham, as it is written, "And he blessed him, and said: Blessed be Abram to G–d Most High, Acquirer of heavens and earth."[107] Israel, as it is written, "Till Your nation, O G–d, shall pass, till this nation You have acquired shall pass"[108]; and it says, "To the holy who are upon earth, the noble ones, in whom is all My delight."[109] The Holy Temple, as it is written, "The base for Your dwelling that You, G–d, have achieved; the Sanctuary, O L-rd, that Your hands have established"[110]; and it says, "And He brought them to His holy domain, this mount His right hand has acquired."[111]

11 Everything that G–d created in His world, He did not create but for His glory. As it is stated: "All that is called by My Name and for My glory, I created it, formed it, also I made it."[112] And it says: "G–d shall reign forever and ever."[113]

> *Rabbi Chananiah the son of Akashiah would say: G–d desired to merit[114] the people of Israel; therefore, He gave them Torah and mitzvot in abundance. As it is stated, "G–d desired, for the sake of his righteousness, that Torah be magnified and made glorious."[115]*
>
> Makot 3:16[116]

(1) Isaiah *60:21. (2) Introductory reading to* Ethics of the Fathers. *It is customary to study the* Ethics of the Fathers *on the Shabbat afternoons of the summer months, from the Shabbat after Passover to the Shabbat before* Rosh Hashanah. *Each weekly chapter is prefaced with this* mishnah *from the talmudic tractate* Sanhedrin *and followed by a* mishnah *(quoted here at the end of Chapter Six) from the tractate* Makot. *(3) From Shimon the Righteous and Antignos of Socho. (4)* Assei l'cha. *Also: "make for yourself"; "enforce upon yourself." (5) The belief that G–d rewards the righteous and punishes the wicked. (6) A position of authority over others. (7) See footnote 4 above. (8)* Zachariah *8:16. (9) Rabbi Judah HaNassi, compiler of the* Mishnah, *is referred to in the Talmud as "Rabbi." (10) Lit: "Do not say something that cannot be understood that ultimately it will be understood." The Hebrew word* l'hishoma, *translated here as "to be understood," also means "to be heard," and the Hebrew prefix* sheh—*can mean both "that" and "for." Thus, another reading of Hillel's saying is, "Do not say something that ought not to be heard, (even in the strictest confidence,) for ultimately it will be heard"* (Bartinoro). *(11)* Chassid—*see introduction to this book. (12) See* Jerusalem Talmud, Yevamot *1:6. (13) See introduction to this book. (14) Out of one's actions. See* A Fearful Sight *on pg. 121 and* Existence As Birth *on pg. 124. (15) Psalms 37:21. (16) "Rabbi Eliezer would say: Repent one day before your death. Asked his disciples: Does a man know on which day he will die? Said he to them: So being the case, he should repent today, for perhaps tomorrow he will die; hence, all his days are passed in a state of repentance. Indeed, so said Solomon in his wisdom* (Ecclesiastes *9:8): 'At all times, your clothes should be white, and oil should not lack from your head.'"* (Talmud, Shabbat *153a). (17) Joel 2:13. (18) See* Subjective Judge *on pg. 143. (19) Psalms 1:1. (20) Malachi 3:16. (21) Lamentations 3:28. (22) Idolatrous sacrifices. (23) Isaiah 28:8. (24) Ezekiel 41:22. (25) That is, the community bears these responsibilities in his stead. (26) Psalms 82:1. The Hebrew word* eidah *("community") is applied to groups numbering from ten individuals— e.g., "This wicked community"* (Numbers *14:27) in reference to the ten evil-*

speaking spies. (27) Amos *9:6. "Band"* (agudah) *connotes a group of five (see Maimonides' commentary on this* mishnah*). (28)* Psalms *82:1. The* beth-din, *or court of Torah law, consists of three judges. (29)* Malachi *3:16. (30)* Exodus *20:21. The Hebrew words "to you"* (eilecha) *and "I will bless you"* (u'veirachticha) *in this verse are in second person singular. (31)* Chronicles I *29:14 (32) At Sinai.* Deuteronomy *4:9. (33) Animals or produce consecrated as offerings to G–d in the Holy Temple (lit., "holy things"). (34) A young person. (35)* Genesis *9:6. (36)* Deuteronomy *14:1. (37)* Proverbs *4:2. (38) Benevolently. (39)* Derech Eretz, *lit., "the way of the world." Also translates as "worldly occupation," that is, the earning of a living by conventional means, or, in the broader sense, secular pursuits (see* mishnah *five of this chapter and* mishnah *two of the previous chapter). (40)* Jeremiah *17:6. (41) Ibid., 17:8. (42) "Nests"—the complex laws of bird sacrifices contained in the mishnaic tractate of that name. (43) Numeric values of words. (44)* Psalms *119:99. (45)* Proverbs *16:32. (46)* Psalms *128:2 (47)* Samuel I, *2:30. (48) When judging; cf. chapter 1,* mishnah *8. (49) Or: There are many neglecters like you for you to contend with* (Me'iri). *(50) That is, a misdeed resulting from one's ignorance or misunderstanding of a point of law. (51) So that you have no need to pursue it yourself at a center of Torah study* (Bartinoro). *Or: "Exile yourself to a place of Torah—do not say that it will come after you—for it is your colleagues who will help you retain it"* (Rashi). *(52)* Proverbs *3:5. (53) According to Torah law, a vow can be annulled if it is determined that the vower had not envisioned the full ramifications of his vow. For example, the Rabbi may ask, "Had you known of such and such difficulties in fulfilling your vow, would you have vowed?" If the answer is "No," the vow is null and void, on the grounds that it was entered into on a mistaken assumption. But if the vow-taker were to be so questioned immediately upon his vowing, when still possessed by the fervor of his vow, he would, in all likelihood, only reaffirm his commitment. Thus, the questioner may ruin his chances for a later annulment. (54)* Proverbs *24:17-18. (55) i.e., "Let there be light," "Let the earth sprout forth vegetation" etc. (*Genesis *1). (56)* Numbers *14:22. (57) Offered on* Shavuot. *(58) The twelve breads* *placed each Shabbat on the Table in the Sanctuary. (59) To swallow Korach (Numbers 16:32). (60) The "Well of Miriam"—the miraculous stone which provided water to the Jewish People during their journeys in the desert (Exodus 17:6, Numbers 21:16-18). (61) Of* Bilaam *(Numbers 22:28). (62) A worm which split stones for the construction of the Holy Temple in Jerusalem (see* Talmud, Gittin *68a). (63) Offered instead of Isaac (Genesis 22:13). (64) See introduction to this book. (65)* Deuteronomy *33:21. (66)* Kings I *15:30. (67) Or "ascetic soul"* (Bartinoro). *(68) Proverbs 8:21. (69) Psalms 55:24. (70) The tractate* Ethics of the Fathers *in Rabbi Judah HaNassi's* mishnah *consists of five chapters only. This sixth chapter is comprised of* braitot *(lit., "externals"), mishnaic teachings that were not included in Rabbi Judah's edition of the* Mishnah. *(71) See introduction to this book. (72) Proverbs 8:14. (73) Sinai. (74) Proverbs 11:22. One who fails to properly study and apply Torah insults it, as the insulted beauty of a jewel in the snout of a swine and the comeliness of an insane woman. (75) Exodus 32:16. (76) Mount Sinai, where Israel was given the Torah. (77) "Heritage of G–d." (78) Numbers 21:19. (79) Psalms 55:14. (80) Proverbs 3:35. (81) Ibid., 28:10. (82) Ibid., 4:2. (83) Psalms 128:2 (84) There are actually two corresponding sets of "thirty virtues," enumerated in the eighth chapter of* Samuel I *and in the 2nd chapter of the talmudic tractate* Sanhedrin *respectively. See* Biurei HaGra *on our* mishnah. *(85) See* Talmud, Bava Kama *110b. (86) Esther 2:22. (87) The words of Torah. (88) Or: "he who articulates them"* (Talmud, Eruvin *54a). (89) Proverbs 4:22. (90) Ibid., 3:8. (91) Ibid., 3:18. (92) Ibid., 1:9. (93) Ibid., 4:9. (94) Ibid., 9:11. (95) Ibid., 3:16. (96) Ibid., 3:2. (97) Ibid., 16:31. (98) Ibid., 20:29. (99) Ibid., 17:6. (100) Isaiah 24:23. (101) Psalms 118:72. (102) Or: "it shall speak for you"* (Rashi); *"it shall speak with you"* (Metzudat David). *Proverbs 6:22. (103) Chaggai 2:8. (104) Proverbs 8:22. (105) Isaiah 66:1. (106) Psalms 104:25. (107) Genesis 14:19. (108) Exodus 15:16. (109) Psalms 16:3. (110) Exodus 15:17. (111) Psalms 78:54. (112) Isaiah 43:7. (113) Exodus 15:18. (114)* L'zakot. *Also: "to refine." (115) Isaiah 42:21. (116) Studied at the conclusion of each weekly lesson of* Ethics.

THE THIRD LINK

G–d, Jew and Torah: The Dynamics of a Relationship

All Israel has a share in the World to Come, as it is stated: "And your people are all righteous; they shall inherit the land forever. They are the shoot of My planting, the work of My hands, in which I take pride."[1]

Talmud, Sanhedrin 90a[2]

Moses received the Torah from (G–d at) Sinai and gave it over to Joshua. Joshua gave it over to the Elders, the Elders to the Prophets, and the Prophets gave it over to the Men of the Great Assembly.

Ethics of the Fathers 1:1

Is there such a thing as a "Torahless" Jew? Can one still be "Jewish" without observing the edicts and ethos of Torah in his daily life?

Jews defy the conventional definitions of a "people" or "nation." We lack a common race, culture or historical experience.[3] While we all share our eternal rights to the Land of Israel, for the greater part of the last 4,000 years the overwhelming majority of Jews have not lived or even set foot in the Jewish homeland.

What defines us as Jews is a relationship. We are Jews because the Almighty chose us to be His "cherished treasure from all the nations.... a kingdom of priests and a holy people."[4] We are Jews because the Almighty chose us to implement His purpose in creation: to orient our lives in accordance with His will, and to develop a society and world community that reflects His goodness and perfection.

The Essence of a Transgression

The substance of this relationship, the charter of this commitment, is the Torah. The Torah is G–d's concept of reality as communicated to man, the blueprint that describes the perfected world envisioned by its Creator. The Torah details the manner in which the Inventor of life wishes it to be lived.

This would seem to define our Jewishness as a "religion": we are Jews because we adhere to the beliefs and practices mandated by the Torah. However, the Torah itself says this is not so. Torah itself proclaims that G–d "dwells amongst them in the midst of their impurities,"[5] that His relationship with His people remains unaffected, regardless of their behavior.

In the words of the Talmud, "A Jew, although he has transgressed, is a Jew."[6] According to Torah law, one's Jewishness is not dictated by lifestyle or self-perception: one may be totally unaware of his Jewishness and still be a Jew, or, one may consider himself Jewish and observe all the precepts of the Torah and still not be a Jew.[7]

In other words, it is the relationship between the Jew and his Creator that defines his Jewishness, not his acknowledgment of this relationship or his actualization of it in his daily life. It is not the observance of the Torah's *mitzvot* (divine "commandments") that makes him a Jew, but the commitment that the *mitzvot* represent.

This is the deeper significance of the axiom that "A Jew, although he has transgressed, is a Jew." The simple meaning of these words is that a Jew is still a Jew *despite* his transgressions. But on another dimension, it is precisely *because* he has transgressed that he is a Jew. A non-Jew who eats *chametz* (leavened bread) on Passover has done nothing wrong; likewise, his eating *matzoh* on the *seder* night has no moral or spiritual significance. But for a Jew, the *mitzvot* of Passover are a component of his relationship with G–d: by observing them he is realizing this relationship and extending it to his daily life; if he violates them, G–d forbid, he is *transgressing*—he is acting contrary to the commitment which defines his identity. Thus, in a certain sense, the fact of a Jew's transgression is no less an expression (albeit a negative one) of his relationship with G–d than his observance of a *mitzvah*.

Indeed, the Hebrew word *mitzvah* means both "commandment" and "connection." The relationship between the word's two meanings can also be understood on two levels. On the behavioral level, we connect to G–d through our fulfillment of His commandments. On a deeper level, we are inexorably connected to Him by virtue of the fact that He chose us as the object of His commandments. Obviously, these two levels of connection are two sides of the same coin, being the inner and outer faces of the same truth: our observance of the *mitzvot* is the manifestation, in our daily lives, of the intrinsic bond between G–d and Israel.

The Six-Dimensional Link

The *Zohar*, the basic text of kabbalistic teaching, expresses this concept in the following manner: *There are three connections that are bound to each other: G–d, the Torah and Israel—each consisting of a level upon a level, hidden and revealed. There is the hidden aspect of G–d, and the revealed aspect; Torah, too, has both a hidden and a revealed aspect; and so it is with Israel, who also has both a hidden and a revealed aspect.*[8]

The *Zohar* goes on to describe the manner in which the Torah serves as the connecting link between G–d and Israel: how the Torah is one with its Divine Author, and how the Jewish people connect to the Torah through their study and observance of its teachings.

But what are the "hidden" and "revealed" elements of G–d, Torah and Israel? And what is their relevance to our connection to G–d through His Torah?

The *Zohar* is intimating that these three "connections" are interlinked on two levels, both on a "hidden" and on a "revealed" plane. For each of the three interconnected "links" possesses both an explicit and an implicit dimension.

There is the so-called "revealed" aspect of G–d—those expressions of His reality which He chooses to manifest within the created existence—and there is His "hidden" unknowable essence. The Jew, too, has his revealed and manifest self—the manner in which he expresses himself through his behavior—and his hidden, quintessential self. And the Torah, as outlined above, has both a more pronounced as well as a more implicit significance as the connecting link between G–d and Israel.

On the "hidden" plane, the soul of the Jew is bound to the very essence of G–d through the underlying relationship and commitment which Torah represents. Even if the Jew's life, on the conscious-behavioral level, is inconsistent with the revealed will of the Almighty, he is no "less" a Jew, G–d forbid: regardless of whether or how he manifests his identity, the "hidden" intrinsic bond that defines his Jewishness is unaffected. But in order to express this relationship on every level of his being, in order for his life to be in harmony with his essence, the Jew must reiterate this connection on the "revealed" level. This he does by studying G–d's Torah and observing its *mitzvot*.

The Third Juncture

There is, however, another, yet deeper meaning to the *Zohar*'s words.

The above-cited passage speaks of "three *connections* which are bound to each other." The Aramaic word translated here as "connections" is *kishrin*, which literally means "knots."[9]

At first glance, this seems to be an inaccurate usage. If Torah is the link between G–d and Israel, then what we have are three *entities* (G–d, Torah and Israel) linked via *two* connections (Israel's connection to Torah and the Torah's connection with the Almighty). Where are there *three* knots/connections?

This brings us to a second definition of the "hidden" and "revealed" dimensions of the relationship between G–d and Israel. The *Midrash* states: "Two things preceded G–d's creation of the world: Torah and Israel. Still, I do not know which preceded which. But when Torah states 'Speak to the Children of Israel...,' 'Command the Children of Israel...,' etc., I know that Israel preceded all."[10]

In other words, G–d created the world in order that Israel might implement His divine plan for existence, as outlined in the Torah. So the concepts of "Israel" and "Torah" precede the concept of a "world" in the Creator's "mind." Yet, which is the more deeply rooted "idea" within the divine consciousness, Torah or Israel? Does Israel exist so that the Torah be implemented, or does the Torah exist to serve the Jew in the fulfillment of his mission and the expression of his relationship with G–d? If the Torah describes itself as a communication to Israel, this presumes the concept of "Israel" as primary to that of "Torah."

This means that G–d's relationship with Israel "predates" (in the conceptual sense) the Torah, for the Torah comes to serve that relationship. In this sense, Israel is the "link" between the Torah and G–d: the Torah's existence, as the embodiment of the divine wisdom and will, is a *result* of Israel's existence and its connection with G–d.

Thus, we have *three* connections linking G–d, Israel and the Torah:

On the revealed level, the Torah serves as the link between G–d and Israel: the Torah is connected to G–d, and Israel is connected to the Torah. (This includes both levels of connection outlined above—the connection achieved through the performance of a *mitzvah* and the connection defined by the commitment itself).

But on a deeper, more quintessential level, there exists a third connection: the "direct" connection between G–d and His people which precedes the very concept of a Torah. On this level, Israel's involvement in Torah is what connects the Torah to the Almighty, what causes Him to extend His infinite and wholly undefinable being into a medium of "divine wisdom" and "divine will." On this level, it is not the Jew who needs the Torah in order to be one with G–d, but the Torah who needs the Jew to evoke G–d's desire to project Himself via the Torah.

Nevertheless, the Torah is crucial to the Jew's relationship with G–d. The essence of the Jew, as it is rooted within the essence of G–d, is indeed one with its Source. But then it "descends" to become part of the created existence, assuming a distinct identity as a soul and then as a human being. So the Almighty provides the Jew with His Torah. Through Torah, the Jew touches base with his own quintessential self, and makes his intrinsic oneness with his Creator a reality in his daily life.

Beginning Before the Beginning

Ethics of the Fathers, the Talmud's summation of the Jew's ethical code, opens with the statement that "Moses received the Torah from (G-d at) Sinai, and gave it over" to all successive generations of Jews. This is meant to underscore that the entirety of Jewish Law and the Jewish way of life stem from G–d's communication of the Torah to us at Mount Sinai.

Yet, when we study the *Ethics* (a chapter on each Shabbat afternoon of the summer months) we do not begin from the beginning, with Moses's receiving the Torah. We preface each chapter with the attestation that *"All Israel has a share in the World to Come,"* that *"Your people are all righteous; they shall inherit the land forever"* because G–d considers them all *"the shoot of My planting, the work of My hands, in which I take pride."* That each and every Jew, regardless of present behavior or spiritual status, is bound by an invincible knot to his Creator.[11]

(1) Isaiah 60:21. (2) It is customary to study the Ethics of the Fathers *on the Shabbat afternoons of the summer months, from the Shabbat after Passover to the Shabbat before* Rosh Hashanah, *one chapter each Shabbat, thus reviewing the six chapters of the* Ethics *several times in this period. Each weekly chapter is prefaced with the above-quoted* mishnah *from* Sanhedrin *and followed by a* mishnah *(quoted on page 334) from the tractate* Makot. *(3) Many Jews are converts or the descendants of converts to Judaism, and segments of the Jewish people have had little or no contact with each other for tens of generations. (4)* Exodus *19:5-6. (5)* Leviticus *16:16. (6)* Talmud, Sanhedrin *44a. (7) Torah Law* (halacha) *specifies the criteria that identify those whose souls stood at Sinai and are included in G–d's choice: anyone who is born of a Jewish mother or who has converted to Judaism in accordance with the guidelines of* halacha. *(8)* Zohar, *part III, 73a (as quoted in the teachings of Chassidism. See the Rebbe's note of page 61 of* Sefer Hama'amorim *5700). (9) See note referred to in above footnote. (10)* Tana D'vei Eliyahu Rabba, *chapter 14. (11) Based on the talks of the Rebbe,* Adar II *16, 5725 (March 20, 1965),* Simchat Torah *5734 (October 19, 1973),* Iyar *3, 5750 (April 28, 1990), and on numerous other occasions.*

FIVE STEPS TO SINAI

> Moses received the Torah from (G–d at) Sinai and gave it over to Joshua. Joshua gave it over to the Elders, the Elders to the Prophets, and the Prophets gave it over to the Men of the Great Assembly.
>
> Ethics of the Fathers 1:1

On the surface, the *Ethics* is giving us a generalized listing of the first 23 generations of Torah's unbroken chain of tradition from Sinai to our day.[1] On a deeper level, it is imparting the five primary qualities which are crucial to anyone who approaches the study of Torah.

"Moses"—Humility

Moses certainly knew who he was. He knew that he was the one human being chosen by G–d to communicate His wisdom and will to man. Nevertheless, the Torah attests: "And the man Moses was the most humble man upon the face of the earth."[2]

Indeed, a lesser man, or a man less aware of his greatness, could not as poignantly exemplify the essence of humility: the understanding that man attains what he does with the gifts bestowed upon him by his Creator. "Had any other man been given what has been granted me," Moses would have said, "he most certainly would have accomplished far more than I."

To study Torah, a person must engage his mind and maximize its prowess—an experience that often inflates the ego and increases a person's sense of self-importance. So the example of Moses is cited as a prerequisite to the proper study of G‑d's wisdom: apply your intellectual gifts to the utmost, but remember that these are indeed gifts, and the purpose for which they have been granted to you.

"Joshua"—Devotion

"The young man, Joshua the son of Nun, would not budge from the tent."[3] Faithfulness, diligence and perseverance were the traits that characterized Joshua; these traits deemed him worthy to assume the mantle of leadership after the passing of Moses and to serve as the second link in the chain of the Torah's transmission from master to pupil.

The greatest mind, the most pious of hearts, cannot hope to master Torah without years of devoted days and sleepless nights; "You shall study it day and night" for only then will your efforts meet success.[4]

"Elder"—It has to cost you

The Hebrew word for "elder," *zakein*, is related to the word *kanah*, to purchase; thus, the Talmud defines an "elder" as "one who has purchased wisdom."[5] Our sages advise, "If someone tells you, 'I have not toiled, but I have accomplished,' do not believe him."[6]

They also have stated, "The Torah is attained only by one who kills himself over it."[7]

"Prophet"—You cannot do it on your own

Torah is the wisdom and will of G–d. To comprehend Torah is to know the infinite mind of the Creator, which is, by definition, unknowable. So the Torah must be *granted* to us, as we say in the blessing recited prior to its study, "...blessed are You G–d, Who *gives us* the Torah."[8] It is only because G–d desires that the human mind should comprehend Him, only because He chooses to violate the line He had drawn at creation between the finite and the infinite, that we are capable of understanding a single word of Torah.

Thus, the study of Torah is unlike any other science. While mastery of any field of knowledge is strictly a matter of intellectual ability, a person's moral and spiritual qualifications are paramount when it comes to the study of Torah. For ultimately, every one who acquires the wisdom of Torah is a "prophet," one whom G–d has chosen to allow a glimpse of His truth.

"The Men of the Great Assembly"—Make it real

The "Men of the Great Assembly" were a council of 120 sages who led the Jewish people at the time of their return to the Holy Land in the 4th century B.C.E., after three generations of exile in Babylonia. Ravaged by 70 years of displacement and assimilation, the fragile, recovering nation faced many challenges. The Men of the Great Assembly applied their knowledge of Torah to address the specific needs of their time, instituting a unified text for daily prayer and many other statutes and ordinances.

This is the final of the five principles upon which one's approach to Torah must be based: Torah must never be studied as a theory. The most lofty of its concepts must be evidenced in the nitty-gritty of everyday life.[9]

---

(1) The Torah, and the system of interpretation, application and extrapolation that accompanies it (the Torah SheBaal-Peh *or "Oral Torah"—see* Written and Relayed *on pg. 266), has been handed down through the generations from master to pupil. From Moses it passed to his disciple Joshua, from Joshua to Pinchas and his fellow Elders (the 70-sage council established by Moses), from Pinchas to Eli the Prophet, and so on (In the introduction to his* Mishneh Torah, *Maimonides enumerates 40 generations of "conveyers of the tradition" from Moses to Rav Ashi and Ravina, editors of the Talmud). Of course, the Torah is available to all who seek to study it and plumb its depths; but each generation has had its one or several ultimate Torah authorities and decisors, individuals who form a chain of tradition linking us to Sinai. In our* mishnah, *the first 23 generations of this chain are generalized as five phases: Moses, Joshua, the Elders, the Prophets and the Men of the Great Assembly. (2)* Numbers *12:3. (3)* Exodus *33:11. (4)* Joshua *1:8. (5)* Talmud, Kiddushin *32a. See* Property Rights *on pg. 133. (6)* Talmud, Megillah *6b. (7)* Talmud, Berachot *63b. (8) See* Property Rights *on pg. 133. (9) Based on an address by the Rebbe,* Nissan 26, 5727 (May 6, 1967).

BARRIER AND GATEWAY

> Make a safety fence around the Torah.
>
> Ethics of the Fathers 1:1

The Torah is a living document to be applied to all societies and all generations of history. Thus, the Almighty entrusted the sages and Torah authorities of each generation with the responsibility of interpreting the Torah and implementing it in the specific conditions and circumstances of their time and place.[1]

This also includes the task of constructing "safety fences" around the Torah. Each generation's leaders are to pinpoint the specific vulnerabilities of their community and enact the appropriate ordinances which will safeguard and strengthen the observance of Torah. For example, the Torah forbids transferring objects from a "private domain" to a "public domain" (e.g., from one's home out to the street) on Shabbat. As a safety measure, a rabbinic ordinance prohibits *any* handling of certain types of objects, lest one inadvertently come to violate the Shabbat. Other rabbinic institutions include making a blessing before eating, the mandated waiting period between meat and milk, praying three times a day, washing hands before meals, and the festivals of Chanukah and Purim. In fact, a major part of what we call "Judaism" is rabbinic in origin.

Indeed, a safety fence inevitably encloses more area than the thing it comes to safeguard. Thus, the rabbinic ordinances have the effect of broadening and extending Torah to areas where the strict letter of the law does not apply.[2]

As a result, the sages are often perceived as having made Judaism more "difficult." A common sentiment is that while their ordinances may be necessary for the preservation of Torah, they unfortunately make it less accessible to the Jew who is not yet fully committed to its observance.

In fact, the very opposite is true. One of the most "attractive" things about Torah is its tremendous breadth and scope. Torah deals with virtually every area of life, on virtually every level of human discourse: the mystic, the philosopher and the psychologist will each find that the Torah speaks his language. Whether a person is looking for roots and tradition or transcendence and innovation; whether he seeks a pragmatic guide to life, an authoritative moral code or a spiritual experience, he will find the *mitzvah* or custom to identify with. Even if he is not yet ready to embrace the entirety of Torah, there will always be an insight or observance which will draw him in, stimulate his soul and whet his desire to learn and experience more.

So the more Torah is "broadened" by its application through the generations, the more ground it comes to cover via the fences that are erected to safeguard it, and all the more does it become accessible to the most diverse of its constituents.[3]

(1) "If there arises a matter that is beyond your judgment... you shall inquire of the judge that shall be in those days.... According to the ruling of Torah which they shall instruct you, and according to the judgment which they shall tell you, you shall do; you shall not deviate from what they tell you, to the right or to the left"—Deuteronomy *17:8-11. (2) The fact that every part of Torah—"including anything that a qualified student is destined to discover" (Jerusalem Talmud, Pe'ah 2:4)—is the unequivocal word of G–d, does not preclude human participation in its development; indeed, the Torah itself establishes that "it is not in Heaven" (Deuteronomy 30:12) but a product of "a marriage of mind" between G–d and man. For a broader treatment of this concept, see* The Human Element *on pg. 154 and* Debating Truths *on pg. 264. (3) Based on an address by the Rebbe,* Nissan 26, 5717 (April 27, 1957).

ABSOLUTE RELATIVITY

> The world stands on three things: Torah, the service of G–d and deeds of kindness.
>
> Ethics of the Fathers 1:2

Truth, by definition, is absolute. Man, however, is a finite being, inhabiting a defined, finite world. It would therefore seem that he is only capable of attaining relative truths, that his every experience and accomplishment is valid only in relation to the limits of his perception and the parameters of his reality.

Does this mean that man cannot know or do anything that is truly and objectively significant? And what, indeed, is a "relative truth"? Is this not a contradiction in terms?

The Two-Directional Flow

In our first generation as a nation, we were led by two great leaders: Moses Our Teacher, and Aaron the High Priest. The two played different—and, in a certain sense, even opposite—roles in the formation of the people of Israel. Yet it was the combination of these two countercurrents which forged the relationship between G–d and Israel that is the essence of our nationhood.

At Mount Sinai we entered into a covenant with G–d: In receiving and committing ourselves to the Torah, the Almighty's "blueprint for creation,"[1] we became His "treasured people.... a kingdom of priests and a holy nation"[2]—the nation He chose to play the central role in bridging the "gap" between Creator and creation, infinite and finite, limitless and limited.

The Torah compares the relationship between G–d and Israel to the marital bond between man and woman. It speaks of the event at Sinai as the betrothal of the Divine Groom and the Bride Israel.[3] In the context of this metaphor, the *Zohar* explains the roles of Moses and Aaron.

At a wedding, both the groom and the bride are led to the wedding canopy by their respective *shushvinin* (escorts),[4] whose role is to assist them in reaching the place of their meeting and bonding under the wedding canopy. In the union between G–d and Israel, Moses serves as the "*shushvinin* of the King," the one who "escorts" the Almighty to the wedding, and Aaron as the "*shushvinin* of the queen," the one who assists the people of Israel in attaining their union with G–d.[5]

Moses is the teacher of Torah, the transmitter of the "wisdom and will of G–d" to the human mind. Aaron is the *Kohen Gadol* (High Priest), whose function is to lead each individual in his service of G–d. Torah is G–d reaching to us, conveying His essence in a medium which the intellect of man can grasp. Man's service of G–d (via the *korbonot*-offerings and prayer) is the human striving to elevate himself, to bring himself closer to his Creator.

Truth and Benevolence

Moses embodies "Truth." Aaron embodies "Benevolence."[6] Of Moses it is said, "Moses is true and his Torah is true."[7] For G‑d is infinite, omnipresent and omnipotent; in a word, absolute—the only absolute. Torah is the expression of His absolute truth and Moses is its teacher to the world.

Aaron, however, deals with individuals—finite, equivocal, imperfect individuals. He "loves peace, pursues peace, loves his fellow creatures and draws them close to the Torah."[8] To assist them in their quest for truth, Aaron must speak to each one of them in his individual language. This defines "benevolence": the capacity to relate to the limitations of one's fellow; to appreciate his situation from *his* vantage point and to deal with him on *his* own relative terms.

So both Moses and Aaron, both the revelation of Torah and the service of man, play an indispensable role in achieving the "marriage" between G‑d and his people. With Torah, G‑d reaches toward His creation, conveying His truth in humanly comprehensible terms; while man strives upwards in his service of his Creator, seeking to transcend his subjective reality and connect to the all-pervading truth which underlies all.

But where do the two intersect? Where, in his personal experience, can the individual find truth? At what point does the absolute translate into relative terms? How does truth become benevolent without becoming less true?

The Debate

In the tenth chapter of Leviticus, the Torah tells us of a disagreement on a point of law between Moses and Aaron, a disagreement in which Moses concedes that Aaron is right.

It took place on the first day of *Nissan* in the year 2449 from creation (1312 B.C.E.), the day in which the Sanctuary was erected and dedicated. Actually, the Sanctuary had already been in operation for seven days, but these were "training" days in which Aaron and his sons were initiated into the priesthood. It was on this, the eighth day, that Aaron assumed his role as *Kohen Gadol* and the manifest presence of G–d (the *Shechinah*) came to dwell in the Sanctuary.

But then tragedy struck. Aaron's two elder sons, Nadav and Avihu, "offered an alien fire before G–d, which G–d had not commanded. A fire came forth from before G–d and consumed them, and they died before G–d."[9] Nevertheless, G–d commanded that the dedication of the Sanctuary should not be disrupted. Although Aaron now had the status of a first-day mourner (*onain*) who is ordinarily forbidden to eat the holy meat of the *korbonot*, he was expressly commanded to partake of the special offerings which were brought that day in dedication of the Sanctuary.

This Aaron did. But there was also another offering brought that day, one that was not connected with the dedication *per se*; this was the goat that is brought on the first of every month as a sin-offering. It was over this offering that Moses and Aaron had their disagreement.

Moses saw that the flesh of the goat had been burned, as the law mandates should be done with an offering, which, for whatever reason, cannot be eaten by a priest. He demanded to know why it wasn't eaten as G–d had commanded concerning the other sacrifices. Aaron explained that he had drawn a distinction between *kodshei sho'o*, offerings which G–d commands to bring on a one-time basis under special circumstances, and *kodshei dorot*, regularly scheduled offerings which apply equally to all generations. If G–d commanded something concerning the one-time offerings brought for the Sanctuary's dedication, argued Aaron, one should not deduce that the same is to apply to the monthly sin-offering. Here, the regular laws, which forbid its consumption by a mourner, should apply.

Moses listened to Aaron's argument and conceded that he was right. He freely admitted that the distinction had escaped him and that Aaron had concluded correctly.

Consistency and Change

This difference of opinion between Moses and Aaron reflects their differing roles of "truth" and "benevolence."

As we noted earlier, truth demands consistency. As soon as it bends to accommodate the circumstances, it becomes a relative pseudo-truth. Moses, as transmitter of Torah, saw no reason to distinguish between *kodshei sho'o* and *kodshei dorot*, between something that is a product of the specialty of the moment and that which is routine in man's service of G‑d. After all, what is true is always true, regardless of the circumstances.

Aaron, however, who stood at the forefront of the "bridal," human side of the relationship, understood that man's service of G‑d is an offering of the sum total of what *man* possesses, a giving of the utmost of his subjective self. He understood that there are ups and downs in the capacity of man, and that which is expected of him in his finest, most inspired hours does not necessarily apply to his routine, everyday self.

Here we have the confrontation, the line of conflict. On one side stands Moses, conveying the absolute and unequivocal expression of the divine reality. On the other stands Aaron, guiding the nation-bride's advance toward the wedding canopy, leading an endeavor to come close, an endeavor which has only finite tools and resources to draw upon: a subjective mind with which to seek, a relative heart with which to feel.

And what happens? Moses agrees with Aaron! Absolute truth grants legitimacy to the "sub-truths" of a relative world.

Indeed, what *did* happen? How has this seemingly unresolvable contradiction been resolved?

What happened was that Moses gained an even deeper insight into the nature of truth.

"G–d is truth,"[10] proclaims the prophet—the only absolute. All else is relative, with no inherent reality other than that which He chooses to grant it. But it is *He* who created these subjective realities, and in doing so He has imparted a legitimacy and truth to their existence. So if we find relative "truths" in His creation, they are an expression of His all-pervading truth—as translated into one of the many "worlds" or realities which He has created.

In other words, when a person gives his "all," his ultimate, he has attained a personal absolute. And the very existence of concepts such as "truth," "consistency," or "absoluteness" within his subjective personal world are possible only because this "world" has been created by G–d, who has given it of His truth. So his personal truth touches the truth of G–d.

A "Piece of Truth"

In his *Tanya*, Rabbi Schneur Zalman of Liadi applies this concept to man's daily struggle to refine himself and his character.

There are three categories of individuals, explains Rabbi Schneur Zalman: the perfect individual (the *tzaddik*), the sinning individual (the *rasha*) and the intermediate individual (the *beinoni*).

The "sinning individual" is deficient in his behavior. He fails to control his base instincts and actually commits evil and self-destructive acts.

The "perfect individual" has not only perfected his behavior, but also his nature and character. He has made himself so totally aware of the desirability of good and the destructiveness of evil that he has eradicated the slightest tendency toward evil from his heart. The mere thought of wrongdoing is repulsive to him.

The "intermediate individual" occupies the middle-ground between the *tzaddik* and the *rasha*. The destructive desires and tendencies of his heart, natural to every man, are as powerful as ever. But he does not submit to them. So the *beinoni* has the deficient character of the *rasha* but the perfect behavior of the *tzaddik*: he exercises complete control over his thoughts, speech, and actions, never allowing the evil within him to translate into an actual deed. He does this with a special exercise of the mind and heart— prayer. During prayer, he makes use of a unique gift which has been granted the human being: the natural superiority and sovereignty of the mind over the heart.

The nature and psyche of man is such that if he studies and meditates upon something long and intensely enough, it will affect the way he feels. If one truly appreciates the desirability of something, he will come to desire it; should he dwell upon how abominable a certain practice is, in time it will repulse him, no matter how much he has craved it in the past.

So the *beinoni* contemplates the greatness of G‑d, how all of creation derives its existence from Him. He comes to appreciate how every act which brings him closer to G‑d brings him closer to his own essence and source of life, how every act that is contrary to G‑d's will is destructive to his own self and to the purpose of his existence. In this way he develops a desire to do good and, concomitantly, an abhorrence of evil. He lacks the mental and emotional fortitude to carry this as far as the *tzaddik*, who has effected a permanent change in the very essence of his nature. But it suffices to override his natural inclinations and rule his behavior.

Because the *beinoni* has not changed his basic nature, the effect of his prayer is temporary and fluctuating. When he is immersed in his contemplation of the Divine, during prayer itself, it is at its peak. As the day wears on and his natural self is exposed to a corrupt and enticing world, the effect wanes. It is a constant battle for the *beinoni* to draw from the "memory" of prayer in order to suppress and overpower the evil in himself.

Thus, continues Rabbi Schneur Zalman, from the perspective of the *tzaddik*, the prayer of the *beinoni* lacks truth. The *tzaddik*'s love of G–d is true—it is consistent and unchanging; not so that of the *beinoni*, which suffers from the ups and downs of an erratic heart and must be constantly recreated lest it dwindle away. Nevertheless, since in terms of the *beinoni*'s personal reality this is the ultimate, there is truth, real truth, to his efforts. For echoes of the absolute truth of G–d resound within the many "worlds" and perspectives of His creation.[11]

This is one example of the point at which Aaron's upward leading of the bride and Moses's drawing down of the Groom meet and unite. Man must strive toward the truth, guided by the directives of Torah, and utilizing the talents and resources he has been granted. He need not be disturbed by the relative nature of his understanding and the subjectivity of his feelings: if his efforts are wholesome and true, then "Moses" will concede that his Aaron-like "truth" is part and parcel of the Absolute Truth. In the words of the psalmist:[12] "Benevolence and truth have met...."[13]

(1) Midrash Rabba, Bereishit *1:2. (2)* Exodus *19:5-6. (3) See* Isaiah *54;* Jeremiah *2:2;* Song of Songs *3:11; and numerous other such references throughout the Torah. (4)* Unterfirers, *in the Yiddish. (5)* Zohar, *part I, 266a. (6)* Midrash Rabba, Shemot *5:10. (7)* Talmud, Bava Batra *74a. (8)* Ethics of the Fathers, *1:12. (9) For the deeper significance of* Nadav *and* Avihu's *death, see* Staying Alive *on pg. 217. (10)* Jeremiah *10:10. (11)* Tanya, *chapter 13. (12)* Psalms *85:11. (13) Based on an address by the Rebbe,* Nissan *24, 5729 (April 12, 1969).*

LOVE AND FEAR

A Four-Runged Ladder

Do not be as slaves who serve their master for the sake of reward. Rather, be as slaves who serve their master not for the sake of reward. And the fear of Heaven should be upon you.

Ethics of the Fathers 1:3

You shall love the L–rd your G–d.

Deuteronomy 6:5

The L–rd your G–d you shall fear.

Deuteronomy 6:13

Love is the drive to come close, to connect, to fuse with someone or something outside of one's own being. Love is the ego's impulsion to extend beyond the confines of self, to embrace that which it presently is not and longs for.

Fear is love's diametrical opposite. To fear is to withdraw, to feel diminished before a daunting reality. In fear, the self retreats and shrivels, repelled by the object of its awe.

Love and fear are the two primary forces at play in the heart of man. For all of emotion involves the motion of the ego, either outward, inward, or both to and fro. To feel is to sense an expansion or a constriction of self, or some combination thereof. So love and fear are the two cornerstones upon which thousands of nuances of feeling are built.

Twin-Engined Flight

The life work of man necessitates a partnership between action and emotion. On the one hand, we have the rule that "the deed is the primary thing"[1]; on the other hand, our sages have said that "a deed without direction (*kavanah*) of the heart, is like a body without a soul."[2] A person may experience the most sublime feelings, but unless he translates them into actions he has accomplished nothing. However, an act devoid of feeling is a lifeless act: the deed and its effects exist, but the doer remains unmoved and unchanged by what he has done.

In the words of the kabbalist Rabbi Chaim Vital, love and fear are the "two wings without which the deed cannot fly upward."[3] Without its wings, the bird, though otherwise hale in body, cannot raise itself aloft; likewise, a deed that is not motivated by and imbued with the love and fear of G–d remains earthbound, imprisoned by the gravitational pull of mundanity. The "body" of the deed is there, but it cannot ascend and uplift its doer, who may have accomplished much good but hasn't escaped his material self.

And a person's efforts to uplift himself must include both love and fear—both a reaching outward of self and an inward self-negation. A one-dimensional emotional involvement is as flightless as a one-winged bird.

Two That Are Four

More specifically, love and fear each include both a higher and lower aspect, making a total of four primary elements in our relationship with the Creator.

The lower aspect of "fear" is the emotion associated with the most basic meaning of the word: our intimidation before a being or force because of its potential to harm us. Yet there is also a higher dimension to "fear," a feeling that is better expressed by the word "awe." Awe is the diminution of self that is experienced when in the presence of that which is immeasurably greater than oneself. One recoils not in fear of being hurt, but in recognition of one's inadequacy before so awesome a presence.

Love, too, includes both a selfish love and an altruistic love. The lower level of love is an attraction that is motivated by the ego's quest for self-betterment and self-advancement: one is driven to attach oneself to something because one recognizes that the relationship will result in a more enhanced self. A higher, purer love is one that is motivated solely by the desire to merge with the beloved. Here the objective is not personal gain—on the contrary, it is the obliteration of self and identity.

Chassidic teaching illustrates this higher love with the model of a small flame set beside a great fire. The flame incessantly pulls towards the fire, seeking to be drawn in and consumed by the fire's greater being. Were the flame's desire to be realized, it would cease to exist as a distinct entity; nonetheless, such is the nature of the flame. Similarly, "The soul of man is the lamp of G–d."[4] Although the basic nature of man is embodied by his "animal soul," whose every act and desire is motivated by an underlying drive for self-preservation and self-advancement (a nature it shares with every other creation), man also possesses another, higher self: a soul that is a "lamp of G‑d." This is his "G‑dly soul," a soul whose very "I" is defined as the desire to shed its identity and be nullified within its infinite source.

The Mitzvah

Man serves his Creator and his purpose in life by observing the *mitzvot* (divine commandments) of the Torah. On the most basic level, the mere fulfillment of a *mitzvah*, regardless of one's motivation in doing so, is an end in itself: the divine will has been implemented in the world; the physical existence has been involved in the realization of G‑d's desire, and has been refined and elevated in the process. Thus, G‑d's purpose in creation—that our world be transformed into a vehicle to express His all-pervading reality by serving as the instrument of His will[5]—has been brought that much closer to its ultimate fulfillment.

But simply going through the motions produces a flightless bird of a deed. The world has been changed, but not the doer. The effect of a *mitzvah* on the person who performs it is not a peripheral issue, but integral to its very function. The elevation of the human mind and heart is no less important a part of the divine objective in creation, than is the elevation of the physical world.

If the *mitzvah* of charity is the means by which a mundane coin is reoriented and elevated to serve a higher end, and if the *mitzvah* of *tefillin* does the same for a piece of leather and the *mitzvah* of *tzitzit* for a bit of wool, then the love and awe of G‑d with which these deeds are imbued are what uplift the soul of man, enabling it to transcend the confines of self and ego and connect to a higher reality.

But the soul of man does not lend itself to a single categorization or definition. It includes various dimensions of self and identity. This is why our emotional involvement in the fulfillment of the *mitzvot* should include both "love" and "fear," and their subdivisions "lower fear," "lower love," "higher love," and "higher fear" (in that order). For each of these levels corresponds to and involves another aspect of the human self.

Conquest and Redirection

As mentioned above, the "I" of man is a two-souled affair, consisting of an "animal soul" and a "G–dly soul." The animal soul is the essence of physical life; at its core is the drive for self-fulfillment and self-enhancement. The G–dly soul is the seat of all that is spiritual and transcendent in man; its "ego" (in diametric opposition to the usual sense of the word) gravitates to its Divine Source, striving to be nullified within the all-pervading reality of G–d.

In its initial, most unrefined state, the animal soul is blind to anything save its own existence and survival. It lacks even the minimal transcendence that is necessary in order to recognize a possibility for a greater and more beneficial state of being for itself. It desires only the pleasures of the here and now, only what gratifies its currently defined self.

On this level, the soul is incapable of love. Entrenched in the morass of self, the concept of extending to something outside of itself (even to its own ultimate benefit) is completely foreign to it. The only thing that sways it is a threat to its own well-being. So, if it is to possess any feeling at all in its service of its Creator, that feeling is fear of the most basic sort—the fear of punishment by a being more powerful than itself.

In attaining this level of "fear of G–d," the animal soul has taken its first step in the conquest and refinement of its ego. It has learned that although it may desire otherwise, it must yield to that which is greater than itself. Now, having gained control of its drives, it can proceed to redirect them by arousing itself to a "love of G–d."

The animal soul's love of G‑d is defined by the verse, "to love the Lord your G‑d... for He is your life."[6] The animal soul loves its own life; when it recognizes that "He is your life," that G‑d is the source and sustainer of its very being, the very same ego that craved the basest of pleasures is now drawn to attach itself to the Almighty, for it realizes that such an attachment would constitute the ultimate enhancement and perfection of self. It will thus sacrifice its present material expressions of selfhood for the promise of a higher and more fulfilled self. True, this is a love of the "lower," ego-motivated sort; yet it represents a tremendous transcendental leap for the intrinsically selfish animal within man.

Less Than Not

Man, however, possesses a potential for transcendence that goes beyond anything his animalistic, egocentric self is capable of. By cultivating and expressing the will of his G‑dly soul, he can experience the "higher love" of self-nullifying attachment to G‑d—the "candle flame" love described above.

However, even this higher love is tinged with self-interest, albeit a self-interest of infinite subtlety. For ultimately, this love represents the gratification of the G‑dly soul's ego—an ego unlike any other, but an ego nonetheless. Although its objective is self-nullification, this is what its nature calls for; this is what it *wants*.

But what if G‑d wants otherwise? What if G‑d desires not the soul's dissolution in ecstatic union with the Essence of All, but that it retain its identity and deal with the material world? That it occupy a physical body together with the animal soul, so that the three together form a single entity, the human being?

Even as the animal soul must develop into something higher, transcending the initial definitions of its nature, so must the G‑dly soul. It must graduate from its instinctive "higher love" to a truly self-negating "higher fear." It must learn to balance its yearning to merge with the Divine with a humbling awe that causes it to retreat back to its self and its mission.

In fact, the closer it comes to consummating its love, the more it is driven to recoil in fear. For the closer one approaches the divine truth, the more one recognizes how insignificant one's own spiritual attainments are in the shadow of the only truly meaningful way to relate to G–d: to fulfill His will.[7]

Slaves and Slaves

Our *mishnah* alludes to these four levels of love and fear: "Do not be as slaves," it states, "who serve their master for the sake of reward. Rather, be as slaves who serve their master not for the sake of reward. And the fear of Heaven should be upon you."

At first glance, our *mishnah* appears to contain two unrelated points: serve G–d without any ulterior motives, and fear G–d. Also, the part about not serving one's master for the sake of reward seems needlessly wordy and repetitious. But our sages constructed their words in such a way so as to contain many layers of meaning below their most literal surface. The same is true of the above *mishnah*; on a deeper level it enumerates the four basic drives that motivate the soul(s) of man:

a) *"Do not be as slaves"* is a reference to the initial "lower fear" which marks the very onset of man's spiritual journey: free yourself of the most debased slavery of all—the unconditional surrender to what is lowest and most confining in your own nature.

b) *"Who serve their master for the sake of reward"*—this is the animal soul transformed, its ego directed as the driving force in man's "lower" love for the Almighty. For it has come to recognize that there is no more rewarding life than a life of attachment to G–d.

c) To *"be as slaves who serve their master not for the sake of reward"* is to employ the nature of the G–dly soul and experience the "higher," self-negating love it possesses.

d) Finally, *"fear of heaven shall be upon you."* Attain a state of utter self-nullification, serving Him for *His* reasons, not for yours.

A true "fear of heaven" dictates that, ultimately, all these levels are equally important. True, they constitute four rungs of an ascending ladder of transcendence and attachment to G–d, but at the topmost rung nothing is significant save the selfless quest to do His will. From this vantage point, what is important is not their function as stepping stones to a higher perfection, but that each deals with and refines another element of the human persona and thus plays a crucial role in the fulfillment of the divine purpose in creation.[8]

---

(1) Ethics of the Fathers, *1:17. (2)* Shaloh *vol. I, pg. 249b;* Tanya, *chapter 38. (3)* Shaar HaYichudim, *chapter 11; see* Tanya, *chapter 40. (4)* Proverbs *20:27. (5) See* Essence and Expression, *on pg. 196, and* Debating Truth, *pgs. 274-281. (6)* Deuteronomy *30:20. (7) See* Staying Alive *on pg. 217. (8) Based on the talks of the Rebbe, Cheshvan 29, 5721 (November 19, 1960), Tammuz 23, 5737 (July 9, 1977) and on other occasions.*

MINDING THE CHILD

The Soul of a Metaphor

Assume for yourself a Master.

Ethics of the Fathers 1:6

And they believed in G–d and in Moses His servant.

Exodus 14:31

What was the nature of Israel's relationship to Moses? Moses, after all, was a human being. And yet, the Torah uses the very same word to connote Israel's belief in him and in the Almighty ("they believed in G–d and in Moses"). Indeed, the *Midrash* derives from this that "One who believes in Moses, believes in the Almighty; one who does not believe in Moses, does not believe in the Almighty(!)"[1]

The Talmud goes even further, applying the same to the sages and Torah authorities of all generations. On the verse, "To love the L–rd your G–d and to cleave to Him,"[2] it states: "Is it then possible to cleave to the Divine...? But whoever attaches himself to a Torah scholar, the Torah considers it as if he had attached himself to G–d...."[3]

The Awareness Factor

"So says G‑d: My firstborn child, Israel" (Exodus 4:22).

In what way is G‑d our "father"? There are, of course, the obvious parallels. G‑d created us and provides us with sustenance and direction. He loves us with the boundless, all-forgiving love of a father.

Chassidic teaching delves further into the metaphor. It examines the biological and psychological dynamics of the father-child model, and employs them to better understand our relationship to each other and to our Father in Heaven.

A microscopic bit of matter, originating in the father's body, triggers the generation of a life. In the mother's womb, a single cell develops into a brain, heart, eyes, ears, arms, legs, toenails; soon it emerges into the world to function as a thinking, feeling and achieving human being.

Physically, what began in the father's body and psyche is now a separate, distinct and (eventually) independent individual. But on a deeper level, the child remains inseparable from his begetter.

In the words of the Talmud, "A son is a limb of his father."[4] At the very heart of his consciousness lies an inescapable truth: he is his father's child, an extension of his being, a projection of his personality. In body, they have become two distinct entities; in essence they are one.

One may argue: Perhaps in the child's mind, the seat of his identity, the singularity of parent and offspring lives on. Here, the child's relationship with his father is sensed, here resides the recognition of their intrinsic oneness. But the brain is only one of the child's many organs and limbs. The rest of him may indeed stem from its ancestral source, but is now a wholly separate entity.

Obviously, this is not the case—any more than it would be correct to say that the eyes alone see or that "just" the mouth speaks. The component parts of the human being comprise a single, integrated whole; it is the *person* who sees, the *person* who speaks, the *person* who is aware. The toenail of the child, by virtue of its physical and neurological interconnection with the brain, is no less one with the father than is the brain itself, the organ which facilitates this oneness.

But what if the toenail, or any other limb of the body, severs its connection with the mind? This would cut it off from its own center of vitality and consciousness, and, as a result, also from its parental origins. In other words, the unity of all the child's limbs and organs with the father's essence is dependent upon their maintaining their connection with their own mind, a connection that imbues them all with the awareness of this unity.

The Body Israel

My firstborn child, Israel.

Israel, too, is comprised of many "organs" and "limbs." In each generation there are the great sages who devote their lives to assimilate the divine essence of Torah. These are the mind of Israel, whose entire being is permeated with the awareness of G–d's truth. Israel also has a heart, individuals whose lives exemplify compassion and piety, and hands, its great builders and achievers. Each and every individual, from the "Moses of the generation"[5] to the "ordinary" foot soldier, forms an integral part of the body of G–d's firstborn—each is equally "the limb of the father."

But, as with the physical father-child relationship, it is the mind of the child that cements his bond with his father. As long as the many organs and limbs of his body remain a single integrated whole, they are all equally the father's child. But it is only by virtue of their

Jack of All Trades

Said Rabbi Yosef Yitzchak of Lubavitch:
There are those who question the need of a mentor
to guide them through life. They claim that each
individual can forge his own relationship with
G-d unaided. They argue that since the Jewish faith rejects
the concept of an "intermediary" between man and G-d,
they have no use for mentor or master.
They fail to understand that the entire Jewish people
are a single entity; that every individual soul is, in truth,
but a limb or organ of the general soul of Israel.
Just as each limb and organ of the human body has its
function at which it excels, so, too, every soul has
its role and mission, as well as its limitations: the
"loftiest" of souls is dependent upon the "lowliest"
for the attainment of the single, unified goal. And were
any limb to strike out on its own, detaching
itself from the "head" which provides the entire body
with vitality and direction, the results
are self-understood.
When someone adapts the attitude that he can do
it all on his own, he reminds me of the story told
about the peasant and the *tefillin*. Once, a Jew noticed
a pair of *tefillin* in the house of a gentile peasant.
Upon seeing a holy object in such a place, he began to
inquire about the *tefillin*, wishing to purchase

> them from the peasant. The peasant, who had looted the *tefillin* at a recent pogrom, grew agitated and defensive. "What do you mean, where did I get them?" he blurted out, "Why, I made them myself! *I* am a shoemaker!"[6]

connection to their mind that they possess the awareness which makes their physically "detached" selves one with their source.

The same applies to the "body" that is Israel: it is our life-bond with our "mind" that both integrates us as a unified whole and facilitates our connection to our Creator and Source. True, a Jew cannot ever sever his bond with his G–d any more than even the lowliest "toenail" of the child's body can "choose" to go off on its own and undo its relationship with its father; but while we cannot change what we are, we *can* determine to what extent our identity as G–d's child will be expressed in our daily lives.

We can choose, G–d forbid, to disassociate ourselves from the leaders that G–d has implanted in our midst, thus banishing our relationship with Him to the subconscious cellar of our soul. Or, we can intensify our bond to the minds of Israel, thereby making our bond with the Almighty a tangible and vibrant reality.

---

(1) Mechilta on verse. (2) Deuteronomy 30:20. (3) Talmud, Ketuvot 111b. (4) Talmud, Eruvin 70b. (5) See Midrash Rabba, Bereishit 56:7; Tikkunei Zohar, 114a; Rashi's commentary on Talmud, Chulin 93a. (6) Based on an address by the Rebbe, Sivan 26, 5711 (June 30, 1951).

DOUBLE STANDARD

Judge every man to the side of merit.

Ethics of the Fathers 1:6

On the most elementary level, this means that if you discern a negative trait in your fellow or you see him commit a negative act, do not judge him guilty in your heart. "Do not judge your fellow until you are in his place," warns another of the *Ethics*' sayings, and his place is one place where you will never be. You have no way of truly appreciating the manner in which his inborn nature, his background and/or the circumstances that hold sway over his life have influenced his character and behavior.

However, this only explains why you should not judge your fellow guilty. Yet our *mishnah* goes further than this, enjoining us to "judge every man to the side of merit." This implies that we should see our fellow's deficiencies in a positive light. But what positive element is implied by a person's shortcomings and misdeeds?

Differently Equal

An explanation may be found in another talmudic saying: "Whoever is greater than his fellow, his inclination (for evil) is also greater"[1]—a rule crucial to our understanding of a fundamental principle of Torah, that man possesses "free choice" regarding his actions.

Indeed, how can we consider a person's choices to be free and uncoerced, when there is so much inequality in life? Can we compare the moral performance of an individual whose character was shaped by a loving family, a stable environment and a top-notch education with that of one who has experienced only rootlessness, violence and despair? Can we compare a person who has naturally and effortlessly been blessed with a superior mind and a compassionate heart to one who has not been so privileged? Are their choices equally "free"? Are they equally accountable for their actions?

The answer to the last two questions is "Yes." Certainly, no two human beings are alike. Each has been given a life that is unique to him alone, with his own individual array of challenges and tests on the one hand, and potentials and opportunities on the other. Free choice means that the Creator, who has created each individual and the circumstances of his life, has also fortified him with whatever resources are required for him to face his every moral challenge.

"Whoever is greater than his fellow, his inclination for evil is also greater." One who has been advantaged with superior talents and qualities must struggle against an inclination towards corruption and evil far more powerful than that which faces the more "average" individual. Conversely, one who has been subjected to a greater measure of setbacks and trials in his life, has been granted an equally greater measure of fortitude and achievement potential.

So if your fellow has committed a crime so despicable that you are incapable of even contemplating such a deed; if he is plagued by demons so horrendous that you can hardly envision such evil—know that he is undoubtedly in possession of a potential for good that far exceeds your own. Understand that while he has succumbed to forces far more powerful than anything which you will ever face, he is an invaluable human being, one whose inner resources, if cultivated, could translate into attainments unimaginable by one less inclined to evil.

In other words, look not to what he is but to what he can be. Dwell not on the way in which he has negatively expressed his potential, but on what this potential truly consists of.

A Single Exception

So judge every man to the side of merit—every man, that is, except yourself. For the attitude detailed above, while appropriate to adopt towards other human beings, would be nothing less than disastrous if applied to oneself.

"True, I have done nothing with my life," the potential-looking individual will argue. "But look at what I am capable of! Look at the quality of my mind, the sensitivity of my feelings, the tremendous talents I possess. It's all there within me, regardless of the fact that I have never bothered to realize any of it. This is the real me. The extent to which I actualize it is only of secondary importance."

In our judgment of human life and achievement, we must adopt a double standard. Our assessment of a fellow human being must always look beyond the actual to the potential reality within. On the other hand, we must measure our own worth in terms of our real and concrete achievements, and view the potential in ourselves as merely the means to this end.[2]

Rabbi Yosef Yitzchak of Lubavitch told:

When I was four years old, I asked my father:[3]
"Why did G-d make people with two eyes? Why not
with one eye, just as we have been given a single
nose and a single mouth?"
Said my father: "There are times when one must look with
a right eye, with affection and empathy, and times when one must
look with a left eye, severely and critically.
On one's fellow man, one should look with a right eye;
on oneself, one should look with a left eye."

---

(1) Talmud, Sukkah *52a. (2) Based on an address by the Rebbe,* Iyar 15, *5742 (May 8, 1982) (3) Rabbi Sholom DovBer Schneersohn (1860-1920), fifth rebbe of Chabad-Lubavitch.*

EVIL FRIEND, HOLY FOE

> Nitai the Arbelite would say: Distance yourself from a bad neighbor, [and] do not cleave to a wicked person.
>
> Ethics of the Fathers 1:7

On the surface, Nitai the Arbelite appears to be conveying a simple, if redundant, message: Stay away from bad people. In truth, however, a much deeper lesson is implicit in his words. In fact, a close examination of his phraseology yields an altogether different sentiment.

What is the difference between a "bad neighbor" and a "wicked person"? And why must one go so far as to "distance oneself" from the former, while, concerning the latter it is enough to avoid "cleaving" to him?

A "bad neighbor" means just that: not a bad person, but one whose proximity to yourself is detrimental to you. It may be that he is a righteous person, and that his path in life is, for him, most suitable and desirable; but if for you it is wrong and destructive, keep your distance.

On the other hand, a "wicked person" is not necessarily a bad neighbor if he is not in the position to influence you. From him you need not, and must not, distance yourself: on the contrary, befriend him, draw him close and help him improve himself, all the while taking care not to cleave to him and emulate *his* ways.

In other words: the evil in another is never cause for you to distance yourself from him—only your susceptibility to something in him that is evil for you. On the contrary, the "wickedness" of your fellow is all the more reason to become involved with him, and prevail upon him to cleave to the positive in yourself.[1]

---

(1) From an address by the Rebbe, Tammuz *21, 5723 (July 13, 1963).*

ULTERIOR MOTIVE

> Hillel would say: Be of the disciples of Aaron—a lover of peace, a pursuer of peace, one who loves his fellow creatures and draws them close to Torah.
>
> Ethics of the Fathers 1:12

"Love your fellow as yourself,"[1] never an easy task for the human heart, proves even more difficult when applied to one's "inferiors"—to those who are spiritually and morally lesser than oneself. How can one honestly perceive another as his equal when his fellow's character and behavior are so obviously corrupt? More specifically, throughout the ages a most divisive issue has been: How is a Jew to regard a fellow Jew who has strayed from the path of Torah?

In the first chapter of the *Ethics of the Fathers*, the great sage Hillel directs, "Love your fellow creatures and draw them close to Torah." "Creatures" (*beri'ot*) is the lowliest of the several Hebrew terms for "man"; it connotes the lowest common denominator of the human race—the fact that we are all G–d's creations. Says Hillel: Love also the creatures, also those whose only redeeming quality is that they are G–d's creations, and lovingly draw them to the ethos and ideals of Torah.

But Hillel's policy seems to raise more questions than it answers. What does it mean to "love G–d's creatures and draw them close to Torah"? Is this the unconditional love of tolerance and acceptance, or a love with an ulterior motive, albeit a most selfless and honorable motive? Is this "Love your fellow as yourself" or "love your fellow, so that you can turn him into yourself"?

A Chassid's Approach

Rabbi Schneur Zalman of Liadi, founder of Chabad Chassidism, applies Hillel's saying in the following manner:

Also those who are far from G–d's Torah and His service... one must draw them close with strong cords of love—perhaps one might succeed in bringing them to Torah and the service of G–d. And even if one fails, one has still merited the rewards of the fulfillment of the precept "Love your fellow."[2]

Yet also Rabbi Schneur Zalman's words require clarification—he seems to adopt *both* of these apparently conflicting definitions of "love." In his closing words, he clearly establishes that the precept of loving one's fellow exists independently and regardless of the positive influence it may bring: even if one's efforts accomplish nothing, one has still fulfilled the Torah's injunction to "Love your fellow." On the other hand, Rabbi Schneur Zalman writes that "one must draw them close with strong cords of love" *because* of the chance that "perhaps one might succeed in bringing them to Torah and the service of G–d"!

Uncompromising Compassion

"Be of the disciples of Aaron... who loves his fellow creatures and draws them close to Torah."
Draw them close to Torah—not *vice versa*. Reach out to your fellow man and help him attain the ultimately fulfilling life—a life guided by Torah—but do not think that you will do him a service if you bring the Torah closer to him. Do not think that you will make Torah more palatable to those still distant from it by carving and trimming it to conform to contemporary whims. On the contrary, a compromised version of its timeless truths will only repel anyone who seeks purpose and meaning in life.

On the other hand, Hillel stresses that "loving G-d's creatures" comes first and "drawing them close to Torah" second. Never should your objective, to enlighten and improve your fellow, be a prerequisite to your accepting him. Aaron's love was not motivated by his desire to influence his fellow. Rather, it was the other way around: because of his unconditional love for his fellows, he did everything within his power to fill their needs, both physical and spiritual.[8]

Who Is a Jew?

This apparent dichotomy in the nature of relations between Jew and Jew also appears in the words of our sages which describe the very definition of Jewishness and a Jew's relationship with G–d.

The Talmud states: "A Jew, although he has transgressed, is a Jew."[3] He may violate, G–d forbid, the entire Torah, yet his intrinsic bond with the Almighty is not affected. In the words of the *Midrash*, "Torah preceded the creation of the world... but the thought of Israel preceded all in the mind of G–d."[4]

At the same time, many verses and sayings in Torah imply that a Jew relates to G–d through—and only through—the Torah. In the words of the *Zohar*: "There are three connections that are bound to each other: G–d, the Torah, and Israel.... Israel binds itself with Torah, and Torah with G–d."[5]

Both are true. A Jew is a Jew is a Jew, no matter what. He enjoys an unequivocal relationship with the Almighty regardless of the extent to which he actualizes it in his daily behavior. But the *realization* of this relationship, the manner in which his physical being and daily life can be brought to reflect and actualize his quintessential self, is the Torah way of life.[6]

Furthermore, because a Torah life is the ultimate expression of what a Jew is, it cannot, and will not, remain suppressed indefinitely. Sooner or later, his true self will inevitably come to light.

So love him because of what he is, and love him because your love and concern may prove to be the impetus that will bring him to Torah—the two are one and the same.[7]

---

(1) Leviticus *19:18*. (2) Tanya, *chapter 32*. (3) Talmud, Sanhedrin *44a*. (4) Bereishit Rabba, *1:4*. (5) Zohar, *part III, 73a*. (6) *See* The Third Link *on pg. 34*. (7) *Based on an address by the Rebbe,* Nissan 26, 5727 *(May 6, 1967)*. (8) *Based on the talks of the Rebbe,* Sivan 9, 5723 *(June 1, 1963)* and second day of Shavuot, *5736 (June 5, 1976)*.

SUPER PHYSICS

> If I am not for myself, who is for me? And if I am only for myself, what am I?
>
> Ethics of the Fathers 1:14

The Talmud relates that the Ark in the *Beit Hamikdash* (Holy Temple) in Jerusalem, which held the Two Tablets inscribed with the Ten Commandments, possessed most unusual physical qualities. The Torah specifies the Ark's dimensions: "Two cubits and a half should be its length, a cubit and a half its breadth, and a cubit and a half its height."[1] Nevertheless, says the Talmud, the Ark did not occupy any of the space of the chamber that housed it. Miraculously, "The area of the Ark was not part of the measurement."[2]

What was the point of this amazing miracle?

Man, in his quest to better himself, is forever faced with a dilemma. Should he strive to break free of his nature and its limitations? Or, is it preferable to work within the parameters of his natural self, to make the most of what he is?

Each goal has its advantages and shortcomings. It would seem that to attain perfection man must reach beyond what he is, as every individual has his inherent limits and deficiencies. Yet lofty, spiritual "experiences" often remain outside of a person's reality, failing to translate into anything tangible in his daily life.

The Ark's "physics" teach us that the two goals are not mutually exclusive. The Ark transcended the spatial, yet retained all of its qualities. In the same way, no matter how high a person reaches, his attainments always can, and must, be made part of his pedestrian, human self.

A life lived according to Torah (which the Ark, container of the Ten Commandments, represents) enables man to reach beyond the confines and dictates of his physical environment and society. At the same time, it insists that he make this greater reality *his* reality — that it become an integral part of his own nature, character and everyday behavior.[3]

---

(1) Exodus 25:10. A cubit is approximately 20 inches. (2) Talmud, Yoma, 21a. (3) Based on an address by the Rebbe, Nissan 29, 5751 (April 13, 1991).

11:59:59

If not now, when?

Ethics of the Fathers 1:14

"**O**ur world is a banquet," proclaims the Talmud. "Grab and eat, grab and drink."[1]

Those who arrived during the early hours of the banquet went about their feasting and dining in a most professional and methodical manner. First, they sampled the appetizers—just enough, mind you, to properly whet their appetites. They then proceeded up the ladder of courses and wines, carefully negotiating their way to gastronomic satisfaction par excellence.

But what of the group who arrived a few scant minutes before midnight, the hour when the tables were to be cleared, the chairs stacked and the doors bolted shut? For them to attempt to follow the course outlined by the intricate rules of dinner etiquette would only guarantee that the doors would slam on their empty stomachs. "Just grab!" we tell them. Grab meat, salads, soup, wine and fish—never mind the order and proportion. It's a race against the clock: Grab and eat, grab and drink....

In earlier generations, there was a well-defined "Standard Operating Procedure" for those who consulted the Torah's spiritual menu for the banquet of life. No one, for example, would have ventured to sample the esoteric wine of creation's secrets before filling his belly with the "meat and potatoes" of Talmud and *halacha*.[2] No one would have been so presumptuous as to believe that he could refine his nature and character before he had perfected his behavior and made his every act, word and thought utterly conform to Torah's directives.

All this, however, was a luxury of generations bygone. Today, we are rapidly approaching the climax of history—the day when Moshiach will herald a new era of goodness and perfection, yet will also bring down the curtain on the struggles and attainments that stem from our currently imperfect state. So grab! Grab another *mitzvah*, master another, yet deeper, facet of Torah. Never mind the "Standard Operating Procedure"—strive for the ultimate, now.[3]

---

(1) Talmud, Eruvin 54a. (2) Jewish Law. (3) Based on a letter by the Rebbe, Kislev 5, 5717 (November 9, 1956).

A THING OF SILENCE

[Rabban Gamliel's] son, Shimon, would say: All my life I have been raised among the wise, and I have found nothing better for the body than silence.

Ethics of the Fathers 1:17

The Talmud goes even further, with the amazing statement: "What is man's task in the world? To make himself as silent as the dumb."[1] Obviously, one can think of many cases in which silence is advisable. But is there no greater virtue? And is this indeed the purpose of life?

Essentially, the world is words—divine words. "G–d said: 'Let there be light!' and there was light." G–d said: "May there be a firmament..." "May the waters gather..." "May the earth sprout forth...,"[2] and our world, in all its infinite variety and complexity, came into being. As chassidic teaching explains, these divine utterances not only caused these creations to materialize; they were, and continue to be, the very stuff of their existence. What we experience as physical light is, in truth, G–d's articulation of His desire that there be light. Grass is our physical perception of the divine words "May the earth sprout forth greenery." And so on.[3]

Obviously, what emanated from G–d's "mouth" was not a "voice" in any human or physical sense. The Torah uses terms from our experience so that by delving into their significance we can learn something of how G–d relates to our existence. In our case, the Torah wishes to describe an existence which, on the one hand, is distinct from its source, yet on the other, is utterly dependent upon it and possesses no reality other than that dependence. This is the significance of the metaphor "speech" in regard to creation.

When a person speaks, he creates something that extends beyond his own being. The thought that he had conceived, and which, up until now, has existed only within his mind, is now translated into words that depart his person to attain an existence distinct from his. Nevertheless, they are utterly dependent upon him for existence: the moment he ceases to speak, the entity we refer to as his "speech" no longer exists. In other words, their existence can only be defined in terms of his ongoing involvement to create them.

So it is with the world. On the one hand, G–d desired that a world *exist*, that it constitute a reality that (at least in its own perception) is distinct from His. On the other hand, the world has no independent existence, possessing no reality other than G–d's constant involvement to create and sustain it. What model have we, in the human experience of reality, for such an entity? Speech. So what is the world? The closest we can come to answering this question in humanly comprehensible terms is to say: The world is G–d speaking.

There is, however, a single exception to this model for the essential nature of all created things: the soul of man. Every single creation is described by the Torah as having come into being by a divine utterance, except for the soul. The *Zohar* explains that the soul is not a divine word, but a G–dly thought.[4]

Referring to the above interpretation of the metaphor of speech, this means that the soul is a creation which does not "depart" from the all-pervading reality of G–d: a creation that not only senses its total dependence upon its source (as, deep down, every creation does), but one that does not even see itself as an "entity" distinct from its Creator.

Alone in a verbose world, the soul of man is a thing of silence. And its mission in life is to impart this silence to the world about it.[5]

---

(1) Talmud, Chulin *89a*. *(2)* Genesis *1*. *(3) See* Words and Names *on pg. 222*. *(4)* Zohar, *part II, 119a;* Ohr Torah *(by Rabbi DovBer of Mezeritch), 2c;* Tanya, *chapter 2. (5) Based on an address by the Rebbe,* Nissan 24, 5719 *(May 2, 1959).*

WOOD SUBMERGED IN STONE

Joseph, Judah and the Servant King

The essential thing is not study, but deed.

Ethics of the Fathers 1:17

The Talmud relates: *Rabbi Tarfon and the sages were assembled on the second floor of the Nitzah House in Lod, when the query came before them: "Which is greater, learning or deed?" Said Rabbi Tarfon: "Deed is greater." Said Rabbi Akiva: "Learning is greater." Concluded all: "Learning is greater, because learning brings to deed."*[1]

So it seems that deed, after all, is the more important element of man's mission in life. Learning may take precedence, but only because one must first learn what to do and how to do it.

But several ambiguities remain. Does this mean that there is no intrinsic difference between the views voiced by Rabbi Tarfon and Rabbi Akiva? And if the conclusion reached by the assembled sages is that, ultimately, doing is more important than learning, why express this in a statement that begins with the words "Learning is greater"? Would it not have been more appropriate to say "Deed is greater, because learning brings to deed"?

Growth and Abnegation

Learning involves the development and perfection of self, while doing entails the servitude of self to the task at hand. So the question presented to the sages assembled in Lod can be phrased in different terms: What should a person strive for—personal growth, or the abnegation of self in the commitment to a higher ideal? Why was man created—to better himself or to serve his Creator?

Man was created to serve his Creator. But in order to do he must learn, and in order to serve he must grow. For not only was man created to serve the Almighty, but everything about him exists only to this end. If man has a mind, a heart, a will, and a faculty for pleasure, then the service desired of him is not a robot-like servitude of the hands and feet. To properly serve G-d he must grow to understand, experience, desire and enjoy his mission in life.

This explains the statement "Learning is greater, because learning brings to deed." Indeed, the underlying truth of life is that man exists only to serve his Creator. This is the foundation and purpose of all. But, as the chassidic saying goes, "the foundation is buried in the ground"—the nature of foundations is that they are submerged and invisible. What is the visible edifice of life? Learning, growth, self-improvement—an endeavor which underscores and develops, rather than abnegates, a person's ego, ambitions, faculties and talents. So although our ultimate commitment is to deed and self-nullification, the "greater" and more emphasized element of our lives—at least in the initial stages of our spiritual development—is the quest for perfection.

Such is the nature of the *quest* for perfection, which is the prominent feature of our currently defined lives. But what about the individual who does attain this perfection? For him, the very opposite is true. The dominant element of his life is "deed," the selfless service of the Almighty. True, his "self" and its various faculties are also employed—he serves his Creator also with his mind and heart—but these are completely "submerged" in his doing. What he understands and experiences is not the issue. What concerns him is only that the ultimate purpose of creation be realized. His life affirms the unequivocal supremacy of deed voiced by Rabbi Tarfon: his ego is utterly nullified before the imperative to do and serve.

These two scenarios express not only the difference between the self-perfecting and the self-perfected individual, they also describe two distinct stages in the development of humanity and creation as a whole. To our currently imperfect existence applies Rabbi Akiva's statement that "Learning is greater." True, we know that this is not an end in itself, that the purpose of "learning" is that it "bring to deed"; but personal growth remains at the fore of our life's work.

In the era of Moshiach, however, when evil and ignorance will cease and our potential for goodness and perfection will be realized, the deed will be paramount. This is not to say that man will become a mindless robot; on the contrary, our understanding and appreciation of the divine reality will be infinitely greater than anything conceivable today. Yet we will not relate to our intellectual and emotional experiences as "achievements." Everything will be an act of divine service, simply another way in which to realize G–d's will. Then, Rabbi Tarfon's vision of life will hold sway: "Deed is greater."[2]

The Model Home

Two structures, the first built largely of wood and the second primarily of stone, embody these two phases of man's mission in life.

"They shall make for Me a Sanctuary, and I shall dwell within them."[3] According to chassidic teaching, these words express the divine purpose in creation: G–d created the world because, in the words of the *Midrash*, "He desired a dwelling within the lowly (i.e, the physical) existence."[4]

On the individual level, this is achieved when man performs the *mitzvot* of the Torah, utilizing the various elements of the physical world to serve the Almighty. Physical money is given to charity. Grain is made into *matzoh* for Passover, animal hide into *tefillin*, wool into *tzitzit*, and so on. Furthermore, when a person devotes his life to the fulfillment of the *mitzvot*, everything which supports this life—the food he eats, the clothes he wears, the energy he consumes—is involved in the realization of the supernal goal.

Thus the physical reality becomes a "dwelling" for G–d. Instead of the "lowliness" which previously defined its relationship to its Creator (for the physical world, with its apparent independence and concreteness of being, can be the greatest concealment of the divine truth), it is now transformed into a "home" for G–d, an environment that serves His will and expresses His all-pervading reality.[5]

On the communal level, the Jewish people built a "home" for G–d in the form of the Sanctuary. By the command of G–d, various materials were used to construct an edifice to serve as the focus of G–d's manifest presence in the physical world. Although G–d is equally everywhere, this was the place where He chose to visibly permeate the material; this was a "dwelling" that represented the ultimate function of every physical thing.

And just as there exist two phases in the life's work of man, so it is with the collective expression of humanity's mission, the Sanctuary.

First there was the *Mishkan*, the temporary, portable Sanctuary that the Jewish people carried in their wanderings through the Sinai Desert. Then, when Israel had finally settled and established themselves in the Holy Land, the permanent *Beit Hamikdash* was built on the Temple Mount in Jerusalem.

The difference can be seen in the construction. The *Mishkan* had an earthen floor, atop which were placed heavy foundation-sockets of silver. Into these sockets were set the wall sections, made of gold-covered cedar wood. The roof consisted of three layers of tent-coverings: tapestries of wool and goat-hair, and a covering of animal hides.

The *Beit Hamikdash*, however, was made almost entirely of earth and stone, from its marble floor to its mortar roof. The *Beit Hamikdash* did include some wood, in the form of support beams, but these were imbedded within the stone and cement. In fact, it was specifically forbidden for even the smallest bit of wood to protrude and be visible.

Thus, the *Mishkan* included both inanimate minerals (earth, silver, etc.) and the products of plant and animal life: the ground and foundation being of the former, the walls and roof consisting primarily of the latter. On the other hand, the *Beit Hamikdash* was built almost exclusively of inorganic materials; the little wood it did contain was secondary and supportive in function, and completely covered up by the stone.

In the "small world" that is man,[6] the inanimate element is our capacity for self-negation ("May my soul be as dust to all"[7])—our capacity for devotion, servitude and deed. Plant and animal life are representative of the capacity for growth and development, of our emotional and intellectual life.

Thus in the *Mishkan*, which represents the initial stages of our mission in life, all these elements are visibly stressed. In fact, the emphasis is on the "higher" faculties of man. True, everything rests upon the foundation of servitude to the divine will, but the edifice which is built on this foundation is the development and realization of human potential.

Ultimately, however, we grow to visibly exemplify the purpose of it all—to serve the Creator. The *Beit Hamikdash*, too, contains elements of growth, but growth of an utterly egoless nature: a growth that is submerged within self-negation, a growth that is solely an instrument to better fulfill G–d's will. In the entire edifice, from top to bottom, one sees only the "stone" and "dust" of deed.

The Historical Rift

Historically, these two aspects of man's mission in life are represented by two different, and often conflicting, parties in the Jewish people.

In the founding family of the Jewish nation, there already existed this dichotomy in the persons of Joseph and Judah. Joseph exemplified learning and self-improvement, while Judah was the epitome of self-sacrifice and self-effacement. Their very names convey their differing natures: Joseph (*Yosef* in Hebrew) means to "add on," Judah (*Yehudah*) to "submit."

Initially, Joseph's brothers, led by Judah, rejected him. But then Judah conceded to Joseph,[8] acknowledging not only the necessity of the growth which Joseph represents but also Joseph's more dominant role in the initial stages of Israel's development.

But later in history, the schism between Joseph and Judah reappeared. While Joseph was the uncontested leader of his brothers in Egypt, and descendants of Joseph (Joshua and Gideon) led the people of Israel during the initial stages of their conquest and settlement of the Holy Land, the predominance of Judah was firmly established with the crowning of David as the king of Israel. But a descendant of Joseph, Jeroboam, refused to accept the sovereignty of the royal house of David. After the death of David's son, Solomon, Jeroboam led a mutiny against the Davidic dynasty and established himself as king in the northern part of the Holy Land. For the next three centuries the Jewish people were split into two kingdoms: Judah in the south, and the Joseph-dominated kingdom of Israel in the north.

The deeper significance of this rift was the unreadiness of the "personal growth" element, represented by Joseph, to yield to the "servitude" of Judah[9]—as Judah, centuries earlier, had acknowledged the predominance of "Joseph" in the initial stages of Israel's mission. In other words, Israel was not yet ready for the ultimate realization of its mission—utterly selfless service of G–d.[10] The resolution of this rift is the key for the ultimate redemption of Moshiach and the perfection of the world in the harmonious service of its Creator.

It is therefore most appropriate that, on the same Shabbat in which the Torah section[11] which describes Judah's approach to and reconciliation with Joseph is read, we also read a section of the Prophets which describes the ultimate reunion of the two, this time with Joseph's acknowledgment of Judah's sovereignty and leadership. Here, the basis of Judah's right to the kingship is also emphasized: because he is G–d's *servant*, he is the eternal leader of Israel. In the words of the prophet Ezekiel:[12]

And the word of G–d came to me, saying: Son of man! Take one stick and write upon it "For Judah, and for the children of Israel his companions"; and take another stick and write upon it "For Joseph, the stick of Ephraim and for the house of Israel his companions."

And join them one to the other to make one stick, and they shall become one in your hand....

Behold, I will take the children of Israel from among the nations into which they have gone, and I shall gather them from all around and I shall bring them to their land. I will make them into one nation in the land, in the mountains of Israel, and a single king shall be over them all; no longer shall they be two nations, no longer shall they be divided into two kingdoms....

And My servant David shall be king over them, and they shall all have a single shepherd. They will follow My laws and observe My statutes and do them.... and David My servant shall be their prince forever.[13]

---

(1) Talmud, Kiddushin *40b. (2) This reflects Rabbi Akiva's membership in the House of Hillel, whose opinions we follow today, and Rabbi Tarfon's membership in the House of Shammai, the school of Torah thought and law that will hold sway in the Messianic Era (see* Midrash Shmuel *commentary on the* Ethics *5:17). (3)* Exodus *25:8. (4)* Midrash Tanchuma, Naso *16;* Tanya, Chapter *36. (5) Cf. the truism quoted by German-Jewish author Moritz Alsberg, "The dwelling provides an instrument for measuring the degree of civilization a people has attained" (*Die Gesunde Wohnung, *1866). (6)* Midrash Tanchuma, Pikudei *3. (7) From the daily prayers, conclusion of the* Amidah. *(8) See the various* Midrashim *regarding Joseph's persecution by his brothers and the confrontation between Judah and Joseph in Egypt, particularly Judah's approach to Joseph related in* Genesis *44:18. (9) "G–d Himself grabbed Jeroboam by the robe and said to him: 'Repent, and I, you and the Son of Jesse (King David) will stroll together in the Garden of Eden.' Asked Jeroboam, 'Who will walk first?' 'The Son of Jesse,' (answered G–d. Said Jeroboam,) 'If so, I am not interested'" (*Talmud, Sanhedrin *102a). (10) The "Joseph" and "Judah" phases are closely interre-*

lated with the Mishkan *and* Beit Hamikdash *periods. Until the descendants of Judah ascended the throne, the* Mishkan *continued to serve as Israel's spiritual epicenter. And for most of the four centuries from the time that the Jewish people entered the Holy Land until the* Beit Hamikdash *was built, the* Mishkan *stood at Shiloh, in the territory of the tribe of Joseph. It was David, the first Judaic King, who dug the foundations for the* Beit Hamikdash, *and his son, Solomon, who built it. And it was the split between Judah and Joseph/Israel which ultimately led to its destruction. (There was, however, a marked difference between the* Mishkan *which accompanied Israel in the desert and the one which stood at* Shiloh: *in Shiloh, the wooden wall sections were replaced by walls of stone, though the woolen and animal-skin roof remained. This would signify an intermediate stage between the almost completely growth-oriented* Mishkan *of the desert, and the utter servitude and self-abnegation represented by the* Beit Hamikdash.*) (11)* Vayigash (Genesis 44-47). *(12)* Ezekiel 37. *(13) Based on the talks of the Rebbe,* Tevet 7, 5732 *(December 25, 1971); Shavuot 5742 (May 29, 1982); and* Tevet 9, 5746 *(December 21, 1985).*

ON THE ESSENCE OF THE *ETHICS*

Rabbi (Judah HaNassi) would say: Which is the right path for man to choose for himself? Whatever is harmonious for the one who does it, and harmonious for mankind.

Ethics of the Fathers 2:1

[Rabban Gamliel the son of Rabbi Judah HaNassi would say:] Make that His will should be your will, so that He will make your will to be as His....

Ethics of the Fathers 2:4

On the surface, Rabbi Judah HaNassi's statement appears to go against the grain of the rest of the *Ethics* and, indeed, the essence of Judaism itself.

Simply stated, the basis of the Jewish faith is the belief that the Torah is G–d's blueprint for existence. In the words of the *Midrash*, "An architect who builds a palace does not do so on his own. He has scrolls and notebooks which he consults on how to place the rooms, where to set the doors. So it was with G–d: He looked into the Torah and created the world."[1]

Furthermore, G–d did not complete His "palace" in the initial six days of creation; all He did was to provide the raw material which man, His "partner in creation," is to develop in accordance with the vision contained in the "scrolls and notebooks."[2] At Sinai, the Architect (G–d) delivered His plans to his contractors (man); He imparted His concept of reality (the Torah) to those whom He had charged to implement it in His creation.

So how can Rabbi Judah say that the "correct path" is defined by "whatever is harmonious for the one who does it, and harmonious for mankind"? Imagine the worker who consults the original state of his materials rather than the architect's plan. "The blueprint calls for a square plank," he muses, "but the log I have is round. Perhaps we can edit the plans a little?" This is what man is doing when he refers to the "way things are" in his own nature, in society or in the world at large for guidance as to how to live his life. Indeed, why labor to change the world if we can conform our moral vision to it?

To the Jew, the "correct path for man to choose" is determined by the divine revelation at Sinai, not by what is comfortable or what goes down well in the prevailing moral climate. To be a partner in creation means that one must, at times, contest the opinion polls as well as one's own nature.

This is why the *Ethics*, which is the Talmud's summarization of the Jew's moral philosophy, opens with the words, "Moses received the Torah from (G-d at) Sinai." Morality, for the Jew, is not the product of man's subjective thinking, but of divine revelation.

So how are we to understand the opening words of the *Ethics'* second chapter?

Within the Line

The answer is: by understanding its place in the Talmud, which incorporates the entire body of Torah law in its sixty-three tractates.

Sixty-two of them deal with the dos and don'ts of life, instructing the Jew how to pray and how to study, how to eat and how to marry, how to observe Shabbat, bury his dead, punish criminals, conduct his business, and so on. The single exception is the *Ethics of the Fathers*, which discusses not the law (*din*) but the area defined as *lifnim mishurat ha-din*—that which is "within the line of the law." "One who wishes to be a *chassid* (pious individual)," says the Talmud, "should study the *Ethics of the Fathers*."[3]

What does it mean to act "within the line of the law"?

On the most basic level, it means going beyond the law's minimum requirements. If the laws of charity mandate that one set aside ten percent of his earnings for the needy, the "pious individual" gives more. He has stricter standards of *kashrut*, dons a higher quality pair of *tefillin* and devotes more time to Torah study than the laws of the Torah require of him.

On a deeper level, the *chassid* is one who goes "within" the parameters of the law in the literal sense: He strives to perfect not only his behavior but also his internal self, his very mind-set and character.

The "letter" of Torah law deals primarily with the conduct, rather than the nature, of man. There is no law that obligates us to be of a generous disposition—only that we actually share our resources with the needy. Nowhere does the Torah demand of us to be revolted by the taste of pork—only that we refrain from eating it. The practitioner of the *Ethics*, however, is one who does not suffice with making his behavior conform to the Torah's directives. He insists that all of him, his outlook, his desires, his feelings—indeed, the very essence of his character—be permeated with the vision contained in the divine blueprint for life.[4]

Precedent at Sinai

Obviously, this represents a more advanced phase in a person's efforts to realize his partnership with G–d in creation. His first objective must be to actually fulfill the directives of the Torah. For man to seek to transform his nature without having first disciplined his behavior is as futile an endeavor as the attempt to train an unbridled horse or to draw energy from an undammed river. First, the "animal" in man must be reined in and controlled. Only then can it be refined and sublimated.

The way we originally committed ourselves to our "partnership" with the Almighty also included both these stages. When we first arrived at Sinai and were told of G–d's desire to give us the Torah, "The entire nation answered together, and said: 'All that G–d has spoken, we will do.'"[5] Several days later, after a period of intense preparation, we reiterated this commitment; this time we said, "All that G–d has spoken, we will do and we will comprehend."[6]

This is how we are to approach Torah. The foundation of the "partnership" must be an unequivocal "we will do." Only then can we proceed to internalize what is already ingrained in our behavior. Only then can we hope to transform the basic drives of our soul so that G–d's will is not only what we actually do but also what we *desire* to do with every fiber of our being.[7]

Chapter Two

Thus, the first chapter of the *Ethics* begins with the words "Moses received the Torah from Sinai." Not "discovered," not "chose," not "learned," but "received"—the basis of Torah being the unequivocal acceptance of and commitment to the divine plan for life on earth.

Chapter *Two*, however, opens with a second, deeper realization of G‑d's purpose in creation: that man himself *choose* the correct path. That his fulfillment of the Torah's commandments be not only an act of submission to the divine will, but also something that is harmoniously consistent with his nature. In the words of Rabbi Judah HaNassi's son, Rabban Gamliel, quoted further along in the chapter, "Make that His will should be your will."

Furthermore, we must not suffice with the transformation of self. We must seek to influence our surroundings, so that the very conscience and character of society come to embody the divine ideal. When the "correct path" of Torah is made to be both "harmonious for the one who does it" as well as "harmonious for mankind," then G‑d and man's joint project of creation will be complete.[8]

Margin of Profit

Other than the question of which comes first, there is another important difference between the external body of the law and its "within" element. Every individual has been given the ability to control and regulate his behavior. If G‑d demands this of us, He has fortified us with whatever it takes to achieve it. Circumstances may, at times, be beyond a person's control; but how he conducts himself in the face of them is entirely a matter of choice and volition.

On the other hand, the ability to transform our character is not necessarily inherent to us; indeed, this is why its achievement is not obligatory. In other words, the choice to *act* in accordance with G‑d's will is in our hands; but to mold our will to be utterly consistent with G‑d's is something that is beyond man's "natural" capacity.

On the Essence of the Ethics

Nevertheless, a *chassid* is one who refuses to settle with what is natural and expected. He wants more, more than the realization of his natural potential, more than to provide the Creator with the "expected" return on His investment in human life. So he toils to transform his inner self, in the hope that his efforts will induce the Almighty to grant him the spiritual resources with which to attain internal as well as behavioral perfection.

In the words of Rabbi Schneur Zalman of Liadi: "Habit reigns supreme in any sphere and becomes second nature. So if one accustoms himself to despise evil, it will, to some extent, become despicable in truth; likewise, if one accustoms himself to gladden his heart in G–d through reflection upon His greatness, his self impulsion will bring on inspiration from On High. If he pursues this path, perhaps a spirit from above will descend upon him and imbue him with the soul of a wholly righteous individual (*tzaddik*)."[9]

This explains the meaning of Rabban Gamliel's words, *"Make that His will should be your will, so that He will make your will to be as His,"* which, at first glance, seems both redundant and contradictory. If it is we who make His will ours, why must G–d subsequently do this for us?

Ultimately, however, this is not something we can do on our own. We can strive for this ideal and we can make significant gains toward its achievement, but in the end, a truly perfected inner self is a gift from Above. So do your utmost to "make that His will should be your will," and the Almighty will respond to your efforts and "make your will to be as His."[10]

(1) Midrash Rabba, Bereishit *1:2*. *(2)* Talmud, Shabbat *119b;* Midrash Rabba, Bereishit *11:7 (see* Etz Yosef *commentary,* ibid.). *(3)* Talmud, Bava Kama *30a*. *(4) See* Absolute Relativity *on pg. 49 (final part of essay) and* Three Times Three *on pg. 137. This is not to say that the* Torah *does not enjoin man to improve his character. Several* mitzvot—*such as the commandment to love G–d, to fear Him, to emulate His ways ("As He is merciful, you, too, are to be merciful; as He is benevolent, you, too, are to be benevolent...."), to love one's fellow as oneself—are addressed to the human heart. Nevertheless, the mandatory element of these* mitzvot *is to do the things which lead to the development of these feelings and traits: to comprehend and meditate upon those ideas which inspire the love and fear of the Almighty, to cultivate positive character traits by consistently acting in a merciful and compassionate manner, and so on. Nowhere does the* Torah *obligate man to transform his basic will. So also, one who must constantly battle his nature to observe the* mitzvot *fulfills every requirement of the "letter" of the law. (5)* Exodus *19:8. (6)* Exodus *24:7. (7) See, however, 11:59:59 on pg. 83. (8) Based on an address by the Rebbe,* Iyar *6, 5748 (April 23, 1988). (9)* Tanya, *chapter 14. In this way, Rabbi Schneur Zalman also explains the significance of the oath administered to the soul prior to its descent into physical life: "Be righteous; do not be wicked"* (Talmud, Niddah *30b). Why the double oath? But there are two separate aspects to a soul's mission in life. "Do not be wicked" is the obligatory, and attainable, endeavor to fulfill, in thought, speech and action, all that G–d has commanded. But the soul is also enjoined to "be righteous"—to also strive to transform its character and essence. (10) Based on an address by the Rebbe,* Iyar *3, 5747 (May 2, 1987).*

ON THE ESSENCE OF THE *MITZVAH*

Commanding, Connection and Refining Deed

> Be as careful with a minor *mitzvah* as with a major one, for you cannot know the rewards of the *mitzvot*.
>
> Ethics of the Fathers 2:1

On the surface, the *mishnah*'s point seems simple enough: do not weigh and categorize G–d's commandments. But upon closer examination, its words seem fraught with ambiguity and contradiction.

Are there or are there not differences between *mitzvot*? The *mishnah* seems to say that there aren't, but it uses the terms "minor" and "major" (*kaloh* and *chamurah*[1])—*mitzvah* categorizations which are used in the Talmud and its commentaries and the various codes of Torah law.

For Torah itself differentiates between *mitzvot*. For example, a leading indicator of the "severity" of a *mitzvah* is the punishment prescribed for its transgression: a penalty of death, *karet* ("a cutting off" of the soul), lashes, a monetary fine, the bringing of a sin-offering to the Holy Temple, etc. Indeed, since these punishments were rarely carried out by an earthly court of law (the conditions the Torah sets for their execution[2] virtually precluded this from ever happening), their main function seems to be to establish the relative values of *mitzvot*. Hence, we know that the observance of Shabbat (whose violation is a capital offense) is "greater" than that of circumcision (whose neglect warrants *karet*), and that an even more "minor" *mitzvah* is the obligation to fence in one's roof (the transgression of which carries a penalty of lashes).[3] These differences also have pragmatic implications, as the severity of a *mitzvah* is often a factor in deciding a question of Torah law.

So when the *mishnah* speaks of "major" and "minor" *mitzvot* it does not mean *mitzvot* that are wrongly considered to be greater or lesser than others; it is referring to their true, Torah-defined status. And yet, in the same breath, it tells us that one should be equally diligent in them all because we "cannot know the rewards of the *mitzvot*"!

One Is All

Furthermore, our sages tell us that G‑d's *mitzvot* all share a singular essence.

It is for this reason that the Talmud rules that "One who is preoccupied with a *mitzvah* is absolved from the obligation of another *mitzvah*."[4] For example, if a person is ministering to the sick during the festival of *Sukkot*, he need not step into a *sukkah* to eat his meals. Since he is already actively performing a *mitzvah*, he need not interrupt it, even for a few minutes, in order to fulfill another.

On the Essence of the Mitzvah

This applies to any two *mitzvot*, regardless of their (apparent) greatness or marginality—*any mitzvah* can take the place of any other! This is because the *mitzvot* are all but the various expressions of a singular essence.[5]

According to this, when our *mishnah* states that we "cannot know the rewards of the *mitzvot*" it does not mean (as we might perhaps have understood it) that we must treat them all with equal reverence *as if* they were all equal, since we cannot presume to know their true value in relation to each other. No—it means that their relative value is intrinsically unknowable, since, in essence, they are all of equal significance.[6]

This even further intensifies the apparent contradiction in our *mishnah*: How can we speak of "major" and "minor" *mitzvot* if the ultimate significance of one *mitzvah* is the same as that of all others?

The Commanding Connection

What is a *mitzvah*? The word means "commandment": Do this, says G–d, and don't do that. Observe Shabbat, give charity, eat *matzah* on Passover. Do not murder, do not steal, do not commit adultery, do not eat cheeseburgers.

But why does G–d care? Can anything we do or refrain from doing affect Him in any way? Can man, finite, mortal and deficient, do or undo something for the paragon of infinity and perfection?

This brings us to another meaning of the word *mitzvah*—"connection."

In commanding us a *mitzvah*, G–d has established that a certain deed constitutes the fulfillment of His will. Strictly speaking, one cannot attribute the phenomenon of "will" or "desire" to G–d, since nothing can contribute to or detract from His perfection. But He wanted to extend Himself to us, to enable us to relate to Him—something that no human endeavor can achieve on its own. So He willed Himself a will; He communicated to man a set of directives which He deemed to constitute His want and desire. He chose to command the *mitzvot* to serve as the vehicle by which we may establish a relationship and connection with Him.

Perfecting Path, Refining Word

But why these particular *mitzvot*? If the entire point of the *mitzvah* is that a human act should become an instrument of the divine will and thereby connect its performer to the Almighty, then any commandment would achieve the same end. What difference does it make *what* G–d commands us to do?

Does this mean that the 613 commandments of the Torah are completely arbitrary? That there could just as well have been 6,000 *mitzvot* or a single *mitzvah*? That we could just as well have been commanded to steal from the poor, rest on Tuesday and eat spinach on Yom Kippur?

Our sages address this issue in the *Midrash*:[7] *"G–d, His way is perfect, the word of G–d is refined...."*[8] *Said Rav: The* mitzvot *were given in order to refine the human being. For what does G–d care if one slaughters (an animal) from the throat or one slaughters from the nape? But the* mitzvot *were given in order to refine the human being.*

In other words, there are two dimensions to the *mitzvot*. On the most basic level, a *mitzvah*, by virtue of its being commanded by the Almighty, binds its performer (as well as the resources which he utilizes in its performance) to its Commander. In this, all *mitzvot* are indeed equal. A *mitzvah* that takes tremendous sacrifice and many years of spiritual development to fulfill, connects us to G–d no more than one which is observed with a single, effortless act.

In the words of Rabbi Schneur Zalman of Liadi, "Had we been commanded to chop wood," we would do it with the same joy and enthusiasm with which we perform the most spiritually gratifying *mitzvot*.[9] For the ultimate significance of the *mitzvot*—that they enable man to connect and relate to his Creator—would be no less realized in the most mundane and mechanical deed—if such was the divine command.

But G–d did more. He not only opened a channel into our lives by which we may connect to Him, He also made this path a "perfect way," a way of life which improves and perfects those who travel it. His word not only conveys His will and command, it is also a "refined" word—a word that refines those who heed it.

This is the second, specific dimension of the *mitzvah*. When we give charity, we not only fulfill a divine command, we also develop in ourselves a sensitivity to the needs of others and learn the proper perspective on the material resources which have been entrusted to us.[10] With our observance of Shabbat, we structure our lives according to G–d's seven-day cycle of creation; thus we not only implement G–d's will, but also ingrain in our minds and lives the source and objective of our own creativity and accomplishments.

The same applies to all the *mitzvot*. The Torah teaches us compassion for all of G–d's creatures with the laws of *shechitah*, which dictate the painless way in which animals are to be slaughtered. From the *mitzvot* that pertain to human sexuality, we gain a sanctity and purity of family life. By observing the *kashrut* dietary laws, we safeguard our moral and spiritual health. Each and every *mitzvah*, in addition to its role as an expression of the divine will, has its particular function as a refiner of the human being—morally, socially, psychologically, and in every other aspect of our lives.[11]

On this level, there will be—and ought to be—differences between *mitzvot*. There will be inherent differences between a *mitzvah* that perfects a major aspect of the human character and one that deals with a more minor area of life. There will also be subjective differences, for each individual responds to Torah in his own unique manner: certain *mitzvot* have a profound effect upon him, while others relate less to his personal talents and aptitudes. If the *mitzvot* refine and develop the entire spectrum of the human experience, they will reflect its diversity and its disparities.

However, warns the *Ethics*, never lose sight of the deeper import of the *mitzvot*. Employ the divine commandments to build a better self and world, thus experiencing them as an entire array of major and minor influences on your life, but remember that they all share a deeper, unified truth. Be equally careful of them all, for their true reward is beyond knowledge and experience.[12]

---

(1) Literally, "light" and "severe." (2) Two witnesses who warned the transgressor immediately prior to the act and informed him of the penalty it carries, and then saw the actual deed being committed. (3) Maimonides' commentary on this mishnah. (4) Talmud, Sukkah 25a. (5) Tzafnat Paane'ach by Rabbi Yosef Rosen ("The Rogatchover"), Klalei Hatorah V'hamitzvah; Yom Tov Shel Rosh Hashanah 5666, pg. 522; B'shaah Shehikdimu 5672, pg. 1081. See Maimonides' commentary on our mishnah, quoted in the following footnote. (6) Indeed, Maimonides considers our mishnah to be the basis for the Talmud's ruling. In his commentary on this mishnah he writes: "Because of this principle, our sages have declared that 'one who is preoccupied with a mitzvah *is absolved from the obligation of another* mitzvah—regardless of which *mitzvah he is involved in and which* mitzvah *is withheld from him....'" Obviously, Maimonides understood our mishnah's*

point to be that all mitzvot *are, in truth, inherently one and the same. (7)* Midrash Rabba, Bereishit *44:1. (8)* Psalms *18:31. (9)* Likkutei Torah, Shlach *40a. (10) See* The Vacuum of Choice *on pg. 152. (11) Although the Torah also includes* chukim, *or supra-rational* mitzvot, *these, too, have a profound effect on the one who fulfills them—despite the fact that he cannot understand their "reason" and utility. In fact, what we understand and appreciate of any* mitzvah *is but a fraction of its true effect upon us. (This lends deeper insight into the above-quoted saying, "Had we been commanded to chop wood...." This is not merely to say that we would joyfully perform a* mitzvah *even if we could not comprehend its beneficial effect upon us. Indeed, many* mitzvot *are no more comprehensible to us than a command to chop wood. Rabbi Schneur Zalman is saying that even if the* mitzvot *had no effect—perceivable or not—upon us, even if they refined our souls no more than the non-*mitzvah *act of chopping wood, we would still enjoy their deepest and most quintessential aspect: an opportunity to fulfill G–d's will.) (12) Based on an address by the Rebbe,* Tishrei 29, 5720 *(October 31, 1959).*

THE LONG BUT SHORT OF IT

[Rabban Gamliel the son of Rabbi Judah HaNassi would say:] Make that His will should be your will....

Ethics of the Fathers 2:4

The Talmud relates: *Rabbi Joshua the son of Chanania said: "Once a child got the better of me.*

"I was traveling and met with a child at a crossroads. I asked him, 'Which way to the city?' and he answered: 'This way is short and long, and that way is long and short.'

"I took the 'short and long' way. I soon reached the city, but found my approach obstructed by gardens and orchards. So I retraced my steps and said to the child: 'My son, did you not tell me that this is the short way?'

"Answered the child: 'Did I not tell you that it is also long?'"[1]

In life, too, there is both a "short but long way" and a "long but short way."

In his *Tanya*, Rabbi Schneur Zalman of Liadi sets down the fundamentals of the Chabad-Chassidic approach to life. On the cover page of this "bible of Chabad-Chassidism" he defines his work as follows:

Based on the verse, "For it (the Torah and its precepts) is something that is very close to you, in your mouth, in your heart, that you may do it"[2]—*it explains, with the help of G–d, how it is indeed exceedingly close, in a long and short way.*

The Torah and its *mitzvot* are the Creator's blueprint for creation, detailing the manner in which He meant life to be lived and His purpose in creation to be fulfilled. But is a life that is ordered utterly by Torah indeed feasible? Can the ordinary Everyman be realistically expected to conduct his every act, word and thought in accordance with Torah's most demanding directives?

The Torah itself is quite clear on the matter: "For the *mitzvah* which I command you this day," it states, "is not beyond you nor is it remote from you. It is not in heaven.... nor is it across the sea.... Rather, it is something that is very close to you, in your mouth, in your heart, that you may do it."[3] Torah's vision of life is not an abstract ideal, nor a point of reference to strive toward, but an achievable goal.[4]

But how? In *Tanya*, Rabbi Schneur Zalman develops the "Chabad" approach, a holistic approach to life in which the mind plays the leading and pivotal role.

First, a person must study, comprehend and meditate upon the quintessential truths of existence: the all-transcendent, all-embracing, all-pervading reality of G–d; the root and essence of the soul and its intrinsic bond with its Creator; man's mission in life, and the resources—both external and internal—that are extended to him to fulfill it. Since these concepts are extremely subtle and abstract, one must toil "a toil of the soul and a toil of the flesh" to grasp them and relate to them.

The next step is to translate this knowledge and identification into emotional drives. In creating human nature, Rabbi Schneur Zalman taught, the Almighty instilled an innate superiority of mind over heart, of reason over feeling. So the proper understanding and assimilation of these concepts will compel the development of the appropriate emotions in the heart: the love and awe of G–d. Love for G–d is the unquenchable desire to cleave to Him and be unified with His essence; awe of G–d brings the utter abhorrence of anything that violates His will and erects barriers between Him and the transgressor.[5]

Finally, when a person has so oriented his mind and transformed his heart, his observance of the Torah's precepts becomes a given. He craves the fulfillment of the *mitzvot* with every fiber of his being, as they are the bridge between him and G–d, the means, and only means, by which he can connect to his Creator. Any transgression of G–d's will, no matter how attractive to his material nature, becomes literally abhorrent to him, for it disrupts his relationship with G–d and runs contrary to his own true self.

But a person may argue: Why spend a lifetime pursuing this demanding regimen of mind and heart? Why must I toil to understand and feel? Why not take the direct approach—open the books and follow instructions? I'm a simple Jew, he may maintain, and the attainment of such lofty spiritual states as "comprehension of the Divine," "love of G–d" and "awe of G–d" are way beyond my depth. I know the truth, I know what G–d wants of me—the Torah clearly spells out the dos and don'ts of life. Yes, I have a material and egocentric nature; an inborn inclination towards evil and self-destructive desires. But I'll control them. My faith, determination and will power will do the job.

This, however, is the short but long way. As the most direct and simple line between two points, it is misleadingly the surest way to town; but in truth, the "direct approach" is a dead end. As with the route which Rabbi Joshua first chose, it seems to lead straight to the city—only somehow it never quite makes it.

For it is a path of never-ending struggle, the scene of a perpetual duel between the self-oriented animal drives of man and his upward-reaching G–dly soul. True, man has been given free choice and furnished with the necessary fortitude and spiritual staying power to meet his every moral challenge; but the possibility of failure, G–d forbid, also exists. No matter how many times he will triumph, tomorrow will bring yet another test. On the short and long road one may win battle after battle, but there is never a decisive victory in the war of life.

On the other hand, the long but short way is winding, steep, tedious, and long as life itself. It is full of ups and downs, setbacks and frustrations. It demands every ounce of intellectual and emotional stamina that the human being can muster. But it is a road that leads, steadily and surely, to the aspired-to destination. When one does finally acquire an aptitude and taste for the G–dly, when one does develop a desire for good and abhorrence of evil, the war has been won. The person has transformed himself into someone whose every thought, deed and act is naturally attuned to his quintessential self and purpose in life.[6]

---

(1) Talmud, Eruvin 53b. (2) Deuteronomy 24:14. (3) Ibid., verses 11-14. (4) See For Real on pg. 297. (5) See Love and Fear: A Four-Runged Ladder on pg. 58. (6) Based on an address by the Rebbe, Kislev 19, 5719 (December 1, 1958). It is important to note that the Chabad-Chassidic approach to life does not preclude the "short but long way"—obviously, doing good and

resisting evil cannot wait until the last curve in the "long but short" road has been turned. Indeed, a person's control of his behavior must come first—one cannot hope to transform his animal self while giving it free reign in his daily life. His actual observance of the Torah must be a given, regardless of his inclinations; it is only upon this foundation that one can hope to build a sublimated inner self (see On the Essence of the Ethics, *pg. 97). So, unlike the metaphorical traveler through physical space, who can only follow a single road at a time, our spiritual journey calls for us to follow both routes simultaneously. In the journey of life, the choice at the crossroads is not an either/or decision, but a question of priority and emphasis.*

THE MIRROR

Do not judge your fellow until you have stood in his place.

Ethics of the Fathers 2:4

Rabbi Israel Baal Shem Tov (the "Besht," founder of the chassidic movement) taught: "Your fellow is your mirror. If your own face is clean, the image you perceive will also be flawless. But should you gaze into this 'mirror' and see a blemish, it is your own imperfections that you are seeing—you are being shown what it is that you must correct within yourself."

We don't need to look to modern psychology for an interpretation of the Besht's outlook. We can find it in another of his teachings, the principle of "Particular Divine Providence" (*hashgacha pratit*).

Nothing is by chance, the Besht would always stress. Every event in a person's life is predetermined and purposeful, and an integral part of his divinely-ordained mission in life. So a person never "chances" upon anything: if he witnesses an event or phenomenon, there is a reason for this experience, a reason that is closely tied to his own path in life. It therefore follows that if divine providence causes him to see his fellow's degradation, it is for a positive and constructive end: to open his eyes to a failing of his own.

In the Eyes of the Beholder

Ultimately, this is the only way a person can truly recognize and deal with his own imperfections. "Love covers up all sins,"[1] said the wisest of men, and what greater love is there than the love of self?

A person's self-kinship blinds him to his own deficiencies. Yet a negative trait or deed, so innocent and justifiable in himself, appears in all its dreadfulness when discerned in others; here, he cannot but be appalled at the depths to which his fellow has sunk.

So the most effective way to open a person's eyes to the negative in himself is to show him what is wrong with his fellow and to then tell him that he, too, suffers from the same lack in one form or another. If he truly wishes to improve himself, if he truly searches his heart until he discovers what it is that the Almighty was pointing out to him by causing him to see what he saw, his self-love will no longer obscure what has been so glaringly presented to him in the person of his fellow.

Still, one may ask: A person's mission in life involves not only the development and perfection of his own self and character but also his responsibility towards his fellow man. So why must he conclude that he is being shown his fellow's failing as a message concerning his own personal state? Perhaps he is being prompted by divine providence to rebuke and rehabilitate his fellow?

Particular Divine Providence

To answer this question, we must first take a closer look at the principle of "Particular Divine Providence." *Particular* divine

The Silver of Self

Rabbi Israel Baal Shem Tov taught:
"Your fellow is your mirror. If your own face is clean,
the image you perceive will also be flawless.
But should you gaze into this 'mirror' and see a blemish,
it is your own imperfections that you are seeing."
To carry the analogy further: A mirror is a clear pane
of glass to which a thin coating of silver has been applied.
When a person's view of another is untainted by selfish
considerations, he can see beyond any surface
imperfections that may exist. His perception is like
a clear glass, allowing him to clearly see what is
on the other side. He is capable of perceiving his fellow
for what he truly is, to recognize the inherent goodness
that is the essence of every man.
However, if a bit of "silver" is involved, his perception
changes dramatically. When a person's view is coated by
self-interest and self-love (*kesef*, the Hebrew word for "silver,"
also means "desire"), he sees not his fellow but himself.
The glass becomes a mirror, in which all of his own failings
are reflected.[4]

providence means that not only is every event purposeful, but also its every aspect and nuance.

For example, the same event can imply different things to different observers, depending on how much they know about the people involved and the events that led up to it. Divine providence is particular in that it shows each observer precisely what is applicable to him. So if you witness an event, it stands to reason that everything about it, including the particular way in which it has affected you, has a specific application to your life.

The same applies to a person's witnessing of a negative act or behavior pattern on the part of his fellow. There are two distinct elements here: a) the *fact* of his fellow's wrongdoing; b) his fellow's guilt, culpability and decadence. The former does not necessarily imply the latter: one may be aware of what his fellow has done wrong, yet such knowledge may be accompanied with understanding, compassion and vindication.

So when G–d makes a person aware of his fellow's deficiency for the sole reason that he can do something about it, this is all that person would perceive—the fact of his fellow's problem and what he could do to resolve it. To also sense another's guilt and lowliness is completely unnecessary; on the contrary, it only hinders his ability to reach out to him in a loving and tolerant manner.

Thus, if he also senses his fellow's degradation, he must conclude that *this* aspect of the experience also serves a purpose. Divine providence has provided him with a mirror with which to discern his own shortcomings.

The Three Sons of Noah

This idea is expressed in the Torah's account of Noah's drunkenness and the response it evoked in his three children:

Noah began to work the land, and he planted a vineyard. He drank of the wine and became drunk, and lay exposed in his tent.

Cham... saw the shame of their father, and told his two brothers outside. Shem and Japheth took the garment, placed it upon their shoulders, walked backwards, and covered the shame of their father; their faces were backward, and the shame of their father they did not see.[2]

What is meant with the words "the shame of their father they did not see"? Do we not already know this from the (twice-repeated) fact that they turned "their faces backward"? But the Torah wishes to stress that the different ways in which the sons of Noah reacted—to the knowledge that their father lay drunk and exposed in his tent—mirrored their own spiritual states.

Cham's own decadence was reflected in his vision of his father's debasement. But when Shem and Japheth were made aware of their father's state, their reaction lay solely in what they must now do to correct the situation: not only did they avoid physical sight of their father's degradation, they also did not perceive his guilt or disgrace. The *shame* of their father, they simply did not see.[3]

---

(1) Proverbs 10:12. (2) Genesis 9:20-23. (3) From an address by the Rebbe, Tishrei 27, 5726 (October 23, 1965). (4) Based on an address by the Rebbe, Tevet 19, 5751 (January 5, 1991).

A FEARFUL SIGHT

Rabbi Shimon the son of Nethanel fears sin.

Ethics of the Fathers 2:9

Which is the best trait for a person to acquire? .... Said Rabbi Shimon: To see what is born.

Ethics of the Fathers 2:10

The second chapter of the *Ethics of the Fathers* includes a description by Rabbi Yochanan ben Zakkai of his five leading disciples. In a few words, Rabbi Yochanan summarizes their predominant qualities. He then conducts a brief survey of each one's outlook on life by asking them a question: "Which is the best trait for a person to acquire?"

Rabbi Shimon, who is described by his teacher as one who "fears sin," answers that the most important component of a person's approach to life is that he "see what is born" out of his actions. This is in keeping with Rabbi Shimon's particular merit: the sinner lives for the moment, but the righteous individual foresees the consequences of his deeds. The instant gratifications of sin cannot entice one who fears its deeper repercussions.

King Solomon also touches on this sentiment when he says, "The wise man has his eyes in his (or its) head; but the fool walks in darkness."[1] Obviously, the physical location of the wise man's eyes is the same as that of the fool's. Explains Rashi: the Hebrew word *b'rosho* should be translated not "in his head" but "in its head"—the wise man is one who, in everything he does, "looks into the beginning ('head') of the deed to see its end."[2]

Now or Later

The verse still needs clarification. If the wise man is simply one who recognizes that, ultimately, all good is rewarded and all evil is punished, why does King Solomon say that "The wise man has his eyes in its *head*"? Would it not have been more correct to say that "the wise man has his eyes in its *end*"?

But the ultimate difference between the "wise man" and the "fool," between the "fearer of sin" who "sees what is born" of his actions and one who "walks in darkness," is not the question of short-term versus long-term considerations.

Ultimately, fear of punishment is not enough to deter wrongdoing. One who desires the act and only fears its promised retribution will often reassure himself that the right lawyer or a proper repentance will get him off the hook. Indeed, one who views the negative consequences of evil in terms of judiciary or Heavenly retribution is hardly one who "fears sin"; he fears only the *consequences* of sin, not the wrongdoing itself.

On the other hand, one who fears sin itself understands the *immediate* effects of a negative act. He understands that such an act runs contrary to the purpose of his life and to the very essence of his being. He understands that even if he truly rectifies his wrongdoing, even if he succeeds in repairing the damage it has wrought upon his moral self, even if the "experience" ultimately makes him a better person, nevertheless, at the moment of his wrongdoing he has disconnected himself from the quintessential good that forms the core of his soul.

It is the true significance of his action, in the here and now, that he sees and fears.[3]

---

(1) Ecclesiastes 2:14. (2) Rashi's commentary on above verse. (3) Based on an address by the Rebbe, Adar 15, 5713 (March 7, 1953).

EXISTENCE AS BIRTH

Which is the best trait for a person to acquire?
.... Said Rabbi Shimon: To see what is born.

Ethics of the Fathers 2:10

A cornerstone of the teachings of Rabbi Israel Baal Shem Tov is the doctrine of "Perpetual Creation." Briefly stated, this means that G–d's creation of the universe, commonly perceived as a one-time event, is a continual act on His part. In each and every fraction of time the world is born anew out of a state of absolute nothingness, as the Creator again imparts life and being to every existence.

Here we have the deeper meaning implicit in Rabbi Shimon's praise of "one who sees that which is born."

Rabbi Shimon is saying: Behold the world's perpetual birth out of utter nothingness. Do not perceive the universe as an existence in its own right—understand that in essence it is nothing, that this seemingly formidable reality of a moment ago is now nought, and must again be brought into being by the Creator. What is real is only the divine will to create.

The implications of this perspective on existence are manifold. Often, the "realities" of our world appear to preclude one's fulfillment of G–d's will: "realistically" one may see no way of earning a living unless one works on Shabbat; "realistically" one's efforts to positively influence one's fellow stand no chance of success. But one who sees the world born anew every instant of time by an act of divine creation understands that "reality" can never be inconsistent with the divine will. It's not even a question of the divine will being more "powerful" than reality; reality is nothing but the fact of G–d's will to create it, as it is, in the present micro-moment.[1]

---

(1) Based on the talks of the Rebbe, Tishrei 24, 5717 *(September 29, 1956).*

THE THIRD PARTY

On the Essence of Ownership

Which is the worst trait, the one from which a person should most distance himself? Rabbi Shimon said: To borrow and not to repay; For one who borrows from man is as one who borrows from the Almighty.

Ethics of the Fathers 2:10

We find the same sentiment expressed in the fifth chapter of Leviticus, where the Torah discusses some of the laws that pertain to one who has violated the integrity of his fellow's property:

G–d spoke to Moses: If a person shall sin and commit a betrayal against G–d, and lie to his fellow concerning an article left for safekeeping, a business venture, a robbery, a withholding of payment, or the finding of a lost object....

Should he sin and be guilty, he must return the theft that he has stolen....

He shall pay back the principal, and shall add its fifth part to it, and give it whom he is owing.... And he shall bring his guilt-offering to G–d....[1]

Talmudic sage Rabbi Akiva points out the amazing implications of G–d's opening words. "Why does the Torah consider him to have 'committed a betrayal against G–d'?" asks Rabbi Akiva. "Because in defrauding his fellow, he is also defrauding the Third Party to their dealings."[2]

Three Owners

How is the offender also defrauding G–d? On the most basic level, we can say that in addition to depriving his fellow of what is rightfully his he is also offending the supernal author of the command "You shall not steal." Another explanation (this one offered by Rabbi Akiva himself) is that although not a single earthly soul may be aware of what really happened, the Almighty is the omnipresent witness to all that transpires. So in addition to lying to his fellow, he is brazenly denying the all-knowing "Third Party to their dealings."

However, the term "Third Party to their dealings" implies more than a witness to and an authority over their transaction. It seems to indicate a common denominator between the three, a three-sided partnership of sorts.

Indeed, such is the case. The three "parties"—the owner, the offender and G–d—share a common relationship to the disputed object: each is in fact its "owner."

The original holder of the object is its "owner" by force of Torah law.

The thief is also exercising a logistical, albeit not rightful, "ownership" over it. In addition to the fact that he has appropriated the *benefits* of ownership (use of the object etc.) for himself, there is also a legal element to his "ownership": he is unconditionally responsible for it. For example, if the stolen object is destroyed by an unpreventible act of G–d—in which case a bailee would not be responsible—the thief must repay the owner; since he has taken it as his own, he cannot claim, as can a bailee, "Your object is no longer in existence."

Finally, the Creator is the object's owner in the ultimate sense of the word. In the words of the psalmist, "The world, and all that fills it, is G–d's."[3]

So the thief, in addition to wronging his fellow, has most literally "committed a betrayal against G–d." He has also violated the property rights of the supreme owner of all.

Ownership By Bequest

Conceivably, the thief may argue: "G–d's ownership of the world transcends whatever rights my fellow or myself may claim. No matter who exercises physical control over the object, it is still in the possession of the Almighty. You may perhaps accuse me of transgressing a commandment of G–d's, or even of misusing His property, but how can you say that I have violated His ownership? Since 'The world, and all that fills it, is G–d's,' can one remove something from His premises? How can one steal from G–d?"

And yet, if we refer to another teaching of Rabbi Akiva's, we find that G–d's "ownership" of the world is indeed violated when man encroaches upon the domain of his fellow human being. Regarding the verse, "The world, and all that fills it, is G–d's," the Talmud quotes Rabbi Akiva's definition of G–d's ownership: "He acquired and bequeathed His world."[4] In essence, Rabbi Akiva is saying that G–d's possession of the world is for the sole purpose of granting pedestrian ownership to human beings!

Another Talmudic sage put it this way: "Everything was created to serve me, and I was created to serve my Creator."[5] G–d created the material resources of our world so that man may utilize them to serve Him—this is *why* He acquired a world, this is *why* He continually provides it with being and life. And in order for man to be able to make use of these resources in accordance with the divine plan, each man's rights over his "share of creation" must be defined and safeguarded. So G–d's "bequest of His world" to man is the very essence of His relationship to it. This is the *raison d'être* of His choice to create and own the universe.

Thus the Torah writes: "If a person shall sin and commit a betrayal against G–d by lying to his fellow...." If you deceive your fellow, you are also betraying the "Third Partner," depriving Him of His ownership as He Himself defines it.

Choice and Responsibility

After establishing that to violate another's property is to "commit a betrayal against G–d," the Divine Legislator proceeds to detail some of the penalties to be exacted from one who is found guilty of "lying to his fellow concerning an article left for safekeeping, a business venture, a robbery, a withholding of payment, or the finding of a lost object."

First of all, he must return the object or sum he has wrongfully withheld. In the case that he denies the charge under oath and is subsequently convicted by the testimony of witnesses, he must pay an additional one-fifth of its value to the owner and bring a "guilt offering" (*korban asham*) to atone for his transgression.

This underscores the other side of the coin. For one who has committed a crime against his fellow may tend to go to the other extreme, categorizing his deed as "something between myself and my G–d" and rationalizing away his guilt and his duty toward his victim.

Indeed, this is the proper perspective for the *victim* to assume. In his *Tanya*, Rabbi Schneur Zalman of Liadi writes: "Our sages have said: 'He who gets angry, it is as if he has worshipped idols.'[6] Why? Because at the time of his anger, faith has departed from him. Were he to truly believe that what has happened to him is of G–d's doing, he would not become angry at all. For although a human being, possessing free choice, is cursing him, or hitting him, or causing damage to his property, and is therefore liable before a human court and before the Heavenly court for the wickedness of his choice— nevertheless, as far as he, the victim, is concerned, this has already been decreed upon him from Heaven, and 'G–d has many agents to do his bidding.' [7] Furthermore, even at the very moment he hits or curses him, he (the perpetrator) is animated by the divine life force which perpetually grants him vitality and being..." [8]

With this approach, Rabbi Schneur Zalman resolves an apparent contradiction between two basic tenets of the Jewish faith: a) the exclusivity of G–d's omnipotent power as the one and only determining force in all of existence; and b) man's freedom to choose between good and evil and his complete responsibility for his actions.

If Joe chooses to strike Moe, it is a choice that Joe has freely made, and which is not influenced by any factor outside of his own self. Joe is thus solely responsible for his choice. But the fact that Moe has been hurt is *not* the result of Joe's choice—to believe so would be to believe in "another G–d," another determining factor to what transpires in the universe. The victim has only one place to look for the responsible party. Had his assailant not made his evil choice, the preordained blow would have been caused by someone or something else. In other words, his anger toward the one who wronged him is simply misdirected.

This is the proper attitude for the victim to take. But how is the perpetrator to view the damage inflicted upon the victim? Is he to see his crime only as a moral issue between himself and G–d?

But the very same section of Torah which teaches us that "if a person shall sin" against his fellow he has "committed a betrayal against G–d," also indicates he is responsible to his victim. This is derived from the fact that, in certain cases, he is sentenced to pay additional compensation to his victim, amounting to one-fifth of the sum (or object value) in question. This, our sages explain, is to compensate for the time in which the victim was deprived of his property.[9]

That he must pay back the principal itself can be understood also in the context of a total disconnection between the two litigants: although the guilty party is guilty only towards G–d, the money is rightfully the victim's. The fact that it was preordained that the victim should suffer a loss does not necessarily mean that it was to be a permanent loss; as soon as we find out that a wrong has been committed, the court must remedy it, restoring the property to its rightful owner. But when the Torah instructs the guilty party to pay the extra fifth, and to pay it not (only) as a fine and punishment but as compensation to the victim for his temporary loss—here we find a direct responsibility on the part of the "wrong-chooser" towards the one affected by his evil choice.

This also explains the otherwise difficult wording of the verse, "He shall pay back the principal, and shall add its fifth part to it, and give it whom he is owing."[10] In his commentary on the verse, Rashi questions the need for the extra words "and give it whom he is owing": would it not suffice to say "He shall pay back the principal, and shall add its fifth part to it"? Rashi explains that this comes to inform us that the thief "must give it to the one whose money it is."

In other words, had not the Torah added these words, I would not have known to whom the added fifth must be given! I would have said: "he shall pay back the principal"—that's clear; after all, the money is rightfully the victim's. But as far as the added fifth is concerned, that's obviously a punishment for the thief's crime—a crime against He who proclaimed "You shall not steal." Perhaps he should give it to charity. The victim? The victim has nothing to do with any of this!

So the Torah must explicitly tell us that the fine is meant as compensation to the victim. True, the perpetrator's evil choice was not the cause of the victim's loss. Nonetheless, the Torah has *made* him responsible for it, in much the same way it has told him to return the principal. In addition to redressing his moral wrong towards his Creator, it is incumbent upon him to feel guilt and responsibility also towards his fellow; to appease and compensate him for his suffering as if he had not merely done him but also *caused* him wrong.[11]

---

(1) Leviticus *5:20-23. (2)* Torat Kohanim, *quoted in Rashi's commentary on the verse. (3)* Psalms *24:1. (4)* Talmud, Rosh Hashanah *31a. (5) Rabbi Shimon ben Elazar in* Kiddushin *82b. (6)* Zohar, part I, 27b. *(7)* Zohar, part III, 36b; see Rashi's commentaries on *Exodus *16:33 and 21:13. (8)* Tanya, part IV, chapter 25. *(9)* Kli Yakar *commentary on verse. (10)* Leviticus *5:24. (11) Based on the talks of the Rebbe,* Adar II 9, 5725 (March 13, 1965) *and* Adar II 13, 5730 (March 21, 1970).

PROPERTY RIGHTS

> Rabbi Yossei would say.... Perfect yourself for the study of Torah, for it is not an inheritance to you.
>
> Ethics of the Fathers 2:12

Surely Rabbi Yossei does not disagree with the Torah's own statement, taught to the Jewish child as soon as he is capable of speech,[1] that "The Torah that Moses commanded us is the inheritance of the congregation of Jacob"?

But our relationship with the Torah is described, again in the Torah's own words, in terms of several different models of ownership and possession:

a) It is our "inheritance," as per the above- and oft-quoted verse (Deuteronomy 33:4).

b) It is an "acquisition" that we have "purchased" ("I have given you a good purchase, My Torah, do not forsake it"—Proverbs 4:2[2]).

c) It is a "gift" that has been granted us ("From the desert, it is a gift"—Numbers 21:18[3]).

Not only are these analogies for our relationship to the Torah categorically different, they are also, in certain respects, contradictory. A "purchase" is something that is paid for, unlike the windfall "inheritance" and "gift." The right of an "inheritance" is determined solely by who you are, a qualification not shared by the "gift" or the "purchase." And the "gift" seems to be in a category of its own. Is it who you are? Is it what you've done? It seems to be a bit of each, but not quite either of them. Obviously, you've done something to deserve it; then again, a gift, by definition, is something that has not been paid for or earned.

The Three-Fold Metaphor

Much of human speech consists of metaphors. We speak of a "deep" feeling, a "lofty" idea, or a "cold" look. Obviously, we don't intend to attribute physical properties to noncorporeal entities; we are merely using the metaphor, an indispensable tool if we are to attempt to make sense of the intangible in our lives.

At times, however, a single metaphor will not suffice. The concept we wish to articulate is simply too unique, too complex, too nuanced to be incorporated in any single model that is part of our concrete reality. In such a case, we enlist two or even several metaphors to make our point. Each model is used for its own properties; together, they piece together a new concept, one that incorporates these various, or even contradictory, elements. This enables us to envision something which has no single counterpart in our experience.

The same is true of Torah. No single phenomenon in our world can serve as a model to convey the nature of our "possession" of it. Only by speaking of it as an inheritance, purchase *and* gift can we gain some insight into our profound, multifaceted relationship with Torah.

Essence and Expression

On the most basic level, Torah is the eternal heritage of every Jew by virtue of his Jewishness. In this, the "inheritance" aspect of Torah, the most accomplished scholar "possesses" no more than the most simple of folk. Two brothers may inherit the fortune of their father; the first may be a seasoned businessman, and the second, a day-old infant. But because an heir is defined by the "who" rather than the "how," the extent of one's aptitude for or interest in the inheritance is completely irrelevant.

Yet at the same time, there is another dimension to our "ownership" of Torah, one in which the "you get what you pay for" maxim applies. True, Torah is yours regardless. True, your "inheritance" is a function of who you are and of your quintessential bond to your heritage, even if you never draw a cent from your "trust" or are even unaware of its existence. But what does it mean to you in practical terms? How does it affect your daily existence? In this sense, the Torah is yours to the extent of your investment and sacrifice—a "purchase" acquired with the currency of time and toil. The more you study and observe, the more you will experience your heritage as a consciously meaningful element in your life.[4]

Toiled and Found

But the combination inheritance-purchase model still does not sufficiently describe the nature of our relationship with Torah. A third mode of acquisition, the "gift," must also be introduced.

A gift often seems to arrive out of the blue, without regard for the identity of the beneficiary or the extent of his investment. But, as the Talmud points out, there is really no such thing as a completely "unearned" gift. Some thing or act on the part of the beneficiary must have evoked the benefactor's desire to give: "Had he not caused him satisfaction in some way, he would not have granted him a gift." For this reason, many of the laws that govern a sale also apply to a gift.[5]

Yet when it does come, the gift is a true windfall, totally without proportion or any traceable connection to the initial investment. The same is true with Torah: the rewards of its study are infinitely beyond the scope of anything in which the human mind can possibly invest. In the words of the Talmud:

Should someone tell you, 'I have toiled but not found'—do not believe him; 'I have not toiled but I have found'—do not believe him; 'I have toiled and I have found'—believe him.[6]

The choice of the word "found" (rather than "gained," for example) seems inappropriate—a "find" implies an unearned benefit, while the Talmud's message is that toil, and only toil, produces anything worthwhile. But this is precisely the point: without toil and effort, nothing happens; but when one does apply himself, to the full extent of his resources and talents, the result—also on the experiential level—is above and beyond anything he could possibly have envisioned.[7]

---

(1) Talmud, Sukkah 42a. (2) See the Midrash Rabba's *exposition on this verse:* "G–d said to Israel: 'I have sold you my Torah....' *(Shemot Rabba 33:1). (3) See also* Midrash Rabba, Bereishit *6:7: "Three things are a gift to the world: the Torah, the luminaries and the rains." Note also that* Shavuot *is referred to in the festival's prayers as* z'man matan toratainu, *"the time of the granting of our Torah." (4) See* The Third Link *on pg. 34. (5) Talmud, Gittin 50b. (6) Talmud, Megillah 6b. (7) Based on an address by the Rebbe,* Shavuot *5724 (May 17, 1964).*

THREE TIMES THREE

> Akavia the son of Mahalalel would say: Reflect upon three things and you will not come to the hands of transgression. Know from where you came, where you are going, and before Whom you are destined to give a judgment and accounting. From where you came—from a putrid drop; where you are going—to a place of dust, maggots and worms; and before Whom you are destined to give a judgment and accounting—before the supreme King of kings, the Holy One, blessed be He.
>
> Ethics of the Fathers 3:1

On the surface, the meaning of this *mishnah* seems clear: Akavia is presenting us with a few humbling facts about our physical selves, the contemplation of which will help us maintain the proper perspective on life.

But the *mishnah*, known for its concise language, might have made this point in one simple sentence: "To keep yourself from sin, contemplate that you come from a putrid drop, that you are going to a place of dust, maggots and worms, and that you are destined to give an accounting before the supreme King."

Instead, it employs three separate statements:

1) Reflect upon three things and you will not come to the hands of transgression.

2) Know from where you came, where you are going, and before Whom you are destined to give an accounting.

3) From where you came—from a putrid drop; where you are going—to a place of dust, maggots and worms; and before Whom you are destined to give a judgment and accounting—before the supreme King of kings, the Holy One, blessed be He.

But Akavia's words also have a deeper and more detailed interpretation. On this level, the *mishnah*'s three segments are actually three variations on its message, directed to three different types of individual.

Perfection, Control or Enslavement

In his *Tanya*, Rabbi Schneur Zalman of Liadi explores the spiritual and psychological makeup of three classes of people: the *Tzaddik* ("righteous man"), the *Beinoni* ("intermediate man") and the *Rasha* ("sinning man").

The *Rasha* allows his animal nature to take control of his life. He periodically succumbs to that which is egocentric and hedonistic in the human character, transgressing against G–d and his fellow man.

At the other extreme is the *Tzaddik*, who has achieved perfection both without and within: both his behavior and character have been cleansed of evil. On the behavioral level, everything he does, says or thinks is absolutely consistent with G–d's will. Within, the *Tzaddik* has accordingly transformed his interior self as well: he craves only his attachment to G–d, and he loathes anything that may impede this relationship.

The *Beinoni* occupies the middle ground between the *Rasha* and the *Tzaddik*: impeccable behavior coupled with a still unrefined nature. Unlike the *Tzaddik*, the *Beinoni* has yet to transform and sublimate his naturally egocentric drives. Still, he exercises full control over his words and deeds, and even over his willful thoughts. While he may desire to do wrong, he never allows such desires to affect his behavior. While not everyone is capable of attaining the perfection of a *Tzaddik*, concludes Rabbi Schneur Zalman, the level of *Beinoni* is attainable by—and expected of—each and every individual.[1]

Priorities

The *Rasha*, the *Beinoni*, the *Tzaddik*—all require contemplation of "three things" to prevent them from falling "to the hands of transgression." But the nature of these "three things," as well as that of the transgression whose "hands" their contemplation will save one from, differs greatly from the perfect *Tzaddik* to the intermediate *Beinoni* to the sinful *Rasha*.

This is why Akavia gives us three different variations on his recommended meditations, each addressing one of these three general types of individual.

The final segment of our *mishnah* ("From where you came—from a putrid drop; where you are going—to a place of dust, maggots and worms; and before Whom you are destined to give an accounting—before the supreme King of kings, the Holy One, blessed be He") is addressed to the *Rasha*. Although this may seem an overtly "negative" approach, it is the only effective way to motivate the *Rasha*. Contemplating the richness and desirability of a life true to one's Creator and purpose would have little effect on the *Rasha*—the only goal he relates to is the pursuit of the material. To overcome his base desires, the *Rasha* must first be confronted with their shallowness and insignificance.

The *Beinoni*, however, is told, "Know from where you came, where you are going, and before Whom you are destined to give an accounting." We need not impress upon him the lowliness of the physical, for the proper perspective on life is already ingrained in the *Beinoni*'s mind and heart; to surrender to the fears and desires of his animal self is, for him, out of the question. Yet even the *Beinoni* is not entirely unsusceptible to negative influences, as attested to by the fact that he may still desire evil. He, too, must contemplate the truths of life, though for a different reason than the *Rasha*: the *Rasha* must be prevailed upon to change his priorities and behavior, while the *Beinoni*'s challenge is to maintain them, while striving for the inner perfection of the *Tzaddik*.

So to the *Beinoni*, "from where you came" is not the putrid drop of the *Rasha*'s corporeal origins, but the origin of his soul in its Divine Source. To the *Beinoni*, "where you are going" refers not to the dissolutionary destination of the body, but the sublime heights attainable through his service of the Almighty. To him, his accountability to G–d is not the "threat" of retribution for wrongdoing that it is for the *Rasha*, but the responsibility to optimally develop his potential. Instead of dwelling on the lowliness of the corporeal, the *Beinoni* meditates on his holy origins, his purpose, and the One to Whom he is responsible in his mission in life.

You, Him, and the World

Finally, the first segment of our *mishnah*, "Reflect upon three things and you will not come to the hands of transgression," is directed to the *Tzaddik*.

The *Tzaddik* is incapable of actual sin; he is literally revolted by anything that may separate him from his Creator and Source. Nevertheless, he must guard himself against the deeper definition of "sin," which is "lack"[2]—the possibility of falling short of the degree of perfection of which he is capable. This would be considered "coming to the hands [that is, the semblance] of transgression"—not a transgression of the line that separates good from evil, G–d forbid, but perhaps a transgression to a lower level within the realm of good itself.[3]

So the *Tzaddik* is told: "Reflect upon three things." These are not the three things of the *Rasha*, who must dwell on the lowly and transitory nature of the mundane, or even of the *Beinoni*, who is also, in a sense, susceptible to its enticements. The *Tzaddik* is above all that. But there are certain pitfalls that even the most perfect of men must beware of, pitfalls that threaten to detract from his perfect fulfillment of his mission in life.

One of these possible "failings" on the part of the spiritually perfect is the tendency to regard existence as a two-dimensional affair: to view everything in terms of "me" and "Him," seeing nothing of significance save one's relationship with G–d. But such a person fails to fully apply his potentials to the purpose for which they were granted him. He may choose a pious life, forgoing society and surroundings in his quest for spiritual closeness to the Almighty. But he is neglecting to acknowledge what it is that G–d truly wants of him.

To forewarn such "transgression," Akavia tells the *Tzaddik* to "Reflect upon three things." In addition to concerning yourself with "you" and "Him," also remember the third element of your mission in life—the world in which G–d has placed you. At all times, set before your eyes the three basic facts of life: Know your Creator; know your own self, recognizing your strengths and weaknesses, and your talents and vulnerabilities; and bear in mind the manner in which G–d desires that you serve Him—by harnessing the resources of the material world and developing them in accordance with His will.[4]

---

(1) See On The Essence of the Ethics *on pg. 97, and* The Long But Short of It *on pg. 111. For a detailed description of these three classes, and of the many levels they each include, refer to the first twelve chapters of* Tanya. *(2)* Chait, *the Hebrew word for "sin," also means "lack." (3) This also explains why our* mishnah *appears in the third chapter of the* Ethics. *Were it to speak only of avoiding literal "sin," its proper place would be at the very beginning of Chapter One—rejecting evil is the very first step in man's journey towards refinement and perfection. However, the* mishnah *is far more complex, dealing with various phases of the journey and the various levels of "transgression" (see concluding paragraphs of* On the Essence of the Ethics *on pg. 97). (4) Based on the talks of the Rebbe,* Iyar *10, 5750 (May 5, 1990) and* Iyar *13, 5751 (April 27, 1991).*

SUBJECTIVE JUDGE

> Know.... before Whom you are destined to give a judgment and accounting.
>
> Ethics of the Fathers 3:1

Said Rabbi Israel Baal Shem Tov: When a person comes before the supernal court to account for his sojourn on earth, he is first asked to voice his opinion on another life. "What do you think," he is asked, "about one who has done so and so?" After he offers his verdict, it is demonstrated to him how these deeds and circumstances parallel those of his own life. Ultimately, it is the person himself who passes judgment on his own failings and achievements.[1]

This explains the peculiar wording of the above passage of the *Ethics*, "before Whom you are destined to give a judgment and accounting." Is not the verdict handed down after the cross-examination of the defendant? So should not the "judgment" follow the "accounting"? And why are you destined to "*give* judgment" as opposed to being judged? But no judgment is ever passed on a person from above. Only after he has himself ruled on any given deed does the heavenly court make him account for a matching episode in his own life.

The same idea is also implicit in another passage in our chapter of the *Ethics*: "Retribution is extracted from a person, with his knowledge and without his knowledge."[2] As a person knowingly expresses his opinion on a certain matter, he is unwittingly passing judgment on himself.

What we have here is a most profound insight into the specialty of the human soul. In all of creation, nothing is loftier than the "spark of G–dliness"[3] that is the soul of man. This is reflected in the fact that man has been given the power of choice—a power he shares only with the Creator Himself.

Free choice allows him to stumble and err, but it is also what makes his potential for good infinitely greater than G–d's more spiritual creations. So even when a soul comes to stand in judgment, implying that there are perhaps faults and failings in its past performance, no judge, be it the loftiest and most spiritual of heavenly beings, has any jurisdiction over its fate. The only power on earth or heaven that can judge man is man himself.[4]

---

(1) Cf. Nathan's admonishment of King David, Samuel II 12. (2) Ethics of the Fathers, 3:16. (3) See chapter two of Tanya. (4) From an address by the Rebbe, Shevat 10, 5720 (February 8, 1960).

THE CONTEMPORARY CANNIBAL

> Rabbi Chanina, deputy to the *kohanim*, would say: Pray for the integrity of the sovereignty, for were it not for the fear of its authority a man would swallow his neighbor alive. Rabbi Chanina son of Tradyon would say.... Two who sit and exchange words of Torah, the Divine Presence rests amongst them.
>
> Ethics of the Fathers 3:2

The basic meaning of (the first) Rabbi Chanina's words is that for a society to be civilized its members must submit to the rule of government and law.[1] The need for "fear of authority" may seem insulting to our sophistication and intelligence, but the fact remains that without it there would be nothing to check the worst in man and the anarchic rule of the jungle would prevail.

There is, however, a deeper meaning implicit in the words and idioms of our *mishnah* as well.

Alive and Well, But Swallowed

Our world, and all the creatures and phenomena that inhabit it, is an expression of the all-embracing reality of its Creator. By examining the workings of the human being, society, and the natural order, we behold a mirror in which is glimpsed ever more spiritual dimensions of existence, and, ultimately, the face of the Supreme Author of reality.

The same is true of the concepts of "government" and "sovereignty." In the words of our sages, "Kingship on earth is a prototype of the Heavenly Kingship."[2] The principles and guidelines that typify human governments and authority structures reflect the nature of the divine sovereignty (*malchut*) of G–d.

The ego of man is cannibalistic in essence. At worst, it destroys everyone and everything in its path in order to attain its selfish goals. At best, as in the case of a civilized, refined and tolerant individual, it acknowledges its status as one among many, avows its support of the "human rights" of its fellows and concedes the legitimacy of pursuits other than its own. But even the most liberal-minded of men cannot escape the trappings of the ego: he will always see his fellow through the prism of self. His (seemingly) objective mind will point out that he shares the planet with billions of others, that there exist countless perspectives and callings in addition to his own; deep down, however, the self will remain the gravitational center of all, his ultimate point of reference. He will see others as necessary, perhaps crucial, but always secondary cogs to the kingpin of self.

This is the deeper significance of Rabbi Chanina's words. The expression, "a man would swallow his neighbor alive," is meant in the literal sense: his neighbor remains intact and alive, but is swallowed up within his own being. He grants the validity of the other's life and work, but sees his own as the all-inclusive, primary definition of reality.

Praying for Sovereignty

So anyone who views the universe as an ownerless, arbitrary existence will never transcend the moral and intellectual cannibalism of the ego. For without a Supreme Authority that creates, defines and gives direction to all of creation, the self and its perceptions are the sole judge of right and wrong; inevitably, one's vision of others will be tinted with the color of self.

It is only through the fear of G–d, only through the acceptance of the sovereignty of the King Of All Kings, that man can grow beyond the prejudice and anarchy of the ego. It is only by sensing an absolute truth before which all are equally insignificant, but which grants significance to the countless individual roles that fulfill the divine purpose in creation, that an individual can genuinely see his fellow as his equal.

And because the naturally self-centered consciousness of man is, by definition, incapable of truly seeing beyond itself, this truth is not something that one can understand and feel with the contemporary tools of his mind and heart. One must therefore "*pray* for the integrity of the sovereignty" in his life. One must concede that the transcendence of self is beyond his humanly natural capabilities, and humbly request that he be granted a higher, ego-free vision of his fellow.

Equal Sitting

Each *mishnah* of the Talmud expresses a single concept; the next concept always warrants a *mishnah* of its own. Yet the second *mishnah* of the *Ethics'* third chapter seems to contain two wholly unrelated ideas: the saying by Rabbi Chanina (deputy to the *kohanim*) discussed above, and the saying by Rabbi Chanina (son of

Tradyon) in the latter part of our *mishnah*, "Two who sit and exchange words of Torah, the Divine Presence rests amongst them...."

But in the light of the deeper significance of the first Rabbi Chanina's words, the second saying of our *mishnah* reiterates the first—this time speaking in terms of a person's Torah study.

Torah is G–d's communication to man, the expression of His wisdom and will in terms digestible to the human mind. Yet there are many levels in man's comprehension of Torah, from the wage earner who manages only the "one chapter in the morning and the one chapter in the evening"[3] to the lifelong round-the-clock scholar. In truth, however, regardless of the scope and depth of one's knowledge in Torah, all who approach G–d's wisdom are equal: equal in the inability of their human, finite minds to truly grasp anything of an infinite truth, and equal in the fact that they have been *granted* the inherently unachievable gift of comprehending Torah, each at his own level.

So if two study Torah and one towers over his fellow and "swallows him up" intellectually, seeing his own achievements as being beyond and inclusive of his fellow's, then it is not G–d's Torah that he is studying but a self-generated, self-colored perception of the divine truth. But "two who sit" as equals "and exchange words of Torah," acknowledging that they are both but humble recipients of a higher truth, then "the Divine Presence rests amongst them."[4]

---

(1) "The law of the land is the law of the Jew," rules the Talmud in Bava Batra *113a. (2) Talmud, Berachot 58a. (3) Talmud, Menachot 99b. (4) Based on an address by the Rebbe, Sivan 28, 5735 (June 7, 1975).*

ON THE ESSENCE OF EAT

> Rabbi Shimon would say.... Three who eat at one table and speak words of Torah, it is as if they have eaten at G–d's table.
>
> Ethics of the Fathers 3:3

On the surface, Rabbi Shimon's message is simple and straightforward: utilize your mealtimes to share the wisdom of Torah. This way, the mundane activity of eating becomes a lofty and G–dly endeavor.

But surely the same applies to a single diner or to many who eat scattered about the room. Why *"three* who eat"? And why specifically when they eat at "one table"? On a deeper level, Rabbi Shimon is conveying the true significance of our need for food.

Hunger in Two Dimensions

The human being consists of two primary components: the physical body, and the soul that gives it life and direction. The same is true of every created thing: its physicality and substance is but its outer husk. Within is a "soul," an inner, spiritual essence and significance.

Ultimately, the soul of the entire universe is one: the drive to fulfill its Creator's will. At creation, this unified "soul" splintered into a myriad of individual "sparks" that now form the core of every created thing.

But unlike the human soul, which exercises will and choice, all other creatures are passive containers of their purpose and utility. They depend upon man, the crown and apex of G-d's creation, to develop and utilize them in accordance with the Creator's design. It is man to whom the Torah, which outlines this design, has been given, and it is man who has been granted the franchise and the tools to implement it.

So the soul of man descends into the trials and trappings of physical life in order to gain access to these "sparks of holiness." By investing itself within a physical body that will eat, clothe itself, and otherwise make use of the objects and forces of the physical universe, the soul redeems the "sparks" that they incorporate. For when man utilizes something, directly or indirectly, to serve G-d's will, he penetrates its shell of mundanity, revealing and realizing its function within the overall purpose of existence.

This explains a most puzzling fact of life: Why is it that man derives life and sustenance from the animal, vegetable, and mineral worlds? How is it that the highest form of life is dependent upon these lower tiers of creation?

But in truth, man's need for the nutrients that his environment provides him (and the many other material resources that sustain and enhance his life) is the manner in which these elements reach fulfillment. When man makes positive use of the energy he derives from them, they become elevated to a station they could never attain on their own. They become an integral part of a conscious, willful being who elects to serve the Almighty. The meat of the beast, the grain in the bread, the water that quenches our thirst—these become the essence of an act of charity, an hour expended in the study of G‑d's wisdom, a feeling of love for G‑d in prayer.

In this way, Rabbi DovBer of Mezeritch explained the verse: "The hungry and thirsty, in them does their soul wrap itself."[1] A person desiring food may sense only his body's hunger; but, in truth, his physical craving is the external expression of a deeper yen. "Wrapped within" is his soul's hunger for the sparks of holiness that are the object of his mission in life.

Three at One

When a person sits to eat there are three partners to the endeavor: his body, his soul, and the food—the vital glue that keeps body and soul together as a living organism.

But if his eating is dominated by the perspective of Torah, these "three who eat" do so at a single table. Their eating is an act of unification, a revelation of the underlying oneness of creation and its connection to the One Creator.[2]

---

(1) Psalms 107:5. (2) From an address by the Rebbe, Sivan 23, 5742 (June 19, 1982).

THE VACUUM OF CHOICE

> Rabbi Elazar of Bartosa would say: Give Him what is His, for you, and whatever is yours, are His. As (King) David says: "For everything comes from You, and from Your own hand we have given to You."[1]
>
> Ethics of the Fathers 3:7

The gist of Rabbi Elazar's message is clear, and encapsulates the Jewish attitude toward charity: we do not "contribute" that which is inherently our own. Rather, we merely carry out the purpose for which the wealth has been entrusted to us by the Almighty.

But there is more to Rabbi Elazar's words. A vital part of the *mitzvah* of charity–and of all G–d's commandments—is that we choose of our own free will to do them. "All is foreseen," proclaims Rabbi Akiva further on in our chapter of the *Ethics*, and yet, "freedom of choice is granted" to man.[2] For if doing good were to come as naturally and compulsively to us as our breathing and eating, our deeds would be no more significant than any other natural phenomenon.

The granting of free choice to man is the most "revolutionary" aspect of G–d's creation, for it runs contrary to the most basic law of reality: the axiom that "There is none else beside Him," that G–d's omnipresent and all-pervading existence does not allow for any other self-determining element.[3] Nevertheless, G–d chose to overrule this "law," in effect creating a so-called vacuum within His infinite being,[4] in order to give the human being the freedom to choose between right and wrong.

So when man elects to share his wealth, he is giving what is his— G–d has relinquished to him the right of ownership and choice. This is why Rabbi Elazar does not say, "Give Him what is His, for everything is His." Were this to be the case, the act of charity would be devoid of any moral worth. Instead he says: "Give Him what is His, for you, and whatever is yours, are His." Indeed there is a "you" and your money is "yours," for G–d has granted you selfhood and property.

But there is an even more basic truth that underlies your existence: the fact that "you, and whatever is yours, are His"—that G–d has granted you being, independence and ownership for the sole purpose of imparting significance to your fulfillment of His will.

The choice is yours. But when you exercise that choice, bear in mind where your power to choose stems from. Remember He Who has granted you your very being as a creature of volition, and to what purpose He has done so.[5]

---

(1) I Chronicles 29:14. (2) Ethics of the Fathers, 3:15. See the essay Knowledge and Choice *on page 170 for a broader treatment of this topic. (3)* Deuteronomy 4:35; See Maimonides' *Mishneh Torah, Laws of the Foundations of Torah, Chapter 1. (4) Referred to, in the* Kabbalah, *as the* Tzimtzum. *(5) Based on an address by the Rebbe,* Sivan 28, 5736 (June 26, 1976)

THE HUMAN ELEMENT

Rabbi Elazar of Modi'in would say: One who profanes the *kodoshim* (sacred things), who degrades the festivals, humiliates his friend in public, abrogates the covenant of our father Abraham or who interprets the Torah contrary to its true intent—although he may possess Torah knowledge and good deeds, he has no share in the World to Come.

Ethics of the Fathers 3:11

What is it about these five transgressions that distinguish them from other violations of the Torah? At first glance, Rabbi Elazar's list seems a collection of unrelated offenses, pertaining to things as diverse as the Temple service, the Jewish calendar, interpersonal relations, circumcision and Torah study. Yet obviously there is something about these things that places them in a category of their own—something that makes their transgression so grave an offense against the very essence and purpose of our lives.

Preserver or Creator

A person may view the commandments of the Torah as a set of instructions from on high. G–d created the world (so goes this line of thinking) and in His Torah He defined its boundaries and parameters. He established what is permitted and what is forbidden and distinguished the holy from the mundane. The role of man is to preserve these borders: to avoid the profane and safeguard the sanctity of that which is holy and G–dly in the world.

But to see our life's mission in these terms is to miss the point entirely. G–d gave us the Torah in order to enable us to become His "partners in creation"[1]—that we build upon and extend His work. That we take our presently imperfect world—a world dichotomized by holiness and mundanity—and transform it, in its entirety, into a harmonious expression of its Creator's goodness and perfection.

This is the "World to Come" that results from our implementation of the *mitzvot* in today's "Present World." If the Present World consists both of the material-dominated workweek and the spiritual sanctity of Shabbat, the World to Come will be "a day that is wholly and eternally Shabbat."[2] If the Present World both reveals and obscures its Creator, the World to Come represents a reality in which every entity and element is suffused with an awareness of the Divine.

If the Present World is the world as G–d created it, divided between the hallowed and the profane, the World to Come is the product of man's contribution to the partnership, the product of his efforts to sublimate the ordinary and sanctify the mundane.

Five Examples

The five transgressions singled out by Rabbi Elazar as detrimental to a person's realizing his share in the World to Come all indicate, each in its own way, the same misguided approach to the essence and function of the *mitzvot*. They describe an individual who, "although he may possess Torah knowledge and good deeds," sees them merely as preservers of a cosmic status quo rather than as the tool for human achievement and partnership in G–d's creation.

A. One who profanes the kodoshim:

Kodoshim is the halachic term for animals that have been designated as an offering to G–d. From the moment its owner expresses his intention to offer it, an animal is *kodosh*, consecrated to the Almighty. It is now a severe prohibition to make use of it for any purpose or to inflict a wound on it; it must be slaughtered in the courtyard of the Holy Temple and eaten under conditions of ritual purity.

The principle of the "consecrated animal" is a prime example of how the Torah empowers man to sanctify his "mundane" possessions by devoting them to the service of the Creator. Thus, one who violates the sanctity of *kodoshim* demonstrates a contempt for the human ability to sanctify. In effect, he is saying: "Holy is what G–d deems holy. But if Farmer Joe points his grubby finger at some calf, and states his intention to bring it as an offering, does this change anything? Is this animal now different from any other?"

B. Who degrades the festivals:

If *kodoshim* exemplify man's ability to endow a physical object with sanctity, the festivals offer him an opportunity to transform and sublimate the substance of time itself. For the Torah establishes that the Jewish calendar be set not by any predetermined cycle or system, but by the monthly "Sanctification of the Month" by the *beth din* (court of law).[3]

To set the new month, at least two witnesses must behold the new moon; the *beth din* must cross-examine them and then officially proclaim the commencement of a new month. So it is human initiative and human actions that determine which day shall be *Yom Kippur*, which day Passover, etc. In fact, the Torah explicitly states that even if the *beth din* erred or was misled, the holiness of the festivals is nonetheless effected by their proclamation.

Again, one who sees Torah merely as the implementation of G–d's instructions for daily living will inevitably fail to properly appreciate the sanctity of the festivals. The holiness of Shabbat he can relate to: after all, G–d Himself consecrated it from the very start—He created the world in six days and rested on the seventh, thereby making this cycle of six days of work and involvement, followed by a day of sublimation and transcendence, integral to the very nature of time. The timing of festivals, however, is humanly determined, and subject to the shortcomings and vulnerabilities of all human products. One who belittles the human side of the "partnership" may view the festivals as days devoted to special activities, designed to commemorate important historic events, because G–d so commanded; yet to say that the nature of the day is more lofty than any other? What has transformed an ordinary Wednesday into a holy day—the finite and error-prone acts of men?

C. Who humiliates his friend in public:

Here, Rabbi Elazar addresses human relationships. For man is not only empowered to sanctify those elements of his environment that he involves in his service of G–d, but also to create hallowed entities in the purely social and interpersonal areas of his life.

Obviously, it is forbidden to humiliate any individual, in any setting. But Rabbi Elazar refers specifically to one who humiliates his friend in public as one who rejects the process that creates the World to Come out of our present-day existence. A person who publicly humiliates his friend effectively says: "*We* created the friendship between us, so it has no more value than either of us cares to attribute to it. There is nothing 'sacred' about it. How can there be, if it's of our own creation? If I am angry with you, I will not refrain from humiliating you in public—at this moment, you mean no more to me than does anyone in this crowd of strangers on the street. You say that I am 'violating' our friendship? What is that supposed to mean? A 'friendship' is not a thing—it is the relationship between two people. And now our relationship is such that I am angry at you and I wish to humiliate you!"

The *mitzvot* of the Torah are of two general types: those that govern the relationship "between man and G–d" and those that apply "between man and man." Our mandate to transform and sanctify our existence is not confined to the "between man and G–d" area of life; also "between man and man" we create realities that are holy and inviolable, and that are part of our "improvement" upon G–d's creation.

D. Who abrogates the covenant of our father Abraham:

The first three examples deal with things whose "sanctity" is indeed initiated and created by man: the animal consecrated as an offering, the day imbued with holiness by an act of *beth-din*, a friendship formed by two individuals.

But what of the *mitzvot* that are wholly ordained from above? Is our observance of them to be defined only in terms of obedience to the divine will, or do they, too, include an element of creative input on our part?

Rabbi Elazar addresses this issue by referring to the *mitzvah* of circumcision as "the covenant of our father Abraham." The use of this elaborate idiom for circumcision seems not only unnecessary but also problematic: G–d commanded Abraham to circumcise himself; it is a covenant between G–d and Israel, first established with Abraham but then reinitiated with each individual Jew. In fact, as Maimonides is careful to point out, "...everything that we avoid doing or that we do today, we do only because of G–d's command to Moses at Sinai, not because of any communication by G–d to earlier prophets... (For example,) we do not circumcise ourselves because our father Abraham circumcised himself and the members of his household, but only because G–d commanded us through Moses that we should circumcise as did Abraham...."[4] And yet, at every Jewish circumcision, the infant's father recites the blessing: "Blessed are You, G–d... Who has sanctified us with His commandments and commanded us to enter him into the covenant of our father Abraham."

We attribute the *mitzvah* of circumcision to Abraham in order to underscore the human element involved. Although the covenant is defined by divine command, each Jewish infant enters it as a pioneering "Abraham," forging a bond with the Almighty that is uniquely and distinctly his own.

True, the *mitzvah* is a divine institution, a command that expresses the desire of G–d. True, the Torah commands "Do not add to what I command you, neither shall you diminish from it,"[5] for how can man presume to rationalize, much less tamper with, the divine will? At the same time, we know that the act of doing a *mitzvah* is a realization of our cosmic partnership with the Almighty. So we may, and must, involve our mortal selves in the deed: our finite comprehension of its significance, our subjective emotional response to it, our innovative ways of enhancing and beautifying the object and the experience of the *mitzvah*.

E. Who interprets the Torah contrary to its true intent:

The partnership which G–d entered into with man includes not only the actual observance of the *mitzvot* but also the Torah itself, the process by which G–d communicates His will to humanity.

Instead of simply presenting us with a set of instructions, G–d chose to embody His wisdom and will in the Torah and to entrust the human mind with the task of deducing the divine laws and commandments it contains. The very notion seems incredible: how can the human intellect possibly fathom the divine "mind"? But the Torah itself proclaims that the "Torah is not in heaven" but has been given to man to study and comprehend.[6] Consider the following incident related by the Talmud: Rabbi Eliezer and his colleagues were debating a point of Torah law. Rabbi Eliezer maintained that a certain type of oven was not susceptible to ritual impurity, while the others disagreed.

"On that day," the Talmud recounts, "Rabbi Eliezer brought them all sorts of proofs, but they were rejected.... Finally, he said to them: 'If the law is as I say, may it be proven from heaven!' There then issued a heavenly voice which proclaimed: 'What do you want of Rabbi Eliezer—the law is as he says....'

"Rabbi Joshua stood on his feet and said: 'The Torah is not in heaven!'"

(What does this mean? Explained Rabbi Jeremiah: We take no notice of heavenly voices, since You, G–d, have already, at Sinai, written in the Torah to "follow the majority."[7])

"(Subsequently,) Rabbi Nathan met Elijah the Prophet and asked him: 'What did G–d do at that moment?' (Elijah) replied: 'He smiled and said: "You have triumphed over Me, My children, You have triumphed." '"[8]

For so G–d desired: that when man applies his rational faculties to the words and principles of Torah, the resultant conclusions are nothing less than His own will!⁹

Hand in hand with so awesome a privilege comes the tremendous responsibility to be faithful to the terms of this partnership. One who departs from the Torah's guidelines on how to interpret and apply it, regarding it as some nebulous theory to be formed and deformed at will, obviously has no appreciation of what Torah truly is: a marriage of minds between man and G–d.¹⁰

---

(1) See Talmud, Shabbat 10a and 119b. (2) Grace After Meals (Shabbat addendum). (3) In 4119 (359 C.E.), about 300 years after the Romans destroyed the Holy Temple in Jerusalem and exiled much of the Jewish nation from their land, the then president of the central beth din (Sanhedrin), Hillel Nessi'ah, *realized that the growing dispersion of the Jewish community would soon make it impossible for the calendar to be centrally set on a monthly basis. He therefore established the 19-year cycle by which the start of each new month on the Jewish calendar can be calculated. His* beth din *then sanctified all the months to come until the coming of the Moshiach, when we will resume the monthly interactive calendar. Thus, our present months are also humanly set, although we eagerly await the reestablishment of the* Sanhedrin *and our return to observing the* mitzvah of kiddush hachodesh *(sanctification of the month) in the optimal manner (see Maimonides'* Mishneh Torah, Laws of the Sanctification of the Month, *chapter 5. (4) Maimonides' commentary on the* Mishnah. Chullin 7:6. *(5) Deuteronomy 4:2. (6) Deuteronomy 30:12. (7) Exodus. 23:2 (8) Talmud, Bava Metzia 59b. (9) See* Debating Truths *on pg. 264. (10) Based on an address by the Rebbe, Sivan 26, 5738 (July 1, 1978).*

YOUR VOWING DAUGHTER

Dealing with the Gray

Vows are a safety fence for abstinence.

Ethics of the Fathers 3:13

Somewhere between the good deed and the moral wrong is the permissible indulgence. How is one to approach these (seemingly) neutral pleasures?

The Torah's view on the matter appears to be mixed. On the one hand, the Talmud interprets the injunction "Be holy"[1] to mean: "Sanctify yourself also in regard to that which is permissible to you."[2] On the other hand, it chides the *nazir*, who, in his quest for holiness, has forsworn wine: "Is what the Torah has forbidden not sufficient for you, that you must further deprive yourself?"[3]

In the thirtieth chapter of Numbers, these two approaches to worldly pleasures are personified by two characters in the Torah's discussion of the laws of vow-taking. We read of a daughter who pledges to refrain from a particular food or pleasure, and of the father who annuls her vow. As is the case with all of Torah's laws, this scenario reflects a corresponding state of affairs within the "small world" that is the human being: within the soul of man there is a "daughter" who shuns the physical world and a "father" who annuls her vows of abstinence.

Everything in G–d's world was created for a positive purpose. So, unless the Torah explicitly prohibits it, nothing is to be rejected or discounted.[4] But man has his vulnerabilities. Instead of using the resources and opportunities of the physical world for a higher end, he may be overwhelmed and seduced by that which he comes to develop and redeem.

So if and when he realizes that he is in danger of succumbing to his baser instincts, he must take the necessary steps to curb them. He must erect "safety fences" of further restriction and disavowal, lest the surface glitter of the material world overshadow its inner potential.

Yet even as he vows to restrict his involvement with the physical, a higher authority within him is already preparing to annul his vows. This deeper and more transcendent self remains forever unsullied by its mundane environment. As man gains mastery and control over his life, he gradually repeals his self-imposed restrictions, so that he may utilize every one of G–d's gifts in a positive and constructive manner.[5]

---

(1) Leviticus 19:2. (2) Talmud, Yevamot 20a. (3) Jerusalem Talmud, Nedarim 9:1. (4) Those elements that the Torah proscribes also serve a positive function—one that is realized through man's conquest of self in resisting them. (5) Based on an address by the Rebbe, Tammuz 26, 5722 (July 28, 1962).

EXPRESSION, CONNECTION AND UNION

The Threefold Identity of the Jew

[Rabbi Akiva would say:] Beloved is man, for he was created in the image (of G–d); it is a sign of even greater love that it has been made known to him that he was created in the image, as it is stated: "For in the image of G–d, He made man."[1] Beloved are the people Israel, for they are called children of G–d; it is a sign of even greater love that it has been made known to them that they are called children of G–d, as it is stated: "You are children of the L–rd your G–d."[2] Beloved are the people Israel, for they were given a precious article; it is a sign of even greater love that it has been made known to them that they were given a precious article, as it is stated: "I have given you a good purchase; My Torah, do not forsake it."[3]

Ethics of the Fathers 3:14

He was one of the greatest sages the Jewish people had ever known. But, as a descendant of converts to Judaism, he could not even claim Jewish ancestry. And although he grew up as a Jew, for the first four decades of his life he was completely ignorant of Torah. An illiterate shepherd until the age of forty, he eventually became one of the most authoritative figures in the history of the study and transmission of Torah.

So Rabbi Akiva was able to relate, firsthand, to the three dimensions of our identity which he enumerates in the above-quoted *mishnah*: our humanity, our Jewishness, and the specialty we achieve through the study of Torah; or—as expressed in terms of our relationship with G–d—our reflection of, connection to, and union with the Almighty.

Reflection and Connection

On the most basic level, man is an expression of the Divine. His discriminating intelligence, his ability to will and choose freely, are wholly G–dly qualities—qualities that the Almighty imparted to the crown and apex of His creation, making humanity the mortal mirror of His omnipotence.

Our identity as Jews represents a deeper aspect of our relationship with G–d, one that the Almighty compares to the intimate and quintessential bond between father and son. Of all the peoples of the world, G–d chose the nation of Israel to be the purveyors of His immanence in our world. To this end He commanded us the *mitzvot*, providing us with many and diverse avenues—as diverse as life itself—for us to make our lives an abode for His presence.

The word *mitzvah* means both "commandment" and "connection." In commanding us to perform a certain deed, G–d creates an opportunity for us to form a connection with Him. He is willing Himself to want something from us, although He certainly does not "want" for anything in the "lack" sense of the word. He does this so that we may be able to relate to Him by fulfilling His will.

In other words, while our identity as beings created in His image has more to do with what we are than with what we do, our identity as Jews means that we have been imbued with the potential to actively create a connection with Him—by living our lives as instruments of His will.[4]

Clothing and Nourishment

But a person's performance of *mitzvot* can be a wholly "external" act—something in which he is involved only on the behavioral level, with little or no effect on his character and personality. This is not to say that merely going through the motions of a *mitzvah*'s performance is of no significance. These "motions" are acts, words or thoughts whose execution the Almighty chose to define as the implementation of His will. But regardless of the magnitude of what a person's deed is accomplishing, he himself may remain unmoved and unchanged.

Torah, however, introduces a new dimension to our ability to connect to G-d. Like the *mitzvot*, Torah is a channel opened by the Almighty to enable us, confined as we are to our finite and material existence, to form a connection with Him. The difference is in the medium He chose: with the *mitzvot*, He chose that certain (mostly physical) actions should embody His "will"; with Torah, He communicated His "wisdom" in terms digestible to the human mind.

In other words, through the performance of *mitzvot* our daily lives become an exercise in the performance of the divine "will," while through the study of Torah our minds become saturated with G-d's "wisdom."

This is one of the reasons why the Torah is often described as "food" for the soul and the *mitzvot* as the soul's "garments."[5] The hand that dons *tefillin* or dispenses charity, the heart and lips that pray, are immersed in an activity that is an extension of the Divine—an activity in which the Almighty chose to invest His will. But, in a sense, this is a one-way relationship: the limbs and faculties involved in the *mitzvah*'s performance are fully immersed in the act, but the act may not penetrate their being. They are doing the *mitzvah*, but the *mitzvah* may not be doing anything to them—at least not anything internal and permanent. They are effecting a connection with the Almighty, but a connection involving only their conduct and behavior, not their inner makeup and character. This is comparable to the relationship between a garment and its wearer: the wearer is encased in the garment, yet the garment remains something that is outside and distinct of the wearer.

Torah, however, is food for the soul; food that is absorbed by its consumer to become the very substance of his being. The thinking mind is not only absorbed by an idea, but also absorbs it, making for "a wonderful union, like which there is none other, and which has no parallel anywhere in the material world—they (the mind and the idea) attain a complete oneness and unity, from every side and angle."[6]

And when the idea is a Torah idea, the human mind attains this "complete oneness and unity, from every side and angle" with the divine essence which G–d communicated as His "wisdom": on the one hand, the mind immerses itself in G–d's Torah (a quality which the act of Torah study shares with all other *mitzvot*); on the other hand, it also digests and internalizes the idea, making it part of its outlook and identity.

In summation:

a) The human soul, simply by being what it is, mirrors and expresses its Divine Source.

b) A more potent relationship is achieved through the *mitzvot*, with which the Jew actively creates a connection with the Almighty.

c) Through the study of Torah the Jew effects not only a connection with his G‑d, but also a union in the most absolute sense of the word.

History, Biography and a Day in the Life of a Jew

The story of Rabbi Akiva's origins and life is also the story of the Jewish nation. The people of Israel are also descendants of "converts" to Judaism: while G‑d impressed His image on the very first man He created, it was more than two thousand years before He began the process of choosing Israel as His nation. And in its younger years, Israel, too, had yet to taste the full extent of the union with G‑d wrought by Torah. While yet in Egypt, they were already referred to by the Almighty as "My firstborn son, Israel"[7] and commanded to do certain *mitzvot*; but it was only on the sixth of Sivan of the year 2448 from Creation (1313 B.C.E.), as the entire people of Israel stood gathered at the foot of Mount Sinai, that the Almighty gave us His Torah and opened a new and unprecedented dimension of opportunity for relationship with Him.

In a certain sense, we each experience these three phases of growth in the course of our lifetimes and, in microcosmic form, every day of our lives. From the moment of birth, we are full-fledged human beings, reflecting and expressing the divine image in which we were created. But the Jewish dimension to our being is not fully realized until the age of twelve (a girl) or thirteen (a boy), when we assume the obligation to observe the *mitzvot* and fulfill our role as one of G‑d's chosen people. And although we are taught words of Torah from the time we begin to speak, it is only after many years of devoted study, years in which we attain the knowledge and maturity of mind necessary to even begin to truly comprehend Torah, that we come to enjoy the special union with G‑d that only the in-depth study of Torah can bring.

On the daily level, we regain full possession of our distinctly human faculties immediately upon awakening. But our relationship with the Almighty is still a wholly passive one—simply by being what we are, we mirror the divine attributes and qualities which He invested in us. Then, with our acknowledgment of G‑d in the words of *Modeh Ani*[8] and our service of G‑d through prayer, we begin the actualization of our Jewish selves and our "filial" relationship with our Heavenly Father. Finally, we move "from the hall of prayer to the hall of study,"[9] where the mind of the Jew and the "mind" of G‑d fuse into one.[10]

---

(1) Genesis *9:6. (2)* Deuteronomy *14:1. (3)* Proverbs *4:2. (4) Ultimately, "A Jew, although he has sinned, is a Jew"* (Talmud, Sanhedrin *44a). So a Jew who is lax in his observance of the* mitzvot *is no less a "child of G‑d" than his more observant brother. However, this does not mean that the* mitzvot *are irrelevant to our identity as Jews; on the contrary, it is our role as G‑d's chosen people that defines our Jewishness, whether we are faithful to it, or, G‑d forbid, we are not. In other words, we are Jewish because of the unique relationship with G‑d achieved through the* mitzvot, *whether we actually realize this relationship in our daily lives or it remains, for the time being, only a potential that we possess (for a broader treatment of this issue, see* The Third Link *on pg. 34). (5) See* Tanya, *ch. 5 and the various sources quoted there. (6) Rabbi Schneur Zalman of Liadi*, ibid. *(7)* Exodus *4:22. (8) "I offer thanks before You, Living and Eternal King, for having restored my soul to me; great is Your faithfulness"—recited upon awakening. (9)* Talmud, Berachot *64a. (10) Based on an address by the Rebbe,* Sivan 23, 5750 (June 16, 1990).

Expression, Connection and Union

KNOWLEDGE AND CHOICE

All is foreseen, and freedom of choice is granted.

Ethics of the Fathers 3:15

Throughout the generations, many of our sages have expounded on these two cornerstones of Jewish faith: G–d's all-encompassing and all-pervading knowledge, and the freedom of choice He granted to man. Much has also been written on the apparent contradiction between the two: If there are no limits to G–d's knowledge, how can man have real choice in his life? If G–d "already" knows what I will do tomorrow, is not my freedom to choose merely an illusion?

Maimonides writes:

Freedom of choice has been granted to every man.... This concept is a fundamental principle and a pillar of the Torah and its commandments. As it is written: "See, I have set before you life (and good, and death and evil)"[1] *... to say: the choice is in your hands.... For were G–d to decree that a person be righteous or wicked, or if there were to exist something in the very essence of a person's nature which would compel him toward a specific path, a specific conviction, a specific character* *trait or a specific deed...how could G–d command us through the prophets, "do this," and "do not do this," "improve your ways" and "do not follow your wickedness"...? What place would the entire Torah have? And by what measure of justice would G–d punish the wicked and reward the righteous...?*

One may ask: "G–d, of course, knows all that will transpire. Now, before a particular deed was done, did G–d know whether the person would be righteous or wicked, or did He not know? If He knew that the person would be righteous, then it was not possible for that person not to be so. And if you say that He knew that the person would be righteous, but it was also possible that he might be wicked, then G–d's knowledge was not complete!" Know that the answer to this question is "longer than the land is its measure and broader than the sea,"[2] and that many great foundations and lofty mountains hang upon it. But understand well what I am going to say. We have already explained in the second chapter of The Laws of the Torah's Foundations *that G–d does not know with a "mind" that is distinct from His being, as is the case with man whose being and mind are two distinct entities. Rather, He and His "mind" are one and the same—a concept that is impossible for the human mind to fully comprehend. Thus, just as man cannot discover and grasp the truth of the Creator, as it is written, "no man can perceive Me and live,"[3] so, too, man cannot discover and grasp the "mind" of the Creator. In the words of the prophet, "My thoughts are not as your thoughts, nor are your ways as My ways."[4] Therefore, we lack the capacity to know the nature of G–d's knowledge of all creations and all events. But this we know without doubt: that the deeds of man are in his hands, and G–d does not compel him to do anything....*[5]

Rabbi Abraham ben David (the "Raavad"), who wrote many glosses on Maimonides' work, takes issue with the latter's approach:

The author did not act in the manner of the wise: one ought not begin something that one is incapable of concluding. He begins by posing a difficult question, then remains with the difficulty and reverts to faith. It would have been better for him to have left it as a matter of faith for the innocent, instead of making them aware (of the contradiction) and leaving their minds in doubt....

Rabbi Abraham concludes by saying that "although there is no definitive answer to this," he had best offer at least "something of an answer" to the issue raised by Maimonides. The gist of his answer is that G–d knows what man will choose, but that this knowledge has no effect on the nature of man's choice. Rather, it is "like the predictions of the stargazers, who know, by some other means, what the behavior of an individual will be" but in no way determine it.

In his *Tosafot Yom Tov* commentary on our *mishnah*, Rabbi Yom Tov Lippman Heller elaborates on this theme, citing the answer offered by Rabbi Shmuel Uceda in his work, *Midrash Shmuel*:

There is no contradiction in the first place. G–d's knowledge of the future is the result of His observing the deed that the person is doing. Just as a person's observation of the deeds of his fellow in no way compels his fellow's actions, so, too, is it with G–d's observation of one's deeds. One cannot argue that because G–d knows the future actions of man He therefore compels them, since before Him there is no precedence and subsequence, as He is not governed by the laws of time.... There is no "future" in G–d's reality—the whole of time is "present" to Him. So just as our knowledge of the present has no compelling effect, so, too, His knowledge is always in (His) "present" and non-compelling....

The *Tosafot Yom Tov* adds that "Indeed, this is consistent with the conclusion of the Raavad, who compares G–d's knowledge to that of a stargazer."

Some Questions

In light of all the above, several things need to be clarified: How would Maimonides respond to the Raavad's argument? Indeed, why begin a philosophical discussion of an issue to which there is no philosophical answer?

On the other hand, the *Midrash Shmuel*'s contention that "there is no contradiction in the first place" appears to be well substantiated. G–d, as the Creator of time and space, obviously transcends them. From His vantage point, the whole of time is an open book. To say that He "already" knows the future "before" we mortals have reached that juncture in our journey through time, is to speak of His reality in terms that are appropriate only to ours. In His terms, His knowledge does not precede our deeds—on the contrary, it is the result of His seeing them transpire in our future (much like the Raavad's hypothetical stargazer who can read the future).

So why does Maimonides not offer this answer? Is there a reason why he would consider it insufficient? Also, why does the Raavad, who *does* seem to offer this answer, refer to it as only "something of an answer" and concede "that there is no definitive answer" to Maimonides' question? And if there is a flaw in this answer (as both Maimonides and the Raavad apparently felt), was the *Midrash Shmuel*, and the commentaries who quote him, unaware of it?

Another Kind of Knowledge

The key to all this lies in the lengthy "non-answer" expounded by Maimonides. Instead of merely saying that we cannot grasp the nature of G–d's "mind," Maimonides refers to what he wrote earlier in his work that G–d and "His mind" are one. Let us examine his detailed formulation of this point in chapter two of *The Laws of the Torah's Foundations*:

All existences aside from the Creator, from the highest (spiritual) form to a tiny gnat in the belly of the earth, all exist by virtue of His reality. So in knowing His own... reality, He knows everything....

G–d is aware of His own reality and knows it as it is. He does not "know" with a mind that is distinct from Him, as we know. We and our minds are not one; but the Creator—He, His mind, and His life are one from every side and from every angle and in every manner of unity. For were He to...know with a "mind" that is distinct of His being, there would exist several "gods"—He, His mind, etc.... One must therefore conclude that He is the Knower, the Knowledge, and the mind all in one. This concept is beyond the capacity of the mouth to articulate, the ear to comprehend and the heart of man to truly know....

Thus, He does not know the creations by perceiving them, as we know them, but rather, He knows then through His perception of Himself.... By knowing Himself He knows everything, since everything relates to Him for its very being.

In other words, the very attribution of "knowledge" to G–d is problematic. The possession of a "mind" and "knowledge," in our sense of these terms, implies both imperfection and diversity. Imperfection, because something other than myself (i.e., the knowledge) gives me something that I lack on my own. Diversity, because the state of "knowing" presupposes a minimum of three components to my being as a knower: the "I" that is the possessor of the knowledge, the information I possess, and the tool by which I possess it—my mind. And if I know many things, the "parts" that compose my knowing self are multiplied accordingly. True, these components have fused into a single entity (the knowing I), but G–d is a pure singularity, not a composite entity.

Maimonides, therefore, states that if we are to ascribe to G–d the knowledge of all beings and all events, we must conclude that: a) His knowledge of the countless facts that comprise our existence are, in truth, but a single knowing—His knowledge of self (since what we call "existence" is merely the expression of His infinite potential to create); and b) He does not know Himself via a "mind" that is distinct from Him, but that He, His knowledge and His "mind" are an utterly singular unit.

Chassidic teaching takes this a step further. The act of creation is, in essence, an act of divine knowing. In choosing to "know" Himself as the source of the created existence, the Almighty grants this existence validity and being. So ultimately, every created entity is but the embodiment of G–d's knowledge of it.

In the words of Rabbi Schneur Zalman of Liadi: "G–d's...thought and knowledge of all created beings embrace, in actuality, each and every creation; for (this knowledge) itself is its very life and being and that which brings it into existence from nothingness into actuality."[6]

According to this, one obviously cannot describe G–d's knowledge of the future—nor, for that matter, His knowledge of the past—as resulting from the facts and events of our existence. In fact, the very opposite is true: the facts and events of our existence result from G–d's knowledge of them.

The Tzimtzum

But in addition to this singular, all-embracing, creating knowledge, there also exists another level of divine knowledge.

In essence, G–d is wholly untouched by the deeds of man ("If you fail, how do you affect Him? If your sins are many, what do you do to Him? If you are righteous, what do you give Him? What can He possibly receive from you?"—Job 35:6-7). And yet, G–d chose to be "affected" by what we do: to take "pleasure" in our accomplishments and to be "angered" by our transgressions.[7] He chose to give Himself these "traits" in order to enable us to relate to Him in a way that is meaningful to us.

This phenomenon is known as the *tzimtzum* ("contraction")—G–d is projecting Himself in ways that are "confining" to His infinite and feature-free essence, assuming definitive attributes by which to relate to us on our terms.

On this "post-*tzimtzum*" level, G–d knows us in a way that is comparable to the workings of the human mind—with a knowledge that results from what we do. At the same time, He also knows us with a higher "pre-*tzimtzum*" knowledge: a knowledge that is an inseparable part of His "seamless" self-knowledge, a knowledge that is not caused by, but is the cause of, its contents. Chassidic teaching refers to these two levels as G–d's "higher knowledge" and His "lower knowledge."[8]

Knowing the Unknowable

We hear the poet exclaim the "sky for height, the breadth of the earth, and the deep—who can trace them out?"[9] But in light of all the above, we can begin to understand the various approaches of Maimonides, the Raavad and others to the issue of divine knowledge and human choice.

G–d's *manifest* effect upon our existence (as well as His "reaction" to our deeds) is confined to the interaction created by the *tzimtzum*-constriction and the "attributes" He assumes in His relationship to us. So on the most basic level, "there is no contradiction in the first place." G–d's "lower knowledge," although unbounded by time, space or any other limits, otherwise resembles knowledge as we know it. It is the product of His observation of our existence (whether past, present or future), so there is no reason why it should affect our freedom of choice.

Ultimately, however, G–d does not know things because they occur; He knows them by knowing Himself, and His knowledge of them is the source of their very existence.

However, this "higher knowledge" is part of the pre-*tzimtzum* reality and, as such, has no perceptible effect on our experience. (Indeed, any logical examination of G–d's relationship to our existence must, by definition, be confined to the post-*tzimtzum* reality, since all created phenomena, including logic and its laws, are a product of the *tzimtzum*. Obviously, one cannot talk about "definitions" and "contradictions" when discussing the Creator of logic beyond the point at which He chooses to relate to His creation on its terms.) This is why the *Midrash Shmuel* and others feel that it is sufficient to deal with the issue of "divine knowledge and human choice" on the level of "lower knowledge."

Nevertheless, the Raavad considers the "stargazer" explanation as only "something of an answer" for it fails to resolve the "contradiction" as it pertains to the essence of G–d's knowledge. The Raavad, therefore, feels that Maimonides ought not to have begun discussion of an issue that ultimately extends beyond the parameters of logic.

But Maimonides chooses specifically to address the higher level of divine knowledge, the level at which "He and His mind are one" and the workings of "My thoughts" are in no way comparable to those of "your thoughts." For man must believe and comprehend that the Almighty's reality extends beyond what is rationally accessible to the human mind. Indeed, if the question of how G–d's knowledge is to be reconciled with the freedom granted to man does not arise, this means that one's perception of G–d's knowledge is limited to its "lower" aspect, regarding which there is indeed no logical inconsistency. To grasp the truly super-logical nature of G–d's "mind" is to understand that it, as His essence, is affected by nothing and is the ultimate Effector of all.[10]

(1) Deuteronomy *30:15. (2)* Job *11:9. (3)* Exodus *33:20. (4)* Isaiah *55:8. (5)* Mishneh Torah, Laws of Repentance, *ch. 5. (6)* Tanya, *part II, ch. 7. (7)* "'A pleasing fragrance for G–d' *(*Leviticus *1:9)—It is a satisfaction for Me, that I have commanded and My will has been fulfilled"* (Sifri, Numbers 28:8). "They have angered Me with their follies" *(*Deuteronomy *32:21). "Beware, lest your heart be led astray... and G–d's anger will burn"* (ibid. *11:16-17). (8) See* Torah Or *15a. (9)* Apocrypha, Ben Sira *1:3. (10) Based on the talks of the Rebbe,* Iyar *14, 5744 (May 16, 1984) and* Adar *27, 5746 (March 8, 1986).*

BEARING WITNESS

Ben Zoma would say: Who is wise? One who learns from every man. As it is stated: "From all my teachers I have grown wise, for Your testimonials (*eidosecha*) are my meditation."[1]

Ethics of the Fathers 4:1

It would seem that a wiser person is also a more critical person, since he has the insight to see his fellow for what he truly is. So why does Ben Zoma say, "Who is wise? One who learns from every man"? Perhaps to *become* wise, a person should learn from everyone; but the wiser he becomes, would he not find less value in those inferior to himself?

One possible answer is that the wise man gleans positive knowledge and instruction also from negative traits and deeds. (Thus, Rabbi Zusya of Anipoli learned seven things from a thief: a) What he does, he keeps to himself. b) He is ready to take risks in order to achieve his goal. c) The smallest detail is of great importance to him. d) He invests great effort and toil in what he does. e) He is swift. f) He is confident and optimistic. g) If at first he fails, he is back time and again for another try.[2])

Another deeper perception of every man as one's teacher is to be found in the verse from Psalm 119 quoted by Ben Zoma: "From all my teachers I have grown wise, for Your testimonials (*eidosecha*) are my meditation." At first glance, only the first half of the verse pertains to our *mishnah*'s point. What pertinence does the fact that "Your testimonials (i.e., the *mitzvot*) are my meditation" have with learning from every man?

Indeed, the Hebrew word *eidosecha*, "Your testimonials," from the root *eid*, "witness" or "testifier," usually refers to the divine commandments, whose observance attests to G–d's sovereignty over the universe and His relationship with us. But there is also another significance to the term—that it refers to each and every one of us. "'You are My attesters (*eidai*),' says G–d"[3]—every single individual, by virtue of his being, bears testimony to the greatness of his Creator.

It is in this context that Ben Zoma quotes the entire verse. "From all my teachers I have grown wise," says King David, expressing the elementary lesson that to *grow* wise one must learn from every man. Furthermore, the wiser he became, the more teachers David had. Why? Because "Your testimonials are my meditation."

True, wisdom enables one to see past the veneer of conduct and grasp the inner motives and desires of men. But the truly wise individual looks even deeper, beyond personality and character, to perceive the quintessence of humanity: man as a testimonial to G–d, Who created him in His image.

Every human being expresses another of the infinite faces of the Creator, and thus serves as a unique and unduplicated insight into the all-embracing, all-pervading source of all wisdom. It takes a truly wise man to look at his every fellow, including the externally corrupt and despicable individual, and perceive the testimony he bears about his Creator.[4]

(1) Psalms *119:99*. *(2) From* Hayom Yom, *a calendar with quotations from the works and talks of Rabbi Yosef Yitzchak Schneersohn of Lubavitch, compiled and arranged by the Rebbe. (3)* Isaiah *43:10*. *(4) Based on the talks of the Rebbe,* Sivan *30 and* Tammuz *14, 5740 (June 14 and 28, 1980).*

THE HEADLESS INVESTOR

> Who is rich? One who is satisfied with his lot. As it is stated: "If you eat of the toil of your hands, fortunate are you, and good is to you!"[1]
>
> Ethics of the Fathers 4:1

Does this mean that only carpenters and porters can taste fortune and goodness? Is the Psalmist advising all businessmen, lawyers and university professors to abandon their offices and classrooms and "eat of the toil of your hands"?

But our *mishnah* simply states, "Who is rich?—one who is satisfied with his lot," and then proceeds to quote the verse from the Psalms. Obviously, the concept of gaining one's living by the toil of one's "hands" applies to every individual, regardless of vocation.

Patriarchal Precedent

In Genesis 28 the Torah describes the first night in Jacob's journey from the Land of Israel to Charan. When darkness fell, "he took from the stones of the place and placed them about his head" in order to protect himself from wild beasts as he slept.[2] But if Jacob was concerned with the threat of physical beasts, why did he shield only his head, exposing his body to the dangers of the wild?

But the Torah is telling us of a deeper, internal barrier that Jacob was erecting. Jacob knew that he was leaving behind his earlier life as a "wholesome man, who dwells in the tents of study,"[3] for the cannibalistic world of commerce and materialism. After decades of secluded study in the Holy Land, he was to spend twenty years in the company of the corrupt and manipulative Laban, in order to build his family and amass the material means to support it. During this time he labored round the clock ("In the day the heat consumed me, and the frost by night; and my sleep departed from my eyes"[4]) until he was "exceedingly successful," and gained "much cattle, maids, servants, camels and donkeys."[5] Yet he only devoted his "body," his external self, to this necessary but spiritually barren aspect of his life, while jealously reserving his "head," his innermost mind and choice talents, for his higher priorities.

Curious Headgear

A chassid of Rabbi Sholom DovBer of Lubavitch
had opened a plant for the manufacture of galoshes.
Soon his every waking hour and thought
were completely occupied in his new
and flourishing business.
Said the Rebbe to him: "To insert one's feet into
galoshes is a fairly common practice;
but a head in galoshes...?"

So after twenty years in the jungle of Charan, Jacob could look back at a fortune created by much genius and skill and refer to it as but "the toil of my hands."[6]

If you wish to be truly rich, our *mishnah* is saying, expend only the toil of your "hands," the more external elements of your talents and faculties, in your material involvements, reserving the "toil of your head" for the more lofty things in life. Save the best of your mind, heart and self to gain true wisdom, serve your Creator, and fulfill your mission in life.[7]

---

(1) Psalms 128:2. (2) Genesis 28:11; see Rashi's commentary. (3) Ibid., 25:27. (4) Ibid., 31:40. (5) Ibid., 30:43. (6) Ibid., 31:42. (7) Based on an address by the Rebbe, Kislev 9, 5711 (November 18, 1950).

HUMILITY: TWO DEFINITIONS

Be humble before every man.

Ethics of the Fathers 4:10

Let's be realistic. Is there no one out there who is less intelligent, less accomplished or less virtuous than yourself? Okay, discount the half-dozen degrees by which your ego inflates your self-perception. Still, is there no one on earth who is less worthy than you?

So what does it mean to "be humble before every man"? Is the *mishnah* telling us that it is our moral duty to underrate ourselves?

To do so would be a sinful waste of our G–d-given talents, which can never be optimally realized unless we are aware and appreciative of what we have been given and what we have accomplished. In the words of Rabbi Yosef Yitzchak of Lubavitch: "Just as it is imperative that a person recognize his own shortcomings, it is no less crucial that he recognize his advantages and strengths."

How, then, does a person make a true evaluation of himself, for the worse *and* for the better, and at the same time experience a genuine feeling of humility before every other individual?

The Larger Picture

Chassidic teaching offers two approaches to develop a true feeling of humility toward someone whose character or behavior is obviously inferior to one's own: a) the "mutual dependency" approach and b) the "relative expectation" approach.

The first approach begins with the recognition that we are all one, that together we comprise a single organism whose various cells, limbs and organs complement and complete one another. A body includes both the sophisticated brain and the "crass" functional foot; but, ultimately, the brain is dependent on the foot just as the foot is dependent on the brain. If the foot is indebted to the brain for its vitality and direction, the brain is dependent on the foot to realize many of its goals.

The humble man looks at the larger picture rather than the particulars, at the unified purpose of life on earth rather than only at his function within this purpose. No matter how lofty his own role may seem in relation to his fellow's, he is grossly limited without him. The knowledge that his own life's work is incomplete without his fellow's contribution arouse feelings of humility and indebtedness toward his fellow: he recognizes that even the coarsest "limb" of the mutual body fulfills a deficiency in himself.[1]

Defining Humility

In this approach, humility is not equated with a sense of inferiority. Rather, it stems from a feeling of equality and mutual need. In becoming humble, a person first realizes that any greater measure of intelligence, refinement, spiritual sensitivity, etc., that he may divine in himself in relation to his fellow is nothing to feel superior about: these are only the tools that have been granted him for his individual role. He also recognizes the limitations of his own accomplishments, and the manner in which they are fulfilled and perfected by the communal body's other organs and limbs. So he is humbled by the ability of his inferior fellow to extend and apply their shared mission on earth to areas that lie beyond his individual reach.

The second approach, however, defines "humility" in the more commonplace sense—as a feeling of inferiority in relation to one's fellow.

How is this truly and truthfully achieved in relation to *every* man? By conducting a thorough evaluation and critique of his own moral and spiritual standing. In doing so, one is certain to find areas where he has failed to prove equal to what is expected of him. That his fellow may be guilty of the same or worse is irrelevant: concerning his fellow's behavior he is in no position to judge. "Do not judge your fellow until you are in his place"[2] say our sages, for you have no way of knowing how his nature, his background and the circumstances surrounding any given deed may have influenced his behavior. However, regarding your own behavior you *are* "in his (i.e., your own) place" and in a position to know that, despite all the excuses and justifications you may have, you could have done better.[3]

With such an approach, a person will "be humble before every man" in the most literal sense of the term, perceiving his every fellow as superior to himself.[4]

Fighting Fire with Fire

Which approach to take? On the whole, the Torah tells us to accentuate the positive in ourselves. True, soul-searching and self-critique are important, for a person must never delude himself. However,

Good Grief

Nothing is as whole as a broken heart
(Chassidic saying).
*Depression is not a sin. But what depression
does, no sin can do*
(Chassidic saying).
Is sad bad? Chassidic teaching differentiates
between two types of sorrow: *merirut*, a
constructive grief, and *atzvut*, a destructive grief.
Merirut is the distress of one who not
only recognizes his failings but also cares
about them. One who agonizes
over the wrongs he has committed,
over his missed opportunities and over his
unrealized potential: one who refuses
to become indifferent to what is deficient
in himself and his world.
Atzvut is the distress of one who has despaired
of himself and his fellow man, whose melancholy
has drained him of hope and initiative.
The first is a springboard for
self-improvement; the second a bottomless pit.
How does one distinguish between the two?
The first is active, the second passive.
The first one weeps, the second's eyes
are dry and blank.

> The first one's mind and heart are in turmoil,
> the second's are still with apathy
> and heavy as lead.
> And what happens when it passes,
> when they emerge from
> their respective bouts of grief?
> The first one springs to
> action: resolving, planning,
> taking his first faltering
> steps to undo the causes of his sorrow.
> The second one goes to sleep.

excessive dwelling on one's shortcomings and failures leads to a down-spiraling vortex of depression, despair and inertia, resulting in the very opposite of constructive action.

So, generally speaking, the precept "Be humble before every man" should be employed in the first manner outlined above: not by disparaging oneself in relation to another person, but by recognizing the indispensability of each of one's fellows to the completeness of one's own attainments.

But there is also a time and place for the second approach. The soul of man is a "spark of G–dliness," inherently and utterly good; yet man must also contend with the egocentric drives of his "animal soul." Physical life is basically the struggle between these two selves, between the divine-seeking G–dly self and the material-seeking mundane self.[5]

In the course of this struggle, a person may encounter a lack in his character that proves especially resistant to all his efforts. He may find this negative trait reinforced by a sense that "this is the way it is, there is nothing to be done"—a "humility" and a self-depreciating despair that actually stem from the ego-driven arrogance of his animal self.

In such a case, one must "fight fire with fire" and administer a dose of its own medicine to his animal soul. He must humble himself by contemplating the lowliness of his animal nature, and that his compliance with its drives and arguments renders him inferior to even the lowliest of men.[6]

This is the constructive side of the second approach to humility, as a sense of inferiority. For at times, this is the only way for a person to break the arrogant "humility" of his animal self and proceed with the lifelong quest for self-refinement.[7]

---

(1) As one wise man put it, "The test of humility is in your attitude to subordinates" (Orchot Tzaddikim, Sefer Ha-Middot, *15c, ch. 2*). *(2)* Ethics of the Fathers, *2:4. (3) See* Double Standard *on pg. 71. (4) "A sage said: 'I never met a man in whom I failed to recognize something superior to myself: if he was older, I said he has done more good than I; if younger, I said I have sinned more; if richer, I said he has been more charitable; if poorer, I said he has suffered more; if wiser, I honored his wisdom; and if not wiser, I judged his faults lighter.'"* (The Testament of Judah Asheri) *(5) See opening chapters of* Tanya. *(6) See* Tanya, *ch. 30. (7) From a responsum by the Rebbe, 5706 (1946).*

CRIME REPAYS

> Rabbi Eliezer the son of Yaakov would say: He who fulfills one *mitzvah* acquires for himself one advocate; he who commits one transgression, acquires against himself one accuser. Repentance and good deeds are as a shield against retribution.
>
> Ethics of the Fathers 4:11

"Your evil does afflict you,"[1] says the prophet. In other words, punishment for wrongdoing is not a divine "revenge" any more than frostbite is G–d's "revenge" for a barefoot trek in the snow: it is the natural consequence of one's deeds. Just as the Creator has chosen to run His world in accordance with the laws of physics, so too, He has instituted a spiritual "natural order"; the fact that good is beneficial and evil is detrimental to their doers is an outgrowth of their essential natures.[2]

Every positive deed on man's part is a realization of his divine essence and purpose, and thus an intensification of his bond with his Creator. And since the ultimate source of life and bliss is G–d, the obvious result is a more enhanced flow of sustenance and well-being. On the other hand, the person who transgresses the divine will disavows the very purpose for which G–d grants him existence and life. So the suffering and afflictions that consequently befall him are the spiritually "natural" result of his having sabotaged his own link and lifeline to his Divine Source.[3]

Didn't Reach the Ground

In light of this conception of reward and punishment we can better understand the Torah's account of the seventh of the Ten Plagues to be visited on Egypt—the plague of *barad*, a devastating storm of rain, fire and ice.

Pharaoh had once again reneged on his promise to let the Jews go; the divine response was to unleash "thunder and hail, and fire which ran down upon the earth...the likes of which there was not in Egypt from when it had become a nation" and which wreaked havoc on the Egyptians, their cattle and their crops.[4]

"And Pharaoh sent and called for Moses and Aaron, and said to them: 'I have sinned this time; G–d is righteous, and I and my people are in the wrong. Entreat G–d that there be no more divine thunders and hail; and I will let you go....'"[5]

"And Moses went out from Pharaoh, out of the city, and spread out his hands to G–d; and the thunder ceased, and the hail and the rain did not reach the ground."[6]

Suspended or Vaporized

Our sages have stated that "G–d desires to uphold the workings of the world as much as possible; nature is dear to Him, and He does not interfere with it unless it is critically necessary."[7] And yet, almost everything about the plague of *barad*, including the manner in which it ended, was supernatural.

Two sworn enemies, fire and ice, collaborated to create the "hail with fire flaring within it"[8] that rained down on Egypt. And when

Moses lifted his arms, the storm ceased—instantaneously. Even the hail and rain that had already begun its descent from the heavens "did not reach the ground."

What happened to these orphaned raindrops and hailstones? A careful reading of the commentaries[9] yields two versions of their fate: a) they remained suspended in midair; b) they ceased to exist altogether.

The need for supernatural plagues is self-evident. As G‑d told Moses, "I will multiply My signs and My wonders.... And Egypt will know that I am G‑d." But why the miraculous end to the plague of *barad*? Why not allow the already falling raindrops to reach their natural groundward course?

Past Revisited

Punishment, as we've noted, is not a divine revenge, but the spiritually natural result of a person's wrongdoing.

The fire and ice that rained down on Pharaoh's Egypt was in punishment for his enslavement of the Jewish people and his repeated defiance of the divine command, "Let My people go." But when Pharaoh repented his crime, acknowledging his guilt ("G‑d is righteous, and I and my people are in the wrong") and committing himself to its rectification ("I will let you go"[11]), the root cause for the plague of *barad* no longer was. The dynamics of reward and punishment now dictated that Pharaoh's evil, now repented, would no longer afflict him.

The laws of physics may have mandated the continued descent of the hail and rain already en route. But the laws of physics are but the implementors of a higher nature. For a single hailstone or raindrop to now strike Egypt would have been a violation of the spiritual "natural order" that the Creator has established to govern our reality.

Crime Repays

This also explains the two versions of what happened to those hailstones and raindrops which Pharaoh's repentance disarmed in mid-flight: did they halt in mid-air or did they cease to exist entirely?

Basically, there are two levels of *teshuvah* (repentance): *teshuvah* that affects only the future, and *teshuvah* that reaches back into the past.

A person who has acted contrary to his ordained mission in life has turned his back on His Creator. As long as he does not repent his deed, he remains in a state of "estrangement" from the Almighty. But when he expresses true regret for his crime and commits himself henceforth to be faithful to his G–d, he repairs the damaged relationship; all is forgiven as he turns a new leaf in his life.

This is your basic, forward-effective *teshuvah*. None of this, however, changes the fact that, prior to his repentance, this individual had been disconnected from his Divine Source and his own intrinsic goodness. His evil deed remains a past reality; all he has done is discontinue its negative effects on his life.

But there also is a higher level of *teshuvah*: a *teshuvah* which reaches back in time to change the past.[12] This is the *teshuvah* of a penitent who succeeds in exploiting his past wrongs as an impetus for good; who garners from his spiritual descents the momentum to achieve otherwise unattainable heights; whose estrangement becomes a source of yearning for His G–d, a yearning with a depth and intensity that far surpasses anything the spiritually pristine soul can feel; and whose negative past is transformed into positive force.

This is the difference between the two scenarios for the suspended *barad*. If Pharaoh's repentance was of the first, "from now on" sort, his past evil, and what it had caused, remained in existence. Only its future *effects* on him were neutralized. The hail and rain remained—only they did not continue their punishment of the now repentant sinner.

But if Pharaoh were capable of achieving the higher level of *teshuvah* that rectifies the past, the negative cause of the *barad* would have been retroactively undone. And since it is "your evil that does afflict you," the utter erasure of his evil would have spelled the immediate unbeing of all that ever resulted from it,[13] including the physical water, fire and ice that came to afflict its perpetrator.[14]

---

(1) Jeremiah 2:19. (2) Shaloh, Bayit Acharon, 12a. (3) Our sages also explain that "punishment" is the by-product of G–d's rehabilitation of an unrepentant soul. The analogy is the removal of an infective splinter from a person's body: the pain that is experienced is not a "punishment" for the person's carelessness, but an inevitable part of the healing process itself. The fact that a foreign body has become imbedded in living flesh and has caused its decay makes its removal a painful experience. Similarly, one who fails to eject the alien element that has infiltrated his soul must undergo the spiritually painful process in which the corruption wrought by his negative deeds is exorcised from his body and soul. (4) Exodus 9:22-25. (5) Ibid., 27-28. (6) Ibid., 33. (7) D'rashot HaRan, pg. 8. See also Genesis 8:22; Talmud, Shabbat 53b. (8) Exodus 9:24. (9) Based on the two possible interpretations of the Hebrew word nitach; see Rashi's commentary on Exodus 9:33. (10) Exodus 7:3-5. (11) Thereby meeting the three requirements of teshuvah (repentance): regret, verbal confession and the resolve to never repeat the offense in the future. (12) This is the deeper significance of the Hebrew word teshuvah, which means "return." (13) At first glance, this may seem the less physically "supernatural" scenario. In truth, however, the very opposite is true. If a hailstone's midair halt violates the law of gravity, its nonexistence would defy a far more fundamental tenet of physics: the law that nothing can ever produce something, and that no thing can ever become nothing. (14) Based on an address by the Rebbe, Tevet 28, 5725 (January 2, 1965).

ESSENCE AND EXPRESSION

Rabbi Yaakov would say: This world is comparable to the antechamber before the World to Come. Prepare yourself in the antechamber, so that you may enter the banquet hall.

He would also say: A single moment of repentance and good deeds in this world is greater than all of the World to Come. And a single moment of bliss in the World to Come is greater than all of the present world.

Ethics of the Fathers 4:16-17

The Talmud relates that Rabbi Yaakov once witnessed the tragic death of a young man who, at that very moment, was engaged in fulfilling the very two *mitzvot* for which the Torah promises "long life."

"Honor your father and your mother," reads the fifth of the Ten Commandments, "that your days be lengthened, and that good befall you."[1] The one other *mitzvah* for which the Torah specifically promises reward is *shiluach hakan* ("dispatching the nest"): "If you happen upon a bird's nest ... and the mother bird is sitting upon the young or upon the eggs, do not take the mother bird along with the young. Send away the mother bird, and you may then take the young for yourself, that good may befall you and that your days be lengthened."[2]

And yet, here was a man who was fulfilling both these commandments simultaneously. At his father's request, he had climbed a ladder to chase away a mother bird from her nest and collect the chicks. But no sooner had he done so that he slipped from the ladder and fell to his death.

"Where are this person's 'long days'?" asked Rabbi Yaakov. "Where is the 'good' he was promised? But, when the Torah says 'that your days be lengthened,' it is referring to a world that is wholly long; and when the Torah says 'that good befall you,' it is referring to a world that is wholly good."[3]

"Rabbi Yaakov," concludes the Talmud, "is of the opinion that there is no reward for *mitzvot* in this world"—a view expressed in the *Ethics* by Rabbi Tarfon ("Know that the reward of the righteous is in the World to Come"[4]) and reiterated by Maimonides in his codification of Torah law, the *Mishneh Torah*.[5]

Another talmudic sage, Rabbi Joshua ben Levi, quotes the verse "You shall keep the *mitzvah*, the decrees and the laws which I command you today to do them"[6]—"today to do them," Rabbi Joshua reads in the verse's meaning, "and not to do them tomorrow; today to do them, and tomorrow to receive their reward."[7]

In other words, "the present world" and "the world to come" represent two entirely different modes of existence, which, for some reason, must each be confined to a world all its own. Our present existence is the environment for deed and achievement, but lacks the possibility to enjoy the fruits of our labor. On the other hand, the

Essence and Expression

"world to come" is a world of ultimate reward, bliss and perfection, but one that precludes any further achievement on the part of man. The Talmud goes so far as to quote the verse, "There will come years of which you will say: I have no desire in them,"[8] and declare: "This refers to the days of the Messianic Era, in which there is neither merit nor obligation."[9]

Why this dichotomy? On the most basic level, this is a function of G–d's granting freedom of choice to man, without which our deeds would be devoid of moral significance. A world in which the benefits of obeying the Almighty's commandments are self-evident would obviously lack the challenge and the sacrifice which makes their observance worthy of reward. So in this world, G–d created an environment in which neither He nor the divine nature of His commandments are openly manifest: a world in which surface appearances shroud and distort the divine truth—a world in which people engaged in life-lengthening *mitzvot* fall off ladders—challenging us to choose between good and evil, between faithfulness to our mission in life and its corruption. Only such a world can serve as the arena for meaningful accomplishment.

The Physics of Will

However, our material world's concealment of the divine truth is much more than an orchestrated moral challenge. On a deeper level, this concealment is significant to the nature of the *mitzvot* themselves.

The *mitzvot* are primarily physical deeds performed with physical objects: animal hides are fashioned into *tefillin* and wrapped around one's head and arm; flour and water become the instrument of a *mitzvah* in the form of the *matzah* eaten on Passover; a ram's horn is sounded on Rosh Hashanah; a citron and palm frond are taken on

Sukkot. For the physical world is ultimately the most appropriate environment for the function of the *mitzvah* to be realized.

"*Mitzvot* relate to the very essence of G–d"[10] is a mainstay of chassidic teaching. But the very notion of something relating to another thing's essence is a philosophical oxymoron. The "essence" of something is the thing itself, as opposed to the manner in which it affects and is perceived by that which is outside of it. Hence the axiom: "The essence of a thing does not express itself or extend itself."[11] In other words, if you see it, it is not the thing itself that you see, only the manner in which it reflects light and imprints an image on your retina; if you understand it, then it is not the thing itself that you comprehend, only a concept which your mind has pieced together by studying its effect on other things, and so on.

Nevertheless, G–d desired to project His essence into the created reality. This is the function of the *mitzvot*: through observing His commandments and fulfilling His will, we "bring" the very essence of G–d into our lives. And this is why He chose the physical object as the medium of the *mitzvah*'s implementation.

Spiritual entities (i.e., ideas, feelings, etc.) intrinsically point to a source, a cause, a greater reality which they express and serve. Unlike the physical, whose deeper significance is buried deep beneath the surface of its corporeality, the spiritual readily serves as the expression of a higher truth. The spiritual is thus the natural medium for the various *expressions* of the divine reality that G–d chose to convey to us.

But when it comes to the projection of G–d's *essence*, the very "virtues" of the spiritual disqualify it: its capacity to convey, to reveal, to manifest, runs contrary to the introvertive nature of "essence." Here, the physical object, the most non-transcendental element of G–d's creation, is the most ideal vehicle for G–d's essence-capturing *mitzvot*.

A physical object merely *is*: "I am," it proclaims, "and my being is wholly defined by its own existence." As such, the physical object constitutes the greatest concealment of the divine truth.[12] Precisely for this reason, it is G–d's medium of choice for man's implementation of His will.

In other words, the object of the *mitzvah* is not a "manifestation" of the Divine. Were it to reflect Him in any way, were it to reveal anything of the "nature" of His reality, it would, by definition, fail to capture His essence. But capture His essence it does, simply because He willed it to. G–d, of course, could have willed anything (including a manifest expression of His reality) to convey His essence, but He chose a medium that is most appropriate according to logical laws he established in creating our reality—a reality in which "essence" and "expression" are antithetical to each other. He therefore chose the material world, with its virtual blackout on any revealed expression of G–dliness, to serve as the "tool" with which we perform the *mitzvot* and thereby relate to His essence.

Better for Whom?

"The reward of a *mitzvah* is a *mitzvah*,"[13] say our sages. For all pleasures and satisfactions (indeed, the very concepts of pleasure and satisfaction) were created by G–d. So what greater delight can there be than to experience the divine essence, the source of all pleasure? Were it possible for a human being to perceive what transpires each time he fulfills G–d's will in his daily life, he would experience the very essence of bliss.

But the very nature of what is accomplished by the performance of a *mitzvah* precludes the possibility of such "reward": as explained above, the concealment of the divine reality which categorizes our material-bound existence is what makes it the appropriate medium for the drawing down of G‑d's essence. Reward can only come in a future world, a world that reveals rather than obscures its Creator. And yet, the world to come, precisely because of its manifest G‑dliness, can serve only as the environment for the reward of the *mitzvah*, but not for its implementation.

Thus, Rabbi Yaakov states in our *mishnah*: "A single moment of repentance and good deeds in this world is greater than all of the world to come. And a single moment of bliss in the world to come is greater than all of the present world."

Regarding the Almighty's purpose in creation—the drawing down of His essence into the physical creation[14]—a single positive act on the part of man is more meaningful than all the bliss experienced in the World To Come. Yet the performer of the *mitzvah* remains in the dark. Although he may be aware of the value of what he is doing, he is unable to perceive it and experience it. On the experiential level, a single moment of bliss in the World To Come is greater than all the joys of our present world.

The Banquet Hall

In light of this, one may ask: Why bother with the reward at all? If G‑d's purpose in creation is realized in our present-day lives, of what significance is our personal satisfaction?

One possible answer is that the need for a World to Come is a function of G‑d's commitment to justice and fairness. In the words of our sages, "G‑d does not deprive any creature of its due."[15] If man is instrumental in satisfying G‑d's desire in creation, he deserves the satisfaction of enjoying the fruits of his labor.[16]

But this certainly does not describe the ultimate significance of the World to Come. Rabbi Yaakov prefaces his above-quoted saying by comparing our world to an antechamber leading to the banquet hall, which is the World to Come. Clearly, then, the World to Come is not a footnote to our world, but its purpose and goal, a theme that is reiterated by many sayings by our sages.

How, then, do we reconcile this with the concept that "the essence of a thing does not express itself or extend itself"? And that it is, therefore, our present world, *because* of its spiritual darkness and inexpressiveness, that facilitates the drawing down of G–d's essence and thereby realizes His purpose in creation?

Truly Him and Truly Here

In applying terms such as "essence" and "expression" to the Almighty, we must bear in mind that it is He who created logic and its laws. Obviously, He is not governed or limited by any rational "axioms."

Nevertheless, He wishes to relate to our world as it is. So He chooses to make His relationship with us consistent with the basic "truths" that define our reality.

Indeed, since the purpose of creation is that the divine essence be drawn down into the physical reality, the objective is to do so on its (the physical reality's) terms, not by overriding them. So if the logical laws that govern our reality dictate that "expression" is incompatible with "essence," our bringing G–dliness into the world is to be achieved "blindly," without any perceptible manifestations of the divine essence.

On the other hand, however, if G–d's essence is truly to enter our reality, He must enter it as He is, without hindrance or inhibition. If *His* reality tolerates no limits or definitions, "revelation" must be no less conducive to His essence than "concealment."

In other words, for Him to be here implies two (seemingly contradictory) truths: if He is to be truly *here*, then His presence must be consistent with our reality; yet if it is truly *He* who is here, He must be here on His terms.

This is why the created existence has two distinct components: the Present World and the World to Come—the process and its culmination. The process of drawing down the divine essence into the created reality is carried out under an obscuring veil of corporeality, in keeping with the created rule that "the essence of a thing does not express itself or extend itself." At the same time, the product and end result of this process is a world in which G–d is uninhibitedly present, in which also the *expressions* of His reality fully convey the quintessence of His being.[17]

---

(1) Deuteronomy 5:16. (2) Deuteronomy 22:6-7. (3) Talmud, Kiddushin 39b. (4) Ethics of the Fathers 2:16. (5) Mishneh Torah, Laws Of Repentance 9:1. (6) Deuteronomy 7:11. (7) Talmud, Eruvin 22a. (8) Ecclesiastes 12:1. (9) Talmud, Shabbat 151b. (10) Torat Shalom, pg. 190, see also Tanya, part IV, section 20. (11) Guide for the Perplexed, quoted in Ki Shemesh U'magen 5692. (12) Ultimately, however, this "I am, period" quality of the physical reflects on the wholly self-contained quintessence of its Creator. So while the most immediate function of the physical is to obscure the divine truth, a deeper contemplation of its qualities will yield insight into the very beingness of G–d, something that no spiritual expression of Him can convey. (It is told that following the Rosh Hashanah *prayers one year, Rabbi Schneur Zalman of Liadi asked his son, Rabbi DovBer: "What did you think of during your prayers?" Rabbi DovBer replied that he had contemplated the meaning of the passage, "and every stature shall bow before You"—how the most lofty supernal worlds and spiritual creations negate themselves before the infinite majesty of G–d. "And you, father," Rabbi DovBer then asked, "with what thought did you pray?" Replied Rabbi Schneur Zalman: "I contemplated*

the table at which I stood.") (13) Ethics of the Fathers *4:2.* (14) *See* Wood Submerged in Stone, *pgs. 91-93;* Debating Truths, *pgs. 273-281.* (15) Midrash Mechilta, Exodus *20:30.* (16) *See* The Resurrection of the Dead *on pg. 207.* (17) *Based on an address by the Rebbe,* Tammuz *12, 5719 (July 18, 1959).*

THE HUMBLE WITNESS

> Shmuel the Small would say: "When your enemy falls, do not rejoice; when he stumbles, let your heart not be gladdened."
>
> Ethics of the Fathers 4:19

Rabbi Israel Baal Shem Tov, founder of the chassidic movement, taught: Nothing is by chance: every single event or experience in a person's life is predetermined and purposeful. So if a person chances to witness the degradation of his fellow, he must realize that he, too, suffers from the same lack in one form or another. Otherwise, why would divine providence have caused him to see his fellow's failing? Obviously, to open his eyes to something he must correct in himself.[1]

So even if one is your enemy, and justifiably so; even if his moral and spiritual downfall is one of his own making—it could have happened without your having been made aware of it. That you have witnessed it has nothing to do with him: it is a message to you, enjoining you to deal with a similar negative element—be it in the subtlest of forms—within yourself.

Shmuel the Small lived at a time when the Jewish community was threatened by vicious detractors, whose attacks against the very soul of Judaism he was forced to answer in kind. As the Talmud relates, it was he who authored the harshly worded passage *"V'lamalshinim"* ("For the informers, may there be no hope, and may all heretics and wicked ones be immediately lost...."), to be included in the daily prayers.[2]

However, his successful efforts to disenfranchise his "enemies" only humbled him—indeed, his extraordinary humility earned him the title, "the Small." Shmuel's life and leadership truly exemplified the ideal that the more a person triumphs over evil, all the more so must he search his heart and soul for its faintest reflection in his own self.[3]

---

(1) See The Mirror *on pg. 116. (2) Talmud, Berachot 28b. (3) Based on the talks of the Rebbe, Av 15, 5737 (July 30, 1977); Tammuz 2, 5741 (July 4, 1981).*

THE RESURRECTION OF THE DEAD

> Those who are born will die, and the dead will live.
>
> Ethics of the Fathers 4:22

A basic tenet of the Jewish faith is the belief that those who have died will again be brought to life. In fact, the "Resurrection of the Dead" is one of the thirteen cardinal principles, or "foundations," of Judaism.[1]

Common wisdom has it that the idea is more enduring than its incarnation, the concept more perfect than any conceptualization, that spirit is superior to substance. It would, therefore, follow that the soul is eternal and invincible, while its physical vessel, the body, is finite, temporal and destined to dust. This is fairly standard theological thinking. Yet the principle of the Resurrection runs contrary to such reasoning. For, if the body is but a temporary and deficient container for the soul, why recompose and revive it?

The Lame and the Blind

On the most basic level, the future reunion of body and soul is crucial to the realization of another of the Thirteen Foundations, the principle of "Reward and Punishment." In the words of our sages, "G–d does not deprive any creature of its due."[2] There are no loose strings in G–d's creation: Ultimately, all good must be rewarded, all that is negative must be corrected.[3] So because life is a joint enterprise of matter and spirit, the body and the soul will be rejoined in order to experience the results of their failings and attainments.

An analogy from the Talmud illustrates this point: Once there was a king who appointed two handicapped watchmen to guard his orchard. One was blind and the other was lame. The two conspired to rob their master: the lame man rode on the blind man's shoulders and steered him to the fruit. When the king confronted them, the blind man said, "How could I have stolen what I cannot see?" while the lame guard argued, "How could I have taken fruit that I cannot reach?" So the king had the lame man set on the blind man's shoulders and judged them as one.[4]

This is the story of man's mission in life. In this material world, man's physical body is able-bodied but blind. It possesses all the necessary tools to fulfill the purpose of its creation—except the vision to apply these tools in the appropriate manner. The body's selfish, animalistic drives distort its priorities and cloud its perception of the truth.

The vision to discern right from wrong must come from the soul, the spark of divinity within man that never loses sight of its Creator and purpose. Yet the soul is helpless on its own. To realize its mission on earth, it needs a physical mind, heart, hands and feet to deal with the physical reality.

Only when body and soul combine and integrate to form the entity called "man," can they safeguard and develop the "orchard"[5] that has been entrusted to them in accordance with its Master's plans.

In this dark and imperfect world, we cannot yet behold and enjoy the fruits of our labor.[6] But in the Era of Moshiach, the accumulated attainments of all generations of history will reach their ultimate perfection. And since "G–d does not deprive any creature of its due," all elements that have been involved in realizing His purpose in creation will be reunited to perceive and experience the perfect world that their combined effort has achieved.

Three Worlds

All this, however, only explains why the Resurrection must take place at some future time. Yet why is it a cardinal principle of the Jewish faith? The Torah includes thousands of beliefs, practices and ideas; of these, only thirteen merit the designation of "foundation," implying that it is upon them that the entire body of Judaism rests—that without any one of them, there would be something lacking in everything a Jew believes in and does.

To understand the centrality of the Resurrection to the whole of Judaism we must first examine the views of two great Jewish thinkers, Maimonides (Rabbi Moshe ben Maimon, 1135-1204) and Nachmanides (Rabbi Moshe ben Nachman, 1194-1270), on what constitutes the ultimate realization of G–d's purpose in creation.

Generally speaking, the entirety of existence is divided into three periods:

a) Our present reality (*Olam Hazeh*)
b) The Era of Moshiach (*Yemot HaMoshiach*)
c) The World To Come (*Olam Haba*)

Our present world is the scene of a daily struggle between good and evil. As in every struggle, there are ups and downs—times when the animal in man gets the better of him, and times when his inherent goodness triumphs. So ours is a world that allows for the existence of greed, hate and suffering. Although G–d created the world to reflect His infinite goodness and perfection, He also shrouded it in a veil of corporeality—a veil that conceals and dis-

Dusty Ego

"Dust you are, and unto dust you shall return,"[11] decrees the Torah—man is mortal and destined to dissolution. Yet one need not resign oneself to the more literal meaning of the verse; for there is also a deeper, more spiritual sense in which man can "turn to dust."

In the concluding verses of the daily *amidah* prayer we express an aspiration for the gift of humility by saying: "May my soul be as dust to all." Dust, seemingly the most downtrodden and lowly of elements, is the foundation of, and the ultimate source of nourishment for, everything on earth. So, too, in the conceptual sense, a self-perceived "lofty" and "prestigious" individual is forever caught up in his ego-bound self, forever trapped within the limits of its own nature. Only through humility and self-negation can one truly connect to his Creator and source and thus become part of something greater than his own existence, something perfect and eternal.

The World to Come will be a time of eternal life, a time when the physical will shed its disintegrative nature. For all beings will be as the egoless dust, having totally negated their self-defined existence to serve as a pure expression of the all-pervading reality of their Creator.[12]

torts its true nature, giving man the freedom to choose between good and evil. Man can either labor to bring to light the good inherent in himself and the world about him, or he can act to intensify the illusion of evil.

Ultimately, however, every moral victory reflects the quintessential nature of reality and is therefore eternal and cumulative, while our negative deeds are but temporary and superficial distortions of this truth. Hence our present-day lives will yield the second phase of existence, the strife-free Era of Moshiach.

The Era of Moshiach is not a supernatural world; it is the very same world we know today—without the corruptions of human nature. Man will have conquered his selfishness and prejudices; a harmonious world community will devote its energies and resources to the common good and the quest for continued growth in wisdom and perfection. In short, the Era of Moshiach represents man's attainment of the peak of his *natural* potential.

But the laws of nature themselves are finite and confining. So a naturally perfect world cannot be said to truly reflect its Creator's perfection. Death, for example, is a most natural phenomenon, a phenomenon connected with the finite and transitory nature of the physical—and the antithesis of G‑d's infinite and eternal reality. Indeed, the world as G‑d initially created it was free of death and dissolution, which were caused by man's first sin. So there is much in nature itself that is a subtle form of "evil"—i.e., part of the veil which obscures the divine truth.

Thus, the Era of Moshiach is also a period of human labor and achievement, although its challenges differ greatly from our present-day struggles.

Today, our lives are completely taken up with combating the negative: feeding the hungry, enlightening the ignorant, bringing

Tears of Life

Death is temporary. As the prophet promises,
"He will destroy death forever; and the L–rd G–d
will erase the tear from every face."[13] For the mortality
of physical life is but a symptom of the imperfection of man.
The perfect existence of Moshiach will bring eternal life
and the resurrection of all who lived in the past.

The resurrection and renewal of life have a
precedent in the revelation at Sinai, when the
entire Jewish nation gathered at the foot of the
mountain to receive the Torah. Our sages tell us that
so overpowering was man's first (and thus far, only)
total perception of the Divine, that when
the Almighty spoke the Ten Commandments,
"with each and every utterance their souls soared"
from their bodies. After each utterance, G–d restored
their souls with the "dew of life with which He is
destined to revive the dead," enabling them to retain
their physical embodiment even as they experienced
the reality of G–d.[14]

This account offers insight into the true nature
of death. The cessation of life that followed
"each and every utterance" was not a blank void,
but the impetus for yet greater attainment.
This is evidenced by the fact that although the

> "dew of life" fortified those assembled at Sinai
> to experience a communication from G–d,
> it was not sufficient to enable them to stand their
> ground for the next, even loftier utterance. With each
> and every revelation their souls again departed,
> experiencing a new "death" from which they rebounded
> to a yet higher level of consciousness and life.
> This is the deeper significance of Isaiah's equation
> of "the tear" with the phenomenon of death.
> The Torah associates the number 120 with a full life
> ("His days shall be one hundred and twenty"[15]).
> *Dim'ah*, the Hebrew word for "tear,"
> has the numeric value of 119—hence its association
> with death. In other words, death is not the negation
> of life; on the contrary, it is its preemptor and purveyor,
> in the same way that the first 119 components
> of the number "120" comprise its incomplete
> but fundamental predecessors. In the days of
> Moshiach, G–d will provide the additional
> "digit" to the tear of mourning, elevating it to the
> ultimate fullness of life.[16]

peace to warring factions. Then, the more blatant aspects of evil having been overcome, we will strive for the attainment of ever greater heights within the realm of good itself—struggling to overreach the limitations that define our natural existence.

The Era of Moshiach will be followed by the ultimate realization of G–d's vision of His creation—a world that expresses His quintessential perfection. Such a world, by definition, is beyond the confines of nature as we know it. This is the World To Come, the world of eternal life.

Two Definitions of Perfection

Is there a place for physicality in such a world?

This is the substance of the debate between Maimonides and Nachmanides. Maimonides is of the opinion that the ultimate utopia is a world of utter spirituality. "In the World to Come," he writes, "there are no physical forms or bodies—only souls.... So there is no eating or drinking, or any of the things that bodies need in the present world. Nor will there happen any of the events that befall bodies in the present world... (the souls) will enjoy the radiance of the Divine Presence—they will know and comprehend the divine truth, which cannot be known while in the dark and lowly body.... This is a life without death, for death is only an occurrence of the body.... This is the reward of which there is no higher reward, and the good of which there is no greater good...."[7]

Where and how does the Resurrection figure in all this? As Maimonides explains in his *Letter on the Resurrection of the Dead*, the reuniting of the bodies and souls of all who have lived throughout the generations of our present world is an important part of the Messianic Era, when all of the natural creation, including its physical elements, will achieve their ultimate perfection. But this will only be *their* ultimate—not *the* ultimate. The dead will be revived to a perfect life—as perfect as a finitely physical reality can be. But this life will also be subject to the dissolutive nature of all physical matter. This life, too, will come to an end, to be followed by the spiritual perfection of the World to Come.

Nachmanides disagrees. The ultimate realization of G–d's creation is not a spiritual world of souls, but a world in which spirit and matter together express the perfection of their Creator—a perfection that is both all-transcendent and all-embracing. According to Nachmanides, the resurrection of the dead will lead to eternal physical life, and usher in the World to Come—a world populated by souls enclothed within physical bodies.[8]

The teachings of Kabbalah and Chassidism concur with Nachmanides' definition of perfection.[9] Citing the axiom that "the higher something is, the lower it can descend," chassidic teaching explains that the ultimate expression of the divine truth is that there is no aspect of reality in which it cannot be found. To consider the physical too finite and too lowly a place for the perfection of G–d to be realized, is to say that He can extend this far and no further. But the essence of G–d transcends all labels and definitions. To categorize Him as "spiritual" is no less a definition than to attribute physical properties to Him, G–d forbid. He is neither one nor the other (having created them both), and both serve Him equally.

In our present-day reality, the material nature of our world is perhaps the cause of a greater concealment of G–dliness than the spirituality of the soul; but, in the World To Come, nature itself will prove the most potent statement of G–d's all-pervading truth. The intensity of a lamp is measured by the farthest point its light reaches; the true mark of genius is the ability to explain the most profound idea to the simplest mind. In the same way, a physical world that conveys the divine truth is the most powerful indicator of the infinite perfection of G–d.

Indeed, this is the purpose of the entirety of G–d's creation: that man, leading a physical existence, should overcome the imperfections of the material and bring to light its true nature and function—to express the goodness and perfection of its Creator.[10]

(1) As enumerated by Maimonides in his introduction to the eleventh chapter of the talmudic tractate Sanhedrin. *(2) Rashi's commentary on* Exodus 22:30. *(3) For a broader discussion of the nature of "punishment," see* Crime Repays *on pg. 191. (4)* Talmud, Sanhedrin *91a. (5) "And G–d took man, and He placed Him in the garden of Eden to work it and to safeguard it" —* Genesis *2:15. (6) See* Essence and Expression *on pg. 196. (7)* Mishneh Torah, Laws of Repentance *8:2-3. (8) Nachmanides'* Shaar Hagmul. *Such is also the view of R. Saadia Gaon (882-942) in his* Emunot V'deyot, *chs. 47 & 49. (9) See* Zohar, *part I, 114a;* Avodat Hakodesh, *2:41;* Shaloh, *introduction to* Beit Dovid; Likkutei Torah, Tzav, *pg. 30, and* Shabbat Shuvah, *pg. 130;* Derech Mitzvotecho, *pgs. 28-30. (10) Based on two responsa by the Rebbe, on the subject of the Resurrection, written in 5704 and 5705 (1944 and 1945). (11)* Genesis *3:19. (12) Based on an address by the Rebbe,* Iyar 6, 5751 (April 20, 1991). *(13)* Isaiah *25:8. (14)* Talmud, Shabbat *88b. (15)* Genesis *6:3. (16) This is an excerpt of an address delivered by the Rebbe on Monday,* Shevat 22, 5752 (January 27, 1992), *the fourth anniversary of the passing of his wife, Rebbetzin Chaya Mushka Schneerson o.b.m. (1901-1988).*

STAYING ALIVE

> Against your will you live; against your will you die.
>
> Ethics of the Fathers 4:22

"The soul of man is a lamp of G‑d."[1]

The flame knows no rest, for it lives in perpetual conflict between two opposite tendencies. On the one hand, it cleaves to its wick, drinking thirstily of the oil that fuels its existence. At the same time, it surges upward, seeking to tear free of its material tether. It knows that such disengagement would spell the end of its existence as a manifest, illuminating flame; nevertheless, such is its nature.

This is the paradox of the flame's life: its attachment to wick and fuel sustains both its continued existence and its incessant striving for oblivion.

Man, too, is torn between these two contrasting drives. On the one hand, he tends towards self, towards life and existence. At the same time, he yearns for transcendence, to tear free from the confining involvements of physical life, to reach beyond his material self.

"Against your will you live; against your will you die"—the tension created by these conflicting drives is the essence of the human experience. The desire to escape the trappings of physical life is what separates the human from the merely animal; but the escapist nature of man is counterbalanced by the compulsion to be, a compulsion that binds him to material reality. Back and forth, back and forth runs the cycle of life, from being to transcendence and back again.

Consumed

> *And Nadav and Avihu, the sons of Aaron, took each of them his censer... and offered a strange fire before G–d, which He had not commanded. And a fire went out from G–d and consumed them, and they died before G–d. And Moses said to Aaron: "This is what G–d spoke, saying: 'I shall be sanctified by those who are close to Me....'"*
>
> Leviticus 10:1-3

> short/ cir/cuit: an abnormal, usually unintentional, condition of relatively low resistance between two points of different potential in a circuit, usually resulting in a flow of excess current.
>
> The Random House Dictionary

Our sages explain that Nadav and Avihu's act of "offering a strange fire before G–d" was not a "sin" per se. On the contrary, the event prompted Moses to say to Aaron, "When G–d said 'I shall be sanctified by those close to Me,' I thought it referred to me or you; now I see that they are greater than both of us."[2]

Rather, as Rabbi Chaim ibn Attar writes in his *Ohr Hachaim* commentary on Torah, theirs was "a death by divine 'kiss' like that experienced by the perfectly righteous—it is only that the righteous die when the divine 'kiss' approaches them, while they died by their approaching it.... Although they sensed their own demise, this did not prevent them from drawing near (to G–d) in attachment, delight, delectability, fellowship, love, kiss and sweetness, to the point that their souls ceased from them."[3]

In other words, the divine fire that consumed the souls of Nadav and Avihu was the fire intrinsic to every soul: the soul's burning desire to tear free of the physical trappings that distance it from its Divine Source. Nadav and Avihu "came close to G–d" by indulging and fueling this desire to the point that they broke free of the "cycle" of life; to the point that their souls literally severed their connection with their bodies and were utterly consumed in ecstatic reunion with G–d.

Making It Real: From Cycle to Spiral

But this was a "strange fire," a fire that "G–d had not commanded." Man was not created to consume his material being in a fire of spiritual ecstasy. Although He imbued our souls with the drive for self-transcendence, G–d wants us to anchor our fervor to reality. He wants us to "settle" this yearning within our physical self, to absorb it and make it part of our everyday life and experience.

Following the deaths of Nadav and Avihu, G–d specifically commanded that their example not be repeated. As the Torah relates: "G–d spoke to Moses after the death of Aaron's two sons, who came close to G–d and died: '...Speak to Aaron your brother, that he come not at all times into the Holy... so that he die not...'"[4]

However, this divine command did not come to limit the degree of self-transcendence and closeness to G–d that we may attain. On the contrary: the command itself empowered us to accommodate, as physically alive human beings, the very fire that consumed the souls of Nadav and Avihu.⁵ So the "strange fire" they offered was also "strange" in a positive sense: an unprecedented act that opened a new vista in man's service of G–d.

This is the significance of a remark attributed to the founder of the chassidic movement, Rabbi Israel Baal Shem Tov: "It is only out of a great kindness on the part of the Almighty that one remains alive after prayer."

Prayer is the endeavor to transcend the enmeshments of material life and come close to one's essence and source in G–d. When a person truly achieves this closeness (that is, when he truly prays), he can experience an attachment to G–d of the magnitude that "released" the souls of Nadav and Avihu. But G–d has enabled us (in the very act of commanding us to do so) to incorporate such sublime experiences into our daily, humanly-defined lives.

So life's constant to-and-fro movement is more than a cycle that runs from existence to oblivion and back; it is an upward spiral. *Against your will you live*—man escapes his finite self, but is driven back to make his transcendent achievements an integral part of his individual being. *Against your will you die*—man's "escapist" nature now reasserts itself, compelling him to reach beyond the horizon of his new, expanded self as well. *Against your will you live*—again, man's tendency for being draws him back to reality.

Back and forth, upward and on, the flame of man dances, his two most basic drives conspiring to propel him to bridge ever-wider gulfs between transcendence and immanence, between the ideal and the real.⁶

(1) Proverbs *20:27*. *(2)* Rashi *on* Leviticus *10:3*. *(3)* Ohr Hachaim *on* Leviticus *16:1*. *(4)* Leviticus *16:1-2* *(5) Thus, immediately after warning Aaron not to "enter the holy" ("lest he die as his sons died"*—Rashi*), G–d proceeds to outline the process by which he is to enter, on* Yom Kippur, *into the Holy of Holies and experience the highest degree of connection with the Almighty. (6) Based on an address by the Rebbe,* Iyar *10, 5750 (May 5, 1990).*

WORDS AND NAMES

On the Essence of Language

The world was created with ten [divine] utterances.

Ethics of the Fathers 5:1

G–d formed every beast of the field and every bird of the air, and brought them to the man to see what he would call them. And whatever the man called every living creature, that was its name.

Genesis 2:19

Says the *Midrash*: "When G–d came to create man, He consulted with the angels.... Said they to Him: 'This man, what is his worth?' Said He to them: 'His wisdom is greater than yours.' G–d brought before them the beasts, the wild animals and the birds and asked them, 'This, what is its name?' and they did not know. He then brought them before man... and man said, 'This is a *shor* (ox), this is a *chamor* (donkey), this is a *sus* (horse) and this is a *gamal* (camel)....'"[1]

Naming things seems easy enough. One selects a syllable or two, coins a word and attaches it to an object. If one wants to be scientific about it, one selects a distinctive feature or two, transfigures them into a Latin-sounding name of eight or ten syllables, and—presto!—one has a name. Why, then, is the ability to name names indicative of a wisdom greater than that of the angels? And why does the Creator consider this ability on the part of man as the one thing that most characterizes his worth as a human being?

A World of Words

The world was created by divine speech. G–d said, "Let there be light... oceans... trees... fish...." and these words came to constitute the essence of every created entity.

In other words, what we experience as physical light is not merely something that the divine words "Let there be light" caused to come into being; it is the very word *light* being continually articulated by the Creator as a verbal expression of the desire that it exist. The same is true of all other creations: a cow, a fish, a tree, a stone—these are all our physical perceptions of the divine words they embody.[2]

(The "ten utterances," which are quoted in the Torah's account of creation, actually specify only the names of a few primary creations [light, water, land, etc.] and several general categories [stars, trees, fish, birds, etc.]. But these elementary creations contain within themselves—on both the linguistic and physical levels—the myriad particulars of the created existence. Ultimately, every created thing has a name in the Holy Tongue, a name that, if not explicit in the "ten utterances" of the first chapter of Genesis, is nonetheless implicit therein, by the means of *gematria* or one of the several other systems of letter transfiguration of the Hebrew language.[3])

Therein lies the difference between the Holy Tongue (*lashon hakodesh*) and other languages.

In all other languages, a word is assigned to an existing entity. If there was a reason why a particular word was originally married to a particular object, this is not a matter of great relevance. If the English word *ox* were to be chosen for that obstinate, silly-looking animal with the long ears, while the word *donkey* referred to the heavy-set fellow with the horns, this would not make a whit of difference. Language would still be performing its commonly assumed function: identifying objects by some agreed-upon arrangement of verbal sounds and letters.

But language, in its truest, "holy," sense, is far more than that. In the Holy Tongue, a word *precedes* its subject, creates it, and constitutes its very being. It articulates the divine desire that it be, expressing its Creator's perception of its qualities and function—of the end toward which He created it.[4]

So for Adam to call even a single creature by its original, quintessential name, he had to know it utterly. He had to possess the wisdom and insight to penetrate its external form and recognize the "holiness" within—the divine utility and purpose that lies at its heart.[5]

Calling Forth

This ability to recognize and name most expresses the role of man in creation.

Every creature possesses the potential to articulate its Creator's goodness and perfection. But it is man who actualizes this potential through his development and utilization of his fellow creations and his incorporation of them in his service of the Almighty. Only man has been imbued with the essentially divine quality of "free choice";

thus, only his actions have moral significance. All of creation can, therefore, realize its divine purpose only through him.[6]

This is the deeper significance of the Hebrew word *vayikra*, "and he called," used by the Torah in describing Adam's calling the name of every creature. As its English counterpart, the Hebrew word *kara* connotes both "calling" and "calling forth"; Adam's calling of names was a demonstration of his ability to call forth and bring to light the "name" and essence of every created thing, by recognizing and developing its potential to serve him in his service of G–d.

When man harnesses the ox to the plow and uses the proceeds to perform a self-transcending act such as charity, prayer or Torah study, every element of creation that was involved in this act—the energy of the ox, the vegetative potential of the soil, the nourishing water and sunlight—achieves something it could never have on its own. It transcends the limits of its own external being and realizes the purpose for which it was created.[7]

---

(1) Midrash Rabba, Bereishit *17:5*. *(2) See* A Thing of Silence *on pg. 85 for an exploration of the concept "divine speech" as a definition of the physical reality. (3) See* Tanya, part II, ch. 1. *(4) The same is true of a person's name: it forms the channel through which his soul radiates life into his body, doing much to define his nature and character. In the words of Elazar ben Pedat, "One's name has an influence on one's life"* (Talmud, Berachot 7b). *Our sages have therefore said that parents' naming of their child is "a small prophecy." (5) The angels may have been able to know the essence of a creature from the perspective of the spiritual realm they occupy. But to relate to a fodder-chomping ox and discern the way in which its physical, animal qualities can be directed to serve the divine purpose in creation was beyond their spiritually defined (and confined) abilities. (6) In the words of the* Talmud

(Kiddushin 82a): "The entire world was created to serve me, and I was created to serve my Creator." See On the Essence of Eat, pg. 149. Chassidic master Rabbi Mendel of Kotzk thus advised: "A person should always have two pockets in his garment: in one he should keep the verse, "I am but dust and ashes," and in the other, the talmudic adage, "For my sake was the world created." (7) Based on the talks of the Rebbe, Simchat Torah 5731 (October 23, 1970) and Kislev 25, 5750 (December 23, 1989).

A PARTICULAR WORLD

> The world was created with ten [divine] utterances. What does this come to teach us? Certainly, it could have been created with a single utterance.
>
> Ethics of the Fathers 5:1

Chapter five of the *Ethics of the Fathers* begins by listing various things that are distinguished by the number ten: the ten divine utterances of creation ("Let there be light," "May the earth sprout forth vegetation," etc.), the ten tests of Abraham, the ten plagues of Egypt, the ten constant miracles in the Holy Temple, etc.

Ten is the complete number. It is no coincidence that man enumerates the objects and components of his world in sets of ten. In essence, the world is comprised of ten generic elements, its every entity and force falling under one of ten general categories.

Thus we are told that G–d created the world with ten utterances. Of course, He could have merely said, "Let there be a world"; but then, the particulars of our existence would be of only secondary significance. If one person is distinguished by his generosity, another devotes his life to the pursuit of wisdom, and a third raises a child, their individual roles would be devoid of a particular significance in a one-utterance world. In such a world, "existence" would be its only significant reality; everything else would be merely a form or expression thereof. For the only true measure of significance is whether a thing is worthy of a specific involvement on the part of G–d to create it.

The Creator desired a world in which not only "existence," but also concepts such as "kindness," "wisdom" and "femininity" are individually important. So He "took the trouble" to emanate from Himself ten distinct creative forces. One is defined as "benevolence" (*chessed*) and includes such things as the emotion of love, the act of giving, and physical water. Another is "wisdom" (*chochmah*)—a general quality that includes the faculty of intellectual conception, the geometric point, and fatherhood. Leadership, receptiveness, femininity, and earth are all components of "sovereignty" (*malchut*).

Ultimately, then, creation consists of ten basic "things"; our world is an immense canvas, populated by countless millions of colors, all derivatives of the ten basic hues of the divine artist's palette.[1]

This is why G–d created the world with ten utterances—to lend particular significance to the particulars of existence. And when the *mishnah* tells us that there are ten of something, it is saying that its significance is not confined to a certain corner of reality, but touches on its every aspect. Abraham proved his faith not in one but in all areas of life. Our exodus from Egypt freed us of not one, but of ten enslavements—it was an exile and redemption involving the totality of our being. The Holy Temple did not merely transcend the natural norm in this or that manner—it expressed the manifest presence of G–d in every nook and cranny of our world.[2]

---

(1) See Tanya, *part II, ch. 1. (2) From an address by the Rebbe,* Tammuz *12, 5742 (July 3, 1982).*

ONE AND ALL

> The world was created with ten [divine] utterances. What does this come to teach us? Certainly, it could have been created with a single utterance. However, this is in order to make the wicked accountable for destroying a world which was created with ten utterances, and to reward the righteous for sustaining a world which was created with ten utterances.
>
> Ethics of the Fathers 5:1

In other words, G–d chose to "expend" ten utterances on our world to make our life's mission within it more significant and valuable.

Yet this explanation seems somewhat unsatisfactory. If G–d *could* create a world with a single utterance, then this ought to be the true measure of its worth. Any additional "expenditure" on His part seems but an artificial inflation of its value. As the commentary *Midrash Shmuel* puts it: If A pays ten *zuz* for an object worth only a single *zuz*, and B steals it, would B's obligation be for more than the object's true value?

Could and Did

Chassidic teaching explains that the above *mishnah* actually describes two existing dimensions of our existence. When the *Ethics* says that the world "could have been created with a single utterance," it is not merely speaking of a theoretical possibility, but of a particular facet of our present reality; a facet that exists by virtue of the "could" element of G–d's creative power.

In other words, there are two aspects of G–d's creation:

a) The very fact of its existence: before it was not, now it is. G–d brought all created things into being out of a prior state of absolute nothingness. Their "somethingness" is a feature that they all share equally, their individuality fading to insignificance before this fact. This most basic creative power of the Almighty originates in the "could" of G–d, the sublime potential for creation rooted in His essence.

b) The individual nature of the various elements to comprise our world. In addition to the common fact of their existence, G–d imbued each entity with its own unique features and qualities, making for a diverse and multifaceted universe.

Of course, G–d could have created our world, in all its infinite detail, with a singular expression of his desire for a world. But had He done so, the only meaningful aspect of our existence would have been the common denominator of all reality: the fact of its existence and the ultimate purpose of its creation. Since the ultimate measure of a thing's value is the significance imparted to it by the Creator, the particular nature of things, despite their vivid individuality, would have been but a superficial phenomenon, devoid of any true import.

Enter the "ten utterances." They represent the divine creative force that shapes the *specific* nature and function of all things.[1] And because the Creator is involved in creation also on this level, the deeds of man—for better and for worse—are doubly significant. Not only does creation as a whole serve a divine purpose, but each of its parts has its specific utility imbued in it by the divine utterance that creates and sustains it.²

So when man makes use of a specific talent or resource that has been placed at his disposal, he fulfills (or, G–d forbid, abuses) its divine purpose on both levels: on the existential level, where it is defined as an object of G–d's overall objective in creation; and on the particular level, the level on which the Almighty identifies and lends import to its specific features and function.

Four Applications

These two dimensions of existence, the singular and the particular, are likewise present in the "miniature universe" that is man,³ and find expression in many areas of our lives.

The individual human being is a virtual "community" of ideas, character traits, drives and tendencies. And yet, it is the same "I" who experiences them all. This duality is likewise reflected in everything that we do. To cite a few examples, the manner in which we contemplate the mystery and majesty of the Creator, how we develop our environment, how we commune with the Almighty in prayer and how we approach the study of His wisdom, the Torah—all include both an "all-inclusive" approach as well as a localized, particular approach.

In man's perspective of the world and its Creator. Through contemplating the nature of His creation, one comes to appreciate the greatness of G–d and to develop feelings of love and awe towards Him.⁴ This meditation may take the inclusive or the specific approach, each with its own results.

One can contemplate G‑d as the creator of existence per se. The result: a humbling realization of how lofty and removed He is from our reality. For the creation of something out of nothing (*ex nihilo*) is attributable only to a being who transcends the terms and definitions of both "something" and "nothing"—an abstraction beyond the domain of the rational mind.

Or, one may contemplate the intricacies of nature, the amazing individual qualities of every created thing. This causes a more "personal" love and awe of G‑d—something closer to and more digestible by the human mind and heart.

In our utilization of the world's resources. The *Midrash* describes G‑d's desire for a world as a "desire for a dwelling place below."[5] By using the resources of our world to serve the Almighty, we fulfill this divine aim, creating an environment hospitable to His presence.

Here again we employ a dual approach. On the one hand, in everything we do we are guided (not by the dictates of its mundane, self-focusing nature, but) by this single common goal—that "all your deeds should be for the sake of Heaven."[6] On the other hand, this does not result in a homogeneous, featureless approach to life, in which the means are insignificant and only the ultimate goal matters. Rather, the unique characteristics of each element are recognized and appreciated as integral elements of G‑d's creation and purpose.

In *prayer*, we approach G‑d with the recognition of our dependence upon Him for existence and sustenance. Here, too, both the inclusive and specific elements are present.

We begin our day with acknowledgment and gratitude to G‑d as the giver of life—the *Modeh Ani* prayer (see inset). Then, throughout the day, we recite many blessings and prayers, each verbalizing a particular aspect of our relationship with G‑d as it pertains to our specific needs and experiences.

In our study of Torah. Torah is a revelation of G–d's wisdom and will, binding its student to the "mind" of G–d. In this most basic function of Torah, the nature and depth of our understanding is all but irrelevant. As one great chassidic master put it, "There are

I to I

According to Torah law, words of Torah
or prayer may be spoken only in a state of
cleanliness and purity. Thus, upon awakening in the
morning, it is forbidden to study or pray before
one has washed his hands and otherwise attended
to his body's hygiene.
Nevertheless, a Jew's very first act of the day,
while still on his bed, is to say the words
of the *Modeh Ani*: "*I offer thanks to You, living
and eternal king, that You have restored my soul to me;
great is Your faithfulness.*"
The "legal" reason for this is that the *Modeh Ani*
does not contain any of the sacred names of G–d.
We address G–d simply as "You," and as our "living
and eternal king." So it is permitted to utter these
words at any time, in any state.
On a deeper level, the *Modeh Ani* goes beyond all
categorizations and definitions (i.e., "names")
of G–d's holiness.
We are addressing the very "You" and
essence of G–d, which transcends concepts

> such as "holiness" or "purity."
> The same is true regarding the level of self that expresses the *Modeh Ani*. The *Modeh Ani* is our acknowledgment that life itself is a daily gift from G–d. Unlike all other prayers, which address a specific human need or a specific aspect of our relationship with G–d, the *Modeh Ani* relates to our very "I," affirming its source in the quintessential "You" of G–d.
> *Modeh Ani*, then, is the "I" of the Jew communing with the "I" of G–d. As such, it knows no restrictions or inhibitions, existing in all circumstances, at all times. In the words of Rabbi Yosef Yitzchak of Lubavitch, "No impurity in the world can touch the *Modeh Ani* of a Jew."

seventy ways of studying Torah; the first one is silence."[7]

In this, the entire Jewish nation is a unified, singular knower of G–d via the Torah. We see this reflected in the wording of the verse, "...and he (Israel) camped opposite the mountain (Sinai)."[8] As our sages comment on the singular usage ("he camped"), the entire nation of Israel was unified as a single individual in preparation for its receiving of the Torah from the Almighty.[9]

On the other hand, G–d encased His Torah wisdom in rational concepts, designating the human mind as the tool by which to grasp His truth. And the realm of the intellect is a specified and individualized domain: no two minds are identical, and different fields must be approached with differing methods, rudiments and points of reference.

The Torah embraces the entire range of intellectual potential of the human mind. It includes every rational discipline known to man, from the mystical to the analytical, from the legal to the psychological. Its every concept is a virtual universe of multilayered meanings and countless applications to every area of life. We therefore beseech G–d, "Grant us our portion in Your Torah"[10]—enable us to properly employ the specific intellectual talents that You have granted us to discover our individual portion and path to our knowledge of Your truth.[11]

---

(1) See previous essay, A Particular World. *(2) G–d's "utterances" are not a one-time phenomenon, but an ongoing act of creation: G–d is perpetually "speaking" our world into being, constantly supplying it with existence and life (see* Existence As Birth, *pg. 124). (3)* Midrash Tanchuma, *Pekudei 3. (4) See Maimonides'* Mishneh Torah, Laws of the Foundations of the Torah, *2:1-2. (5)* Midrash Tanchuma, Naso *16; see* Tanya, *ch. 36. (6)* Ethics of the Fathers *2:12. (7) The Tchortkover Rebbe, Rabbi Zevi Hirsch HaLevi Hurwitz (d. 1758). (8)* Exodus *19:2. (9)* Mechilta *on verse. (10)* Ethics of the Fathers *5:20, recited three times a day at the conclusion of the* Amidah *prayer. (11) Based on an address by the Rebbe,* Iyar 27, 5751 (May 11, 1991).

A HISTORY LESSON

There were ten generations from Adam to Noah. This is to teach us the extent of G–d's tolerance; for all these generations angered Him, until He brought upon them the waters of the Flood.

There were ten generations from Noah to Abraham. This is to teach us the extent of G–d's tolerance; for all these generations angered Him, until Abraham came and reaped the reward for them all.

Ethics of the Fathers 5:2

With this summation of the first twenty generations of history, our *mishnah* addresses an ever-pressing issue in the micro-history of our individual lives: how are we to deal with the negative we encounter in ourselves and in our surroundings?

The first set of ten wicked generations yielded—nothing. After stretching His tolerance to the limit, G–d wiped the slate clean and rebuilt His world anew from the righteous Noah and his family.

Following Noah, there were another ten generations of wicked and destructive behavior on the part of humanity. But Abraham "reaped the reward for them all"—that is, he succeeded in realizing the potential for good that these ten generations represented. Abraham was able to extract the kernels of good embedded in all this evil. Instead of being lost, their lives and endeavors were redeemed and sublimated in the person of Abraham.

On the individual level, a person must learn to distinguish between two kinds of evil. On the surface, they are both negative, but there is a world of difference between them: the Torah sets clear boundaries to define what is to be rejected outright and what is to be developed and transformed.

There are certain elements, which, if one encounters them in his own character or in the world about him, must be totally eradicated: any attempt to deal with them will prove counterproductive and corrupting. But the Torah also directs us to discern those aspects of our lives that, despite their crude exterior, are rich with potential treasure. To write them off as undesirable is to throw out the baby with the bathwater; often, it is precisely these "lowly" elements that contain the most rewarding gifts. To extract these gems from the rough and treacherous ground in which they are imbedded is the challenge of life on this material earth.

THE FRONTIER OF SELF

> Our father Abraham was tested with ten tests, and he withstood them all—to indicate how great was his love for G‑d.
>
> Ethics of the Fathers 5:3

The tenth and most important test of Abraham's faith was the "Binding of Isaac" (the *Akeidah*), recounted in the twenty-second chapter of Genesis:

And it came to pass after these things that G‑d tested Abraham. And He said to him, "Abraham!"; and he said, "Here I am!"

And He said: "I beseech you: take your son, your only son whom you love, Isaac, and go to the land of Moriah; and offer him there as a burnt offering upon one of the mountains of which I shall tell you."

And Abraham rose up early in the morning and saddled his ass; he took his two attendants with him, and his son, Isaac. And he broke up wood for the burnt offering and rose up and went to the place which G‑d told him....

And Abraham built an altar there, and laid the wood in order; and he bound his son Isaac and laid him on the altar upon the wood.

And Abraham stretched out his hand and took the knife to slaughter his son.

And an angel of G–d called to him out of the heavens: "...Lay not your hand upon the lad, neither do anything to him. For now I know that you fear G–d, for you have not withheld your son, your only son, from Me...."

The Binding of Isaac has come to represent the ultimate in the Jew's devotion to G–d. Every morning, we preface our prayers by reading the Torah's account of the *Akeidah* and then say: "Master of the Universe! Just as Abraham our father suppressed his compassion for his only son to do Your will with a whole heart, so may Your compassion suppress Your wrath against us, and may Your mercy prevail over Your attributes of strict justice...."

On Rosh Hashanah, when the world trembles in judgment before G–d, we evoke the Binding of Isaac by sounding the horn of a ram (a ram replaced Isaac as an offering) as if to say: If we have no other merit, remember Abraham's deed. Remember how the first Jew bound all succeeding generations of Jews in a covenant of self-sacrifice to You.

Why Abraham?

Obviously, the supreme test of a person's faith is his willingness to sacrifice his very existence for its sake. But what is so unique about Abraham's sacrifice? Have not countless thousands of Jews given their lives rather than renounce their covenant with the Almighty?

Yet to sacrifice one's child? This is a far greater demonstration of faith than to forfeit one's own life. But in this, too, Abraham is not unique. Time and again through the generations, Jews have encouraged their children to go to their deaths rather than violate their faith.

Every Jewish schoolchild knows the story of "Chanah and her seven sons." Chanah encouraged her seven children to die a torturous death rather than bow before a Greek idol, and then proclaimed: "My children! Go to Abraham your father and say to him: You bound one offering upon the altar, and I have bound seven offerings...."[1]

Furthermore, while Abraham was *prepared* to sacrifice his son, in thousands of *Akeidot* throughout our history Jews actually gave up their lives and the lives of their entire families. And, unlike Abraham, G–d had not directly spoken to them and requested their sacrifice; their deeds were based on their own convictions and the strength of their commitment to an invisible and often elusive G–d. And many gave their lives rather than violate even a relatively minor tenet of their faith, even in cases in which the Torah does not require the Jew to do so.[2]

Nevertheless, as Don Isaac Abarbanel writes in his commentary on Genesis, it is the Binding of Isaac "that is forever on our lips in our prayers.... For in it lies the entire strength of Israel and their merit before their Heavenly Father...." Why? What about the many thousands who made the ultimate sacrifice in reiteration of their loyalty to G–d?

Of No Substance

The same may be asked in regard to Abraham himself. The *Akeidah* was the tenth and final "test" in Abraham's life. In his first test of faith, Abraham was cast into a fiery furnace for his refusal to acknowledge the arch-idol of his native Ur Casdim, the emperor Nimrod, and for his continued commitment to teaching the world the truth of one, non-corporeal and omnipotent G–d. All this before G–d had revealed Himself to him and chosen him and his descendants to serve as a "light unto the nations"[3] and the purveyors of His word to humanity.

In a certain sense, this early act of self-sacrifice seems to be even greater than the latter ones. All on his own, a man recognizes the truth and devotes himself to its dissemination—to the extent that he is even willing to sacrifice his very life to this end. All this without a command or even sign from Above.

And yet, the Binding of Isaac is considered the most important test of Abraham's faith. The Talmud asks: Why did G‑d, in commanding Abraham on the *Akeidah*, say, "I beseech you...."? Answers the Talmud: "G‑d said to Abraham: 'I have tried you with many tests and you have withstood them all. Now, I beg you, please withstand this test for Me, lest they say that the earlier ones were of no substance.'"[4]

Again we ask, Why? Granting, even, that the *Akeidah* was the most demanding test of all, why are the others "of no substance" without it?

The Trailblazer

Once there was an untamed wilderness. No path penetrated its thick underbrush, no map charted its forbidding terrain. But one day there came a man who accomplished the impossible: he cut a path through this impregnable land.

Many trod in his footsteps. It was still a difficult journey, but they had his charts to consult, his trail to follow. Over the years, there were some who made the journey under even more trying conditions than those which had challenged the first pioneer. While he had done his work in broad daylight, they stumbled about in the black of night. While he had only his determination for company, they made the trip weighed down by heavy burdens. But all were equally indebted to him. Indeed, all their achievements could be said to be but extensions of his great deed.

Abraham was the pioneer of self-sacrifice. And the Binding of Isaac was the first instance of true self-sacrifice in all of history.

Selfishly Altruistic

Sacrificing one's self is not the same as sacrificing one's life. There is a world of difference between the two.

Mankind's story includes many chapters of heroic sacrifice. Every generation and society has had its martyrs—individuals who gave their lives for their faith, for their homeland, and for virtually every cause under the sun.

They did so for a variety of reasons. For some it was an act of desperation: to them, their lives were not worth living unless a certain objective could be attained. Others believed that their deed would be richly rewarded in the hereafter, so they readily exchanged the temporal benefits of physical life for the soul's eternal gain. Finally, there were those for whom their cause had grown to be more significant to them than life itself: they had come to so completely identify with a certain goal that it became more integral to their selves than their existence as individuals.

In all the above cases, the martyr sacrifices his life, but not his self. Indeed, he sacrifices his physical life for the sake of his self—be it the self projected by his obsession, the spiritual self of his immortal soul, or a broader, universal self he has come to identify with. Ultimately, his is a selfish act; "selfish" in the most positive and altruistic sense of the word—here is an individual who has succeeded in transcending the narrow, material definition of "self" that dominates our corporeal world—yet "selfish" nonetheless.

Breakthrough and Revelation

Abraham was a man with a mission. A mission for which he sacrificed everything, a mission more important to him than his own life.

For many years he had agonized that there was no heir to this mission, that his work of bringing the beliefs and ethics of his monotheistic vision of G–d to a pagan world would cease with his passing from the world. Then came the divine promise: miraculously, at the age of 100, he was to have a son, from whom would stem the people of Israel. "You shall call his name Isaac," said G–d, "and I shall establish My covenant with him for an everlasting covenant, and with his descendants after him."[5]

And then G–d told him to destroy it all.

When Abraham bound Isaac upon the altar, it was not in the service of any calling or cause. In fact, it ran contrary to everything he believed in and taught, to everything he had sacrificed his life for, to everything G–d Himself had told him. He could see no reason, no purpose for this act. Every element of his self cried out against it— his material self, his spiritual self, his transcendent, altruistic self. Yet he did it. Why? Because G–d had asked him to.

Abraham was the pioneer of self-sacrifice. Before Abraham, the self was inviolable ground. Man could enlighten the self's priorities, he could even broaden and sublimate it, but he could not override it. Indeed, how could he? Man's every deed has a motive (conscious or otherwise), and his every motive has a rationale—a reason why it is beneficial to his own existence. So how could he be motivated to annihilate his own self? The instinct to preserve and enhance oneself is the source and objective of a creature's every drive and desire. Man could no more transcend it than lift himself up by pulling on the hair of his own head.

Yet Abraham did the impossible. He sacrificed his self for the sake of something beyond the scope of the most transcendent of identities. Had he not done so, no other act of self-sacrifice—previous or subsequent, of his own or of his descendants—could be presumed to be of any "substance," to be anything more than the expression of a higher self.

The Frontier of Self

But when Abraham bound Isaac upon the altar, the heavenly voice proclaimed: "*Now* I know that you fear G–d." Now I know that the will of G–d supersedes even the most basic of your instincts. Now I know that all your deeds, including those which could be explained as self-motivated, are, in essence, driven by the desire to serve your Creator. Now I know that your entire life was of true, selfless substance.

So when we speak of the *Akeidah*, we are also speaking of those who trod the path this great deed blazed. Of the countless thousands who died for the creed of Abraham, of the many millions who lived for its sake. Their sacrifices, great and petty, cataclysmic and everyday, may, on the surface, seem but the outgrowth of their personal beliefs and aspirations—commendable and extraordinary, but only the fulfillment of an individual soul's identity. But the *Akeidah* reveals them to be so much more than that.

For Abraham bequeathed to his descendants the essence of Jewishness: that at the core of one's very being lies not the self but one's commitment to the Creator. And that, ultimately, one's every choice and act is an expression of that "spark of divinity" within.[6]

---

(1) Talmud, Gittin 57b. (2) According to Torah law, a Jew must give up his life rather than commit murder, certain sexual crimes (such as incest or adultery) or idol-worship, or where there is a deliberate attempt to force a renunciation of the Jewish faith. (3) Isaiah 49:6. (4) Talmud, Sanhedrin 89b. (5) Genesis 17:19. (6) Based on an address by the Rebbe, Kislev 21, 5731 (December 19, 1970).

NO GOOD REASON

[From the ten miracles of the Holy Temple:] No woman ever miscarried because of the smell of the holy (meat).

Ethics of the Fathers 5:5

There are those who would limit the number of their offspring for a variety of social and economic reasons. At times, the rationale for family planning assumes positive, even "holy" guises: less children means more time and energy to educate them properly, more money to give to charity, etc.

Says the *mishnah*, "No woman ever miscarried because of the smell of the holy." Nothing, be it the loftiest and holiest of considerations, can ever justify the prevention of the creation of another life.

ON THE ESSENCE OF THE INSTRUMENT

The First Pair of Pliers

Ten things were created at twilight of Shabbat eve. These are: the mouth of the earth,[1] the mouth of the well,[2] the mouth of the donkey,[3] the rainbow, the manna, the staff (of Moses), the *shamir*,[4] the writing, the inscription and the tablets (of the Ten Commandments). Some say also the burial place of Moses and the ram of our father Abraham. And some say also the spirits of destruction as well as the original tongs, for tongs must be made with tongs.

Ethics of the Fathers 5:6

What would you think of the host who begins preparing the food and setting the tables only after his guests have arrived? This, explains the Talmud, is why the human being was created after all other creatures, on the sixth day of creation. Man is G–d's "partner in creation,"[5] charged to refine and develop the world to its Creator's vision of perfection; so G‑d first readied for him the entirety of creation, "so that he may enter immediately into the banquet."[6]

Nevertheless, our *mishnah* tells us that ten (or twelve or fourteen) things were created after man, in the closing moment of the sixth day of creation. It would seem to follow, then, that these objects are not part of the furnishings for man's "banquet" and life's work; that while all the other elements of creation serve as the resources and tools with which man completes G‑d's work, these creations lie beyond the scope of human achievement.

Indeed, the *mishnah*'s list of things created "at twilight of Shabbat eve" is basically one of supernatural phenomena, whereas our development of the world is specific to the natural arena. We use our natural faculties to refine and sanctify our natural environment; the miraculous, on the other hand, is G‑d's involvement in creation in a manner that seems to preclude any participation on the part of His mortal "partner." In fact, our sages have stated that a *mitzvah* that is performed by supernatural means is not valid. The entire point of the divine commandments is that we utilize the *natural* resources of creation to fulfill G‑d's will.

A significant exception, however, is the final item on the *mishnah*'s list—the "original tongs." As the Talmud[7] explains, since the forging of a metal object requires a pair of tongs, how could the first pair of tongs be made? This is why G‑d created the original tongs at the twilight of the sixth day of creation. But assuming that human iron-working could indeed not have commenced without a divinely-fashioned pair of tongs (the Talmud itself goes on to question this premise, pointing out that the first tongs could have been poured out in a mold), why were they created "at twilight of Shabbat eve"? Do not the prosaic tongs fall within the category of the tools and resources used by man to develop the world?

More Questions

Also problematic are the exclusion of the 13 other, miraculous "twilight creations" from the "banquet" prepared for man.

In the opening verse of the second chapter of Genesis, the Torah states:

And G–d concluded, on the seventh day, His work which He had done; and He rested on the seventh day from all His work which He had done. And G–d blessed the seventh day and sanctified it, for on it He rested from all His work which G–d had created to do.

Our sages address the apparent contradiction between the words "And G–d concluded, on the seventh day, His work" and those which immediately follow, "and He rested on the seventh day." Did He or did He not work on the seventh day? Indeed, since our observance of Shabbat is the reenactment, on the human side of the partnership, of G–d's resting on the seventh day, how can we say that G–d concluded His work on the seventh day itself?

In his commentary on the verse, Rashi cites two explanations:

A man of flesh and blood, who does not have absolute knowledge of his times and moments, must add from the mundane (weekday) onto the holy (Shabbat). But G–d, who knows His times and moments, entered into Shabbat by a hairsbreadth, so it seemed as if He concluded His work on the day itself. Another explanation: What was the world lacking? Rest. With Shabbat there came rest, and the work of creation was concluded and finished.

Immediately after telling us that "G–d concluded, on the seventh day, His work which He had done," the Torah establishes man's partnership with G–d in creation by concluding that all the "work which G–d had created" was made "to do." Our sages explain that the phrase "to do" (*la'asot*, in the Hebrew) means "to perfect"; in the words of the *Midrash*, "all that G–d created requires perfection" on the part of man.[8]

Beyond the Letter of the Law

From all this, one thing is clear: the things which G–d created in the last hairsbreadth of the sixth day of creation, and even the phenomenon of rest created on the seventh day itself, are also part of what "G–d created (for man) to perfect." So why were these creations not awaiting Adam when he opened his eyes?

Hovering Upon The Waters

From this we conclude that there are two aspects of man's mission in life:

a) The "banquet" prepared prior to his creation so that he may find everything he needs to refine and develop his environment.

b) Those elements of creation (the "twilight" creations and the "rest" of Shabbat) that followed man's own and that represent a later stage in the fulfillment of his function in G–d's world.

Our Sages compare G–d to an architect who provides his workers with the raw materials, the tools and the blueprint with which to construct the edifice he has designed. The tools and materials are our faculties and our world's resources, the blueprint is the Torah, and the completed edifice is the world of Moshiach.[9]

Thus, when the Torah says in the opening verses of Genesis, "And the world was without form and void, and darkness was upon the face of the deep; and the spirit of G–d hovered upon the waters," the *Midrash* expounds: "'The spirit of G–d hovered'—this is the spirit of Moshiach."[10] The spirit of Moshiach is the soul of creation itself, for the Messianic Era is the realization of the world which G–d envisioned at creation.

But what will we do after this goal has been achieved, after we have eradicated evil and ignorance from the face of the earth? Is history over? Does humanity enter a "golden age" of retirement? G–d is infinite and He has created us in His image. So our potential for perfection is also infinite: after we attain what is to our eyes the ultimate in perfection, we recognize that another, higher perfection awaits beyond our present horizon of achievement.

But there is a major difference between our current quest to perfect our world and the future challenges of a post-Moshiach world. Today, the focus of our efforts lies in combating the negative. Virtually all "achievement" is defined in these terms: a disease cured, a criminal rehabilitated, a street cleaned. Doing good means feeding the hungry, enlightening the ignorant, bringing peace to warring factions. So our vision of perfection is the obliteration of all evil and suffering from the face of the earth.

And yet, there also exists a higher mode of refinement and development: not the development of an evil-free society, but development within the realm of good itself; not the separation of the gold from the dross, but a refinement of the gold itself, to attain a new, unprecedented level of quality.

Snippets Of Future

In his commentary on Genesis, Nachmanides writes that G–d's six days of creation correspond to the six millennia of human endeavor. Just as the six days of creation culminate in a seventh day of divine withdrawal and rest, 6,000 years of human achievement result in the "day of eternal Shabbat and tranquility"—the era of Moshiach.

But, as explained above, the "rest" of the messianic Shabbat is not an absence of achievement, but a new manner of achievement. Our present-day labors, which largely involve the battling of adversaries, are characterized by struggle and toil. Not so the future attainments of the Shabbat-millennium of Moshiach (and, to a lesser extent, those of the present-day weekly Shabbat), which involve only the harmonious progression toward ever-greater levels of perfection.

So the supernatural creations created at the point of time that straddles the six days of creation and Shabbat, and even the element of "rest" created on Shabbat itself, are also elements to be developed in our partnership with the Almighty. Yet these belong to a later phase of our perfection of our world.

All that is part of our present-day efforts preceded our creation, so that the banquet of life's challenges and achievements was laid out when the first human being entered the banquet hall. On the other hand, those elements that represent a toil- and adversary-free mode of development were created later—in order to underscore the fact that, even as we deal with these elements today, they are of a "futuristic" nature.

True, we experience Shabbat for one day of each week of our lives. In contrast to the six workdays of the week, in which we struggle to extricate ourselves from our enmeshment in the corporeal and direct our lives towards positive and holy ends, Shabbat is a day of harmonious refinement. Everything is holier, more spiritual. We withdraw from the challenge to change the world, for the inherent goodness of G–d's creation is a touch closer to the surface on this day. We cultivate this goodness and enrich it, rather than battle the negative visages of the material.[11] The same is true of the "borderline Shabbat" elements that were created at twilight of the sixth day: they all represent points in history and aspects of our lives where we attained and attain a semblance of this higher, harmonious developmental process.

But these are all "tastes" of a future world. The fact that they appear only after man has begun his mission upon earth implies that, in essence, they follow the fulfillment of his initial struggle-rife efforts. That, ultimately, their true time and place is the seventh millennium, the Shabbat that culminates the embattled workday phase of human history.

Means and Ends

The "original tongs" represent a certain aspect of this higher form of refinement. G–d did not create this pair of tongs for the "banquet" that represents the initial stage of man's development of his world— as pointed out above, humanity could have managed to work iron without this divine head start. Rather, they were created in order to establish a certain truth in creation, one that serves as a prototype and "foretaste" for a refinement within the realm of good itself.

The *mitzvah* lies at the heart of our refinement and perfection of the world. A person uses his prowess and expertise to earn money, and then appropriates a part of it to charity; a person eats, and then uses the physical energy derived from the food for prayer and study; animal hide becomes *tefillin*, wool becomes *tzitzit*, flour and water become *matzah* for Passover. Through these acts, we direct our talents and resources to serve G–d's will, thereby implementing His blueprint for creation.

Obviously, not everything we possess or come in contact with is actually made into an instrument of a *mitzvah*. But if only ten percent of a person's earnings are contributed to charity, the other ninety percent enables him to sustain his life and his business so that he may continue to give his annual ten percent. The same applies to all *mitzvot*: while only a relatively small percentage of our energies and resources is directly involved in doing a *mitzvah*, a much greater part of our lives can be utilized as "accessories" to the divine commandments we fulfill. Indeed, a person can transform his entire existence into a vehicle for implementing the divine will: his every act and endeavor is either a *mitzvah*, or an "accessory" that enables or enhances the performance of a *mitzvah*, or "the accessory to the accessory of a *mitzvah*," and so on.[12]

According to this, different components of our lives may be viewed in terms of varying degrees of refinement and speciality. For example, the energies one devotes to help another are seen as "better" spent than those exhausted on earning a living. The first is directly involved in one's "partnership with G–d in creation" while the second plays only a secondary (or third-level or fourth-level) role.

But this grading of areas in our lives by degrees of importance and "holiness" is significant only when the driving force behind one's dedication to G–d's will is the desire to feel a sense of "involvement" and "partnership" with the Almighty. When such is the case, those activities that more directly involve the realization of the divine purpose are deemed more lofty and spiritual than the "secondary" aspects of life, and are the source of greater satisfaction and fulfillment.

However, there is a higher, more selfless approach to life. When a person seeks only the fulfillment of G–d's will, without any thought to his own "achievement" or "involvement," all this is irrelevant. The most spiritual of his attainments and the most mundane detail of his life are equal in his eyes, as they are both vital to the development of creation in accordance with the divine desire.

This is an example of a further refinement within the realm of good itself. After you have eliminated the negative from your life, after you have directed your every act and resource to your partnership with G–d, a further challenge awaits you. Your life, while wholly dedicated to the divine will, now includes elements of "greater good" and "lesser good," measured in terms of the immediacy of their involvement in the fulfillment of a *mitzvah*. Now, your challenge is to further refine these lower tiers of your life. By shifting the focus of your life from your own sense of closeness to G–d to the simple desire to fulfill His will, all elements of your existence, including those farthest removed from any direct participation in an overt command of G–d's, become equally imbued with sanctity and significance.[13]

A pair of tongs, by definition, serves no purpose of its own. Its function is to create other tools that, in turn, will serve some useful function. The "original tongs," formed for the purpose of forging other tongs, is even further removed from any direct utility. The fact that G–d Himself troubled to create them in the hairsbreadth of time that opens the day (and era) associated with harmonious creation and development means that also the accessories and secondary instruments in our lives can be elevated to a level of primary connection to the essence and purpose of existence.[14]

---

(1) To swallow Korach (Numbers 16:32). (2) The "Well of Miriam"—the miraculous stone which provided water to the Jewish People during their wanderings in the desert (Exodus 17:6, Numbers 21:16-18). (3) Of Bilaam (Numbers 22:28). (4) A worm which split stones for the construction of the Holy Temple in Jerusalem (Talmud, Gittin 68a). (5) Talmud, Shabbat 119b; see footnote 8. (6) Talmud, Sanhedrin 38a. (7) Talmud, Pesachim 54a. (8) Midrash Rabba, Bereishit 11:7; see Etz Yosef commentary on this Midrash. (9) Midrash Rabba, Bereishit 1:2. (10) Ibid., 2:5. (11) A prime example is the manner in which we regard physical pleasure on Shabbat. During the week, we seek to divest our physical drives and resources of their corporeal embodiment and transform them into something more altruistic and "spiritual." For example, when we eat, we do so with the intention to utilize the energy we derive from the food for a higher purpose. In this way, the material substance of the food and the physical act of eating are transformed into something that serves and expresses the Divine: transformed into the energy expended in helping the needy, into the fervor of prayer, into the acumen of the mind studying the divine wisdom in Torah—transformed into an instru-

ment of the divine will. On the other hand, eating for no other purpose than for the sake of physical pleasure is not a constructive—much less a holy—act. Instead of sublimating the material, it has the very opposite effect: it sinks the person deeper into the morass of self, even further distancing him, and the material environment he occupies, from his and its quintessential purpose and function. On Shabbat, however, pleasure for the sake of pleasure is itself a mitzvah, a fulfillment of G‑d's will. There is no need to change the nature of the physical or our physical nature: deriving pleasure from the material world is itself an act of holiness, an expression of the divine essence implicit in our existence. (12) Cf. the Talmud's discussion (Shabbat *130a*) of whether one may "cut down trees to make coals to forge a scalpel to perform a circumcision" on Shabbat. (13) The Talmud *relates that Rabbi Chiya himself sowed flax, wove nets, trapped deer, tanned the hides of the deer, made parchment and prepared scrolls. He then journeyed to a city that had no schools. He wrote the Torah and the* mishnah *on his scrolls and taught the children of the town* (Ketuvot *103b*). (14) Based on an address by the Rebbe, Iyar *26, 5737 (May 14, 1977) and on other occasions.*

INSIDE WORK

> There are four types of people. One who says, "What is mine is yours, and what is yours is mine," is a boor. One who says, "What is mine is mine, and what is yours is yours"—this is a median characteristic; others say that this is the character of a Sodomite. One who says, "What is mine is yours, and what is yours is yours," is a *chassid* (pious one). And one who says, "What is mine is mine, and what is yours is mine," is wicked.
>
> Ethics of the Fathers 5:10

As a rule, the *Ethics of the Fathers* deals with the area known as "within the line of the law"—not with establishing what is forbidden or permitted (as do the other 62 tractates of the Talmud), but with the conduct of the pious individual who wishes to go beyond what is mandated by the laws of the Torah.[1]

So the above *mishnah* requires some clarification. According to Torah law, the concept of charity—i.e., to share what one has been given with the less fortunate—is not an optional "pious" practice but an obligation; and to make use of another's possessions as if they were one's own certainly violates the most basic legal precepts of the Torah. Accordingly, one who adopts a policy of "yours is mine" and/or "mine is mine" is not only "wicked" by the pious standards of the *Ethics*, but by the rudimentaries of Torah law as well. So what principle "within the line of the law" is this passage conveying to us?

But when the *Ethics* says, "One who *says*...." it means just that. The issue here is not that it is wrong to steal or that it is mandatory to give, but a matter of attitude. According to the "dry" law, it makes no difference what one thinks or feels or says, as long as one does what is right. But the "chassidic" standards of the *Ethics* demand more than an impeccable exterior.

This is the deeper significance of the term "*within* the line of the law": that the inner environment of a person's character and personality be in line with his actions. A person may be generous in practice; but should he in any way express the attitude that he is giving what is by rights his, he has failed to assimilate the Torah's concept of charity as part of his inner self.[2]

---

(1) See introduction to this book. (2) Based on an address by the Rebbe, Av 25, 5739 (August 18, 1979).

REASONABLE LOVE

> Any love that is dependent on a specific thing—when the thing ceases, the love also ceases. But a love that is not dependent on a specific thing never ceases. Which is a love that is dependent on a specific thing? The love of Amnon for Tamar. And one that is not dependent on a specific thing? The love of David and Jonathan.
>
> Ethics of the Fathers 5:16

At first glance, the difference between these two types of love seems obvious. The first is an attraction and connection between two people that is based on some ulterior motive: the lover wishes to benefit in some way from his relationship with the beloved. But beauty may fade, physical passion wanes, "common interests" grow less interesting; people whose ideas and whose company we once found stimulating can become repetitious and unexciting. Bereft of its cause and basis, such love dissipates. But a truly altruistic love, a love in which two souls bond and fuse for no external motives or reasons, is eternal and invincible.

But a closer examination of the two examples cited by the *Ethics* yields some interesting results. The story of Amnon and Tamar is related in the Book of Samuel: Amnon was stricken by an incestuous desire for his sister Tamar and forced himself on her. His lust sated, "Amnon hated her... with a hatred that was greater than the love with which he had loved her."[1]

As brother and sister, Amnon and Tamar were connected by a bond that is not based on any external factors. The bond between siblings, as that between parent and child, stems from the fact that they are "one flesh"; it is a quintessential bond, one that is not caused by the beloved's goodness, intelligence, physical beauty or any other "reason." Nevertheless, though this bond always exists, it is not always expressed in a person's consciousness and behavior. It may lie dormant in the depths of one's heart for years. Or, it may manifest itself only in the form of a lesser, externally motivated love, one that is limited to an appreciation of the beloved's qualities. In the case of Amnon, his love for his sister was expressed only in the corrupt form of incestuous desire.

So Amnon's love for and subsequent hatred of Tamar illustrates that even a relationship that is in essence altruistic may be expressed in a way that makes it dependent on secondary factors. When this happens, these secondary elements become vital to the relationship. Without them, the love cannot survive, at least not on any conscious level.

By contrast, the love between David and Jonathan began as an ordinary friendship between two people with no intrinsic connection to each other—a friendship that was based on one's appreciation and enjoyment of the other's positive qualities. Yet their friendship developed into a truly altruistic love. "Jonathan's soul became bound to the soul of David, and Jonathan loved him as his own soul,"[2] to the point that Jonathan risked his life for David even though David's very existence was to his detriment: Jonathan, the eldest son of King Saul, was initially destined to succeed his father as king of Israel. When Saul learned that David had been anointed by the prophet Samuel to be the next king, he wished to kill him; it was Jonathan who repeatedly saved David from Saul's plans, telling David, "You shall be king over Israel, and I shall be second to you."[3]

It is, therefore, significant that our *mishnah* speaks of "a love that is dependent" on something, and "a love that is not dependent" on anything, using the term *dependent on* (*t'luyah*) as opposed to "based on" or "caused by."

For as the examples of Amnon and Jonathan demonstrate, the original cause and basis for a relationship does not, in itself, determine the nature of its expression. A quintessential love may be experienced only as something which is dependent on external factors, in which case the nature of the relationship is that of "a love that is dependent" on something. And a relationship that is initially based on "ulterior" motives can develop into "a love that is not dependent" on anything.

From Within

In his *Mishneh Torah*, Maimonides dwells on the significance of the concept of "love of G–d." In the tenth chapter of *The Laws of Repentance* he writes: "One who serves G–d out of love, occupies himself with the Torah and the *mitzvot*, and follows the pathways of wisdom, not for any reason in the world—not out of fear of evil or out of a desire to inherit the good; rather, he does the truth because it is true.... This is the level which G–d enjoins us to attain, as it is written 'You shall love the L–rd your G–d.' When a person loves G–d with a proper love, he observes the *mitzvot* out of love....

"One who occupies himself with the Torah in order to receive reward or to escape punishment is doing it not for its own sake ('*shelo lishmah*'). And one who occupies himself with it... out of a love for the Master of the Universe who has commanded it to us, is doing it for its own sake ('*lishmah*'). Said our sages:[4] 'A person should always occupy himself with the Torah, even if he is doing it not for its own sake; since from doing it not for its own sake he will come to do it for its own sake.'"

Chassidic teaching takes this a step further. Not only is doing the right thing for the wrong reasons desirable because it will ultimately lead to doing it for the right reasons, but even now, before attaining this higher state, a person *is* doing it for the right reasons. While his conscious self may focus on the physical and spiritual benefits of leading a righteous life, deep down, in his heart of hearts, there is a part of him that is intrinsically connected to the truth and desires it "because it is true."

This idea is also expressed in the above talmudic saying quoted by Maimonides. The Hebrew word *mitoch* means "from within"; so a literal translation of the saying would read: "A person should always occupy himself with the Torah, even if he is doing it not for its own sake, since *from within* his doing it not for its own sake he will come to do it for its own sake." In other words, buried within a person's external motives lies a deeper truth: the desire, rooted in the very essence of his soul, to do what is right for its own sake.

However, this quintessential self is not, at the present phase of his spiritual development, expressed in his conscious feelings and day-to-day behavior. So although his desire to fulfill the divine will "contains" a purely selfless love for G–d, his relationship with the Almighty is dependent upon external considerations.

Superficial but Crucial

Thus, our *mishnah*'s discussion of "dependent" and "independent" love holds a twofold lesson.

Never discount the value of what you're doing, even if you find it tainted with ulterior motives. Ultimately, as the love of David and Jonathan demonstrates, a feeling originally born out of external causes can grow into "a love that is not dependent" on anything and ever-enduring.

Know, that at the core of your deeds and feelings lies a pure, altruistic commitment to your Creator and to the purpose of your creation. By being true to this commitment in your daily life, you will ultimately cause it to be realized, in all its purity, as an expressed and tangible feeling in your heart.

But one may take this to the other extreme, and say to himself: "If I indeed subconsciously possess a selfless love and commitment for what is right, why not rid myself of my imperfect feelings? Shouldn't I best banish every self-oriented motive from my heart, so that my true nature may come to light?"

So the *Ethics* cites the case of Amnon as its example for "a love that is dependent" on something. Although a quintessential bond underlay his relationship to Tamar, it did not "come to light" when his selfish love was undone. For though this bond did exist, it did not find expression in his feelings toward his sister. When his "dependent love" lost its basis, it was replaced not by an altruistic love but by hatred and revulsion.

In Amnon's case, his selfish "love" for his sister was corrupt and ruinous. Still, what we can learn from it concerns the *positive* application of "dependent love." It teaches us that our sense of how G–d's Torah is beneficial to our lives must be fostered and cultivated.

One must remember that "a love that is dependent" on something—"when the thing ceases, the love also ceases"; that as long as a person has not yet translated his quintessential love for G–d into a manifest feeling in his heart, these external factors remain vital to his relationship with the Almighty. He must continue to make use of his appreciation of the benefits—both material and spiritual—of leading a righteous and productive life, until such time as the deeper, purer motives that are intrinsic to his soul have matured and have come to be as expressed in his conscious thoughts and feelings and in his day-to-day behavior.[5]

---

(1) II Samuel, *13:16*. *(2)* I Samuel, *18:1*. *(3)* Ibid., *23:17*. *(4)* Talmud, Pesachim *50b*. *(5) From an address by the Rebbe*, Iyar *24*, *5733 (May 26, 1973)*.

DEBATING TRUTHS

On the Essence of the Machloket

> Any dispute that is for the sake of Heaven is destined to endure; one that is not for the sake of Heaven is not destined to endure. Which is a dispute that is for the sake of Heaven? The dispute(s) between Hillel and Shammai.
>
> Ethics of the Fathers 5:17

Why would we want a dispute—albeit one that is "for the sake of Heaven"—to endure?

But first we must understand the nature of the Torah dispute (*machloket*). For the existence of differing opinions regarding the interpretation and application of Torah seems to run contrary to the very essence of what Torah is: the unequivocal word of G–d.

And yet, the Torah itself foresees a situation in which two groups of sages, each applying their knowledge and cognitive powers to an issue, arrive at two differing conclusions. The Torah instructs that, in such a case, one is to follow the majority opinion[1]—an opinion that now assumes the status of *halacha*, a law that is the expressed will of the Almighty.

In other words, a conclusion that is based on subjective human logic, on debatable arguments and proofs—a conclusion that may even be the result of who happened to be in attendance when the matter was put to a vote in the study hall or rabbinical tribunal[2]—represents the absolute and inviolable will of G–d!

Marriage of Minds

For this is what the Almighty desired His Torah to be: a collaboration between divine revelation and human intellect. It is the human mind, with all its inconsistencies and shortcomings, which G–d chose as the instrument of His Torah's translation into the terms of the created reality.[3] When man applies his rational powers to the principles revealed at Sinai, and does so in a manner that is faithful to the guidelines established by the Almighty, the result is nothing less than "Torah"—G–d's communication of His wisdom and will to humanity.

The Talmud takes this a step further, citing the Heavenly voice that proclaimed, regarding a *machloket* between two groups of sages, "These and these are both the words of the living G–d."[4] Not only is the ultimate ruling an expression of divine will, but also the "rejected" view is nothing less than "the words of the living G–d."

Since both opinions are based purely upon the divine will revealed in Torah; since both conclusions have been reached by applying the guidelines and techniques that Torah itself establishes; since both seekers have subjugated their minds to the pursuit of truth without the slightest nuance of personal consideration—both ideas become part and parcel of Torah, products of G–d's "collaboration" with the human mind.

Plural and Singular Expressions

In practice, we can obviously apply only one conclusion. In the concrete and definitive realm of physical action, where two differing rulings are mutually exclusive, only one of them can actually be

Written and Relayed: The Dynamics of a Partnership

The Torah is comprised of two basic parts: the "Written Torah" and the "Oral Torah."
The Written Torah, commonly referred to as the *Chumash*, the Five Books of Moses, or simply the "Torah," encapsulates the entire communication of the divine will and wisdom given to us at Sinai. The Oral Torah is the vast body of interpretation and methodology by which the Written Torah is understood and applied.
The Oral Torah is no less inviolable than the Written: both were communicated by G–d to Moses; both embody the divine absolutes upon which the universe is founded and which constitute the "blueprint" by which the Creator desires that we order our lives. The difference lies in the manner of their transmission: the "Five Books" were written down for posterity by Moses from the Almighty's dictation, while the interpretation of

> these writings, and the rules that govern their extrapolation to address "new" phenomena and situations to be encountered by each generation, were transmitted as an oral tradition. Beginning with Moses and Joshua, the Oral Torah was handed down through the generations from master to disciple, as described in the opening *mishnah* of the *Ethics*.[29]
>
> Why did the Almighty choose to impart His wisdom and will to man via the dual instruments of the Written and Oral Torahs? Obviously, no logical reason can explain a divine "motive," as all phenomena, including "logic" and "motivation," were created by G–d. But we can examine the nature and implications of the manner in which the Almighty elected to relate to us.
>
> One thing we know: Because the Torah consists of a Written Torah and Oral Torah, man has been made a partner to G–d's endeavor of communicating to His creation. When the finite and vincible mind of man, faithful to the guidelines set down by Torah, employs its rational powers to interpret or apply the Torah, its conclusions are a pure and absolute articulation of G–d's desire.

implemented. The hundred dollars belong either to the plaintiff or to the defendant; the piece of meat is either *kosher* or it is not. Hence, the Torah-ordained rule of adopting the majority opinion.

But in the nebulous world of the soul, conflicting perceptions can exist side by side and be constructively applied in unison. Here, the variant opinions in the *machloket* of Torah form the basis for the many dualities which could—and should—be part of our outlook, our feelings and our approach to life.

Thus, we have two dimensions to each *machloket*. On the pragmatic, "bottom line" aspect of Torah, known as *halacha*, only one of the conflicting views becomes law. Only one of the disputing parties merits that, in the words of the Talmud, "'G–d is with him'[5]—the *halacha* is as he says."[6]

But regarding the "soul" of the dispute—the concepts and perspectives that underlie its arguments—we have the dictum, "These and these are both the words of the living G–d."

This distinction can be seen in the different names for "G–d" that the Talmud employs. The phrase, "These and these, are both the words of the living G–d" (in Hebrew, *eilu v'eilu divrei Elokim chayim*), uses the divine name *Elokim*, while the other, "'G–d is with him'—the *halacha* is as he says" (*v'HaVaYaH imo—halacha k'moto*), refers to the Almighty as *HaVaYaH*. *Elokim* describes G–d as He relates to His creation, speaking of His power as expressed by tremendous multiplicity and variety of His work; indeed, the very word "*Elokim*" is plural in its construction. *HaVaYaH*, on the other hand, is the divine name that refers to G–d's transcendence of creation, to His absolute singularity and oneness.

When applied to the divine wisdom and will vested in Torah, *Elokim* connotes G–d's projection of His wisdom into the multifaceted and dichotomous world of human intellect, where it finds expression in differing, even contrasting, ideas. The *HaVaYaH* of Torah is *halacha*, the singular, unequivocal rulings of divine law.

The Anatomy of a Machloket

Many of the famed Torah disputes are contested by the disciples of two great talmudic sages, Shammai and Hillel[8]—indeed, it is regarding a dispute between "The House of Shammai" and "The House of Hillel" (as these two schools of Torah thought came to be known) that the Heavenly voice proclaimed "These and these, are both the words of the living G–d." The Hillel and Shammai schools differed

Maimonides on the Machloket

The question of how two conflicting opinions can both express the word of G–d is further augmented by the fact that for twenty-four generations from when we received the Torah at Sinai, there was not a single *machloket*. Indeed, Shammai and Hillel themselves (who lived in the twenty-ninth generation from Sinai), whose names call to mind dozens of *halachic* disputes, actually differed only on three points. It was only in the following generations that the two schools of thought that they had founded (the "House of Hillel" and the "House of Shammai") gave birth to many disputed issues of Torah law. Can we then say that the phenomenon of *machloket* is a result of human failing? The Talmud seems to say as much: "When the number of insufficiently developed disciples of Shammai and Hillel grew, disputes increased within Israel."[30] And yet, the Talmud also

Debating Truths

maintains, "These and these are both the words of the Living G‑d"!

Maimonides, in his famed introduction to the *Mishnah*, explains: "If two people are equal in the caliber of their minds, in the depth of their study and in their knowledge of the principles from which the cognition is to be derived, there will be no disagreement between them; and even if there would, their differences will be minor, such as we find in the case of Shammai and Hillel who only differed on a few laws.

"But when their disciples' diligence in wisdom slackened and their cognition diminished in comparison to that of their masters, they fell in dispute over the understanding of many issues, as each one's conclusions were based on his mind and on the extent of his comprehension of the principles.

"We are not to fault them in this, as we do not compel two debating sages to debate with the minds of Joshua and Pinchas.[31] We do not doubt the validity of their arguments, for they are not on the level of Hillel and Shammai or those greater than them—and G‑d did not command us to insist on this in our service of Him. Rather, He commanded us to heed the sages of the generation, as He said: 'If[32] there arise a matter that is beyond you to judge.... You shall come... to *the judge who shall be in those days*.'"

Thus, the very phenomenon of the *machloket* underscores the fact that the study and application of Torah involves a marriage of minds between the human and the Divine:

> that the intellect of man, applied to the utmost of its finite and relative abilities, serves as a conduit of the divine wisdom and will.

on a wide range of issues, including criminal law, torts, laws regarding ritual purity, the festival observances, marital law and virtually every other area of Torah. Ultimately, however, their many differences can be traced to a few basic principles which characterize each school's distinct perspective and approach.

Let us consider the following cases:

a) How many lights are to be kindled in the Chanukah *menorah* on each of the eight evenings of the festival? According to the House of Shammai, one is to kindle eight lights on the first evening, seven lights on the second evening, and so on, concluding with a single light on the last evening of Chanukah. The House of Hillel rules that one should begin with a single light on the first evening, increase to two on the second, three on the third, and conclude with eight lights on the eighth evening.[9]

b) Historically, which is to be considered the precise moment of the Exodus? According to the House of Shammai, it is Passover eve (Nissan 15), when the Jews were free to leave Egypt. According to Hillel's disciples, it is midday of the following day, the moment in which our forefathers physically left Egypt's borders. (The practical implication of this dispute is the question of whether Psalm 114 ["When Israel went out of Egypt..."] is to be recited before partaking of the pascal lamb at the *seder*.)[10]

c) The Torah commands the Jew to read the verses of the *Shema* ("Hear O Israel....") twice a day, "when you lie down and when you rise."[11] Our sages differ on how to interpret the phrase, "when you lie down."

Rabbi Eliezer, a member of the Shammai school, understood this as a reference to the time period during which people lie down to sleep—i.e., the first few hours of the evening. Rabban Gamliel and other Hillelian sages interpreted it to include the entire duration of time in which people sleep, and thus allow the reading of the *Shema* at any time of the night.[12]

d) At what point does a fish become susceptible to ritual contamination? One of the rules that govern the laws of ritual impurity (*tum'ah*) is that living plants and animals do not become impure through contact with an impure object. According to the House of Shammai, as soon as the fisherman hauls his net out of the water, his catch is subject to contamination. The House of Hillel disagrees, holding that a fish retains its immunity to contamination up until the moment it actually dies.

These four disputes between the disciples of Hillel and Shammai, and many others as well, are all expressions of a single underlying point of contention: Which is the more basic definition of an object or phenomenon—its potential or its actual state?

What is freedom—the potential to act freely or the actual removal of all constraining and limiting elements? What is the "time of sleep"—the time when people are actually sleeping, or the time when they engage in the activity that results in the state of sleep? Is a creature that is still actually alive, but devoid of all potential to live, to be considered immune from contamination by virtue of the "life" it possesses?

The *menorah*'s lights reflect the number of days embodied by a particular evening of Chanukah. So do we count the days which that evening possesses in potential, or those which have been actualized to date? The first evening of Chanukah represents the actual experience of but (a few minutes of) a single day, yet holds in store the potential eight days to come. The opposite is true of the eighth day. Its value in terms of potential is "one," while it can boast of the realized accomplishments of eight days (seven, plus the opening moments of the eighth).

In each of these cases, we are confronted with two realities, the potential and the actual. Which is to serve as our primary point of reference? Are we to deal with the elements of our world as they exist in actuality and regard the potential they contain as an auxiliary phenomenon? Or, are we to relate more to their essence and potential, while our experience of a certain aspect of this potential as "actuality" is to be regarded as a secondary truth?

"These and these" may both be the words of the living G–d, but only one view can be incorporated into our lives. The fish in question cannot be both ritually pure and impure, the psalm cannot be both recited and not recited before the eating of the pascal lamb, one either can or cannot recite the *Shema* at 2:00 a.m., and the number of lights to be kindled on the first night of Chanukah is either one or eight. Either what is actual in our lives is to take precedence over the potential, or vice versa. They cannot both take precedence over each other. Or can they?

First Things First

Perhaps the most basic *machloket* between the schools of Shammai and Hillel is one that appears in the talmudic tractate *Chagigah*:

The House of Shammai says that first the heavens were created, then the earth. The House of Hillel says that first the earth was created, and then the heavens.[13]

The very first words in the Torah state, "In the beginning G–d created the heavens and the earth." So, obviously, the schools of Shammai and Hillel are not debating which came first in the sequential sense. Indeed, much of kabbalistic teaching centers around the *Seder HaHishtalshelut* (literally, "order of evolution"). This is the process by which G–d first emanated from Himself a series of divine attributes (*sefirot*), out of which He proceeded to evolve a chain of "worlds" and realities, each further "removed" from His utterly abstract and intangible being.

In other words, G–d began by creating all existences in their most sublime and spiritual form; He then caused them to evolve and metamorphose, in many steps and stages, into their more concrete incarnations, ultimately producing our physical world, the final and most tangible embodiment of these realities.

So spirit preceded matter.[14] What the schools of Shammai and Hillel are debating, then, is: Which is the primary focus of G–d's creation? Did G–d create all of existence, including the physical universe, for the sake of the spirituality of the heavens? Or, does the divine purpose in creation lie in the existence of material life on earth, and everything else exist to serve this end?

Final in Deed, First in Thought

Yet, here, too, there seems to be no room for debate. The Torah's view on G–d's purpose in creation is clear: the entirety of the created existence, from the most sublime spiritual entity to the most corporeal creature, was created so that physical man should implement the divine will in the physical world by observing the *mitzvot* of the Torah.[15]

Thus the soul of man, which is "carved out of the heavenly throne of G–d,"[16] "descends" to earth to assume a material body, character and life. Thus the Torah, which originates in the heavens,[17] has not only been revealed on earth, but has been *given over* to man; after Sinai, the Torah "is not in heaven,"[18] but in the hands of its earthly students and observers.

The following passage in the Talmud says it all:

When Moses went up to heaven, the angels said to G–d: "What is a human being doing amongst us?" Said He to them: "He has come to receive the Torah." Said they to Him: "This hidden treasure, which was secreted with You for nine hundred and seventy-four generations before the world was created, You wish to give to flesh and blood...? Place Your glory upon the heavens!"

Said G–d to Moses, "Answer them."

Said (Moses): "Master of the Universe! This Torah that You are giving to me, what is written in it? 'I am the L–rd Your G–d who has taken you out from the land of Egypt.' Have you been descended to Egypt?" asked Moses of the angels, "Have you been enslaved to Pharaoh?

"What else does it say? 'You shall have no alien gods'—Do you dwell amongst idol-worshiping nations...?'Remember the day of Shabbat'—Do you work...? 'Do not swear falsely'—Do you do business...? 'Honor your father and your mother'—Do you have parents? 'Do not kill,' 'Do not commit adultery,' 'Do not steal'—Is there jealousy among you? Do you have an evil inclination?"[19]

The *Midrash* puts it this way: "G–d desired a dwelling place in the lowly realms."[20] He desired that there be a realm that is lowly and distant from Him, a world that is inhospitable to His presence—in other words, a mundane, physical world—and that man transform this world into an abode for His manifest presence.

Debating Truths

"This is what man is all about, this is the purpose of his creation and of the creation of all the worlds, supernal and ephemeral," writes Rabbi Schneur Zalman of Liadi in his *Tanya*.[21]

So the objective of creation lies in our earthbound existence. It is to this purpose that G–d first created the spiritual heavens: so that they yield a physical world that is descendant from a higher, more G–dly reality, and thereby possessive of the potential to transcend its lowliness and corporeality and become a "dwelling" that houses and expresses the Divine.

So which comes first, the heavens or the earth? In sequence, the heavens, in essence, the earth.[22] That much is clear. So what is the dispute between the House of Shammai and the House of Hillel?

The Cosmic Experiment

But there are two ways in which G-d's desire for "a dwelling in the lowly realms" may be understood: the Shammaian way and the Hillelian way; from the perspective of potential or from the perspective of the actual.

A muscular fellow lifts a barbell at a weightlifting competition. A scientist conducts an experiment to prove the accuracy of his calculations. What is the purpose of these acts? Is the objective to lift a few hundred pounds of lead several feet off the ground, or to push up the mercury in the scientist's thermometer so many millimeters? Obviously not. These things are being done not because we wish for certain physical developments to take place, but in order to establish the truths they reflect: the strength of the weightlifter or the validity of the scientist's theory. Here, the actual is not an end in itself, but the means by which to express a potential.

The purpose of creation may be seen in a similar light: as G–d's desire to express His infinite potential. The intensity of a lamp is measured by the farthest point its light reaches. The true mark of genius is the ability to explain the most profound idea to the simplest mind. In the same way, a physical world that conveys the divine truth is the most powerful indicator of G–d's infinity and omnipotence. If G–d is truly infinite, then His light can extend everywhere, even to the darkest corners of finiteness and corporeality; if the divine truth is truly absolute and unequivocal, then it can manifest itself everywhere, even in the brute physicality of our existence.

This is the Shammai perspective on reality. What is the primary element of G–d's creation? The spirituality of the heavens. True, the soul and the Torah descended from heaven to earth, but this is a "descent for the sake of ascent"[23]—a descent whose objective is to manifest their heavenly potential. True, our material world is the arena in which the divine purpose is realized. But what is this purpose, if not that the material itself should be made to express a higher truth?

Rabbi Israel Baal Shem Tov (the Besht) expressed this concept thus: "G–d makes the spiritual physical; the Jew makes the physical spiritual." When a Jew does a *mitzvah*, utilizing his physical faculties and elements of his physical environment to fulfill G–d's will, he is, in effect, reversing the divine act of creation. G–d first projected the spiritual potential of creation from Himself, then embodied it in a physical reality. Conversely, a *mitzvah* penetrates the mundanity of its object to reveal the spirit within; it redefines reality in terms of its divine essence and function rather than its physical husk. Indeed, this is why the physical evolved from the spiritual: so that it may ultimately come to reflect it and prove its infinite extent and scope.

So the question arises, "Which is more real to Torah, the potential of a thing or its actual state?" The Shammai sage's reply is: "The potential." To him, the actual possesses no significance of its own: What is real is creation's potential to express the Divine, while the way that things actually are is merely the "experiment" that proves the underlying truth.

Simple Desire

The House of Hillel disagrees. Does G–d "need" to prove or express His potential? Indeed, can there be any rationale for His desire, any motive that drives Him to want for something? Ultimately, no. If "G–d desired a dwelling in the lowly realms," then this is what He desired, period. No reason or utility can fully describe this desire, much less cause it or define it.

G–d created the heavens and the earth because He desired that His will, as expressed in the *mitzvot* of the Torah, be implemented by our physical selves in a physical world. If this is G–d's desire, then it is an end in itself, not an exercise in the fulfillment of some other goal.

The fulfillment of this desire may also prove the infinity and all-pervasiveness of His truth, but this is certainly not its ultimate source and objective. On the contrary: the spiritual dimension of creation—its potential to express the Divine—ultimately exists to serve this desire, by aiding and inspiring our observance of the *mitzvot*.

So, from the Hillelian perspective, the actual, physical state of a thing is the primary point of reference as to its status in Torah. For ultimately, the purpose of creation (and the function of Torah) is not to "spiritualize" the material existence, but that the material existence, as it is, should serve the divine will. Everything else is of secondary significance.

To Be or Not

These two perspectives are reflected in another philosophical debate between the schools of Shammai and Hillel:

For two-and-a-half years, the House of Shammai and the House of Hillel debated. These said, "It is better for man not to have been created than to have been created"; and these said, "It is better for man to have been created than not to have been created."[24]

Before the soul of man assumes a body and physical identity, it is a wholly spiritual entity—that is, an entity devoid of ego and individuality, one whose very being is defined solely as an expression of its supernal source.

So from the Shammaian perspective, the soul would indeed have been better off not to have fused with a body and become "man." If, as the House of Shammai maintains, our mission in life is to divest ourselves and our world of their material nature, then the initial state of our soul is also its most perfect state. Its corporeal embodiment is truly a "descent"—a departure from its true essence and function.

The soul endures this "descent" in order to carry out the divine objective in creation. But this objective itself is defined as the endeavor to regain its—and the physical universe's—initial spirituality. So there is no intrinsic value to the material: all it is, is the testing ground upon which the divine potential invested in the soul and in creation "proves" itself by making the journey to mundane earth and back.

The stated aim of creation, according to the House of Shammai, is its reversal. Every *mitzvah* is an exercise in nullification: that man "nullify his will before G–d's will,"[25] that he establish the truth that "there is none else beside Him,"[26] by demonstrating that everything exists only to serve the Creator. In a Shammaian world, man is created so that he uncreate himself; spirit evolves into matter only that it revert to its quintessential insubstantiality.

Born to Be

The school of Hillel, however, maintains, "It is better for man to have been created."

True, the soul in its "uncreated" state is more spiritual than when saddled with a materialistic self and character. True, the self-focusing human ego is far less expressive of the divine truth than its selfless pre-incarnation. But only through its "descent" into being and individuality does the soul of man come to relate to its Creator in a far more meaningful way: by implementing His will.

For it is a "dwelling in the lowly realms" that G–d desired. Not a dwelling in what used to be a lowly realm, not a dwelling that transforms the lowly realm into a lofty realm, but a dwelling within the lowly realm itself. The ultimate purpose of creation is realized specifically in the physical reality—retaining its physicality and realness, and specifically by the human being—retaining his humanity and beingness. G–d wanted that this "lowly" world—retaining it's "lowliness" and worldliness—should welcome Him and house His truth.

From the "actual" perspective of the Hillel school, the ultimate function of a *mitzvah* is to involve the physical creation, *as it is*, in the fulfillment of the divine will. Furthermore, a "dwelling for G–d in the lowly realms" means more than physical deeds and materials being used to fulfill G–d's commandments. It also means that the very essence of physicality—the very features that deem it lowly—are also enlisted to serve this end. Ego, individuality, pride—the antitheses of the soul's affirmation of the divine truth—these, too, are forces to be harnessed to drive our efforts to build the world that G–d desires.

The Enduring Dichotomy

Which are we to adopt, the vision of the Shammai school or that of the Hillel?

How are we to view reality, in terms of its potential or its actuality? Which should come first in the "miniature universe"[27] that is man, heaven or earth?

Should we see our world as spirit or as matter? Should we grant validity and significance to the material demands of life or view it all as nothing more than a test of our spiritual integrity? Should we strive for self-abnegation or for the constructive application of ego?

These and these are both the words of the living G–d.

When it comes to deciding how many lights to kindle on the first night of Chanukah, we can either stress the potential number of days or their actual number. We cannot do both. Here, the majority opinion must decide the *halacha*.

Yet when it comes to the manner in which we view ourselves, our world and our mission in life, we have no such limitations. We can embrace both the perspective of Shammai and that of Hillel. Both are valid Torah viewpoints; both are part of the divine blueprint for existence.[28]

---

(1) Exodus 23:2. (2) See Talmud, Shabbat 13b (in mishnah*); Maimonides' Commentary on the* Mishnah, *ibid. (3) See insets. (4) Talmud, Eruvin 13b. (5) I Samuel 16:18. (6) Talmud, Sanhedrin 93b. (7) HaVaYaH* is a transfiguration of the four letters *(Yud, Hei, Vav, Hei) of the ineffable name of G–d (the Tetragrammaton). (8) Hillel and Shammai themselves differed only on three matters of Torah law (see inset). (9) Talmud, Shabbat 21b; see Rashi's commentary. (10) Talmud, Pesachim 116b; Jerusalem Talmud, Pesachim 10:5; see Rashi's commentary on Deuteronomy 16:1. (11) Deuteronomy 6:7.*

(12) Talmud, Berachot *2a. Rabban Gamliel's colleagues, while accepting the principle that the Torah designates the entire night as the time for reading the* Shema, *impose a midnight deadline as a precautionary measure. However, they, too, agree that if midnight had passed and one has not yet read the* Shema, *one may do so until dawn. (13)* Talmud, Chagigah *12a. (14) Time is itself a physical creation of G–d's, evolved by Him from a "prior" conceptual-spiritual state. So when we say that G–d "first" created the spiritual essence of the world and "then" "proceeded" to embody it in a material existence, we are not referring to a sequential progression in terms of physical time, but to a hierarchy of cause and effect. (For example: the fact that 1+1=2 "precedes" and "causes" the fact that 2-1=1. This has nothing to do with durational time—both facts are simultaneously true—but it is purely a matter of logical sequence.) In any case, as far as the process of creation is concerned, the spiritual heavens certainly "preceded" the material earth. The debate between the House of Shammai and the House of Hillel must therefore relate to yet a deeper definition of "first" and "second." (15) In the words of the* Midrash: *"Says the Torah: I was G–d's building tool.... An architect who builds a palace does not do so on his own. He has scrolls and notebooks which he consults on how to place the rooms, where to set the doors. So it was with G–d: He looked into the Torah and created the world"* to which the Zohar *adds, "the Jew looks to the Torah and sustains the world,"* (Midrash Rabba, Bereishit *1:2;* Zohar, *part II, 161b). This is also alluded to by the opening word of the Torah,* Bereishit. *In Hebrew, the letter* bet *is also the number "2"; so* Bereishit *is a reference to the two things described by the Torah as* reishit *("first"): the Torah (Proverbs 8:22) and* Israel *(Jeremiah 2:3) (Rashi's commentary on* Genesis *1:1). (16) Zohar, part III, 29b; see Rashi's commentary on the* Talmud, Shabbat *152b. (17)* Exodus *20:19;* Deuteronomy *4:36; see* Talmud, Sanhedrin *90a. (18)* Deuteronomy *30:12; see the amazing story related by the* Talmud, Bava Metzia *59b (quoted on pg. 160 of this book). (19)* Talmud, Shabbat *89a. (20)* Midrash Tanchuma, Naso *16. (21)* Tanya, *ch. 27. (22) In the words of kabbalist poet Rabbi Shlomo Alkabatz, "Final in deed, first in thought" (from the Friday night* Lecha Dodi *prayer). (23)* Likkutei Torah *(by Rabbi Schneur Zalman of Liadi),*

Balak *73a*. *(24)* Talmud, Eruvin *13b*. *(25)* Ethics of the Fathers *2:2*. *(26)* Deuteronomy *4:35*. *(27)* Midrash Tanchuma, Pekudei *3*. *(28) Based on the Rebbe's* Hadran on the Mishnah *(5748 [1988]) and his* Hadran on Mishneh Torah *(delivered on* Tevet 26, 5748 *[January 16, 1988]) and others. (29) The Oral Torah was finally set down in writing in the 2nd century C.E., in the form of the* Mishnah, *by Rabbi Judah HaNassi. This drastic measure was taken "lest the Torah be forgotten from Israel": the ever-widening dispersion of the Jewish people threatened to disconnect many communities from the Torah centers in the Holy Land and Babylon where the oral tradition was being applied and transmitted to the next generations. The* Mishnah, *and the transcripts of the discussion and analysis of it over the following four centuries (known as the* Gemara), *together comprise the Talmud, which forms the heart of the "written" Oral Torah we have today. Although the Oral Torah has been written down, the essential distinction between the Written and the Oral elements of Torah remains. The Written Torah is defined by its words and letters: every character or nuance of sentence structure is significant and "mounds and mounds of laws" are derived from the "serif of a* yud*"; to the extent that one who recites the words of the written Torah, even if he does not understand what he is saying, has observed the* mitzvah *of Torah study. On the other hand, the Oral Law is primarily defined by its content rather than by its literary rendition. (30)* Talmud, Sanhedrin *88b*. *(31) The primary Torah authorities in the second and third generations after Moses. (32)* Deuteronomy *17:9*.

Debating Truths

DIVISIVENESS, DIVERSITY AND DISTINCTION

Which is a dispute that is not for the sake of Heaven? The dispute of Korach and all his company.

Ethics of the Fathers 5:17

Korach, Moses's mutinous cousin, earned the dubious distinction of father and prototype of all quarrelers and divisors. His very name has become synonymous with disharmony and conflict. The Talmud goes so far as to proclaim: "Anyone who engages in divisiveness transgresses a divine prohibition, as it is written: 'And[1] he shall not be as Korach and his company.'"[2] When the Torah wishes to tell us not to agitate disputes and perpetuate disunity, it does so by saying: Don't be like Korach....

But Korach was no ordinary rabble-rouser. He was a leading member of Kehot, the most prestigious of the Levite families. Joining him in his mutiny against Moses and Aaron were "two hundred and fifty men of Israel—leaders of the community, of those regularly called to assembly, men of renown."[3] Korach's difference with Moses was an ideological one, motivated by the way in which he understood Israel's relationship with the Almighty and by the manner in which he felt the nation ought to be structured.

So how is it that every petty squabbler is included in the prohibition "not to be as Korach"? Obviously, there is something at the heart of Korach's contentions that is the essence of all disunity.

Often, the antithesis of a certain quality is superficially identical to it. This is especially so when it comes to the root of a matter: a hairline distinction between two seemingly similar concepts actually translates into all the difference in the world.

The same is true of "peace" and "divisiveness." The source of all divisiveness is something that misleadingly resembles true peace. It is this pseudo-peace that lay at the heart of Korach's misguided vision and which ultimately led to his corruption and catastrophic end.

What Exactly Did Korach Want?

What is peace? "Just as their faces are not alike, so, too, their minds and characters are not alike."[4] Such is the nature of the human race: individuals and peoples differ from each other, divided by distinctions in outlook, emotional orientation, expertise, vocation, and the many other differences, great and small, which set them apart from each other.

Often, these differences give rise to animosity and conflict. And yet, at the core of the human soul is the yearning for peace. We intuitively sense that despite the tremendous (and apparently inherent) differences between us, a state of universal harmony is both desirable and attainable. But what exactly *is* peace? Is peace the obliteration of the differences between men and nations? Is it the creation of a "separate but equal" society in which differences are preserved but without any distinctions of "superior" and "inferior"? Or is it neither of the above?

But let us examine Korach's dispute. If we understand Korach, we will also understand the fine line that divides true peace from the essence of divisiveness.

What exactly did Korach want? His arguments against Moses and Aaron seem fraught with contradiction. On the one hand, he seems to challenge the very institution of the priesthood (*kehunah*), maintaining that "as the entire community is holy, and G–d is within them, why do you raise yourselves over the congregation of G–d?"[5] But from Moses's response[6] we see that Korach actually desired the office of the *Kohen Gadol* for himself!

This paradox appears time and again in various accounts of Korach's mutiny in the *midrashim* and the commentaries. Korach comes across as a champion of equality, railing against a "class system" that categorizes levels of holiness within the community (Israelites, Levites, Priests and the High Priest). Yet, in the same breath, he contends that he is the more worthy candidate for the High Priesthood.

Heavenly Waters, Earthly Waters

In the Torah's account of G–d's six-day creation of the world, each day's work concludes with the statement: "And G–d saw what He had created, and behold, it was good." Each day, that is, except the second day, the day that "G–d made the firmament (of the heaven), and divided between the waters which are below the firmament and the waters which are above the firmament."[7]

Explains the *Midrash*: "Why does it not say 'it was good' on the second day? Because on that day divisiveness was created; as it is written 'it shall divide between water and water.'"

However, the *Midrash* then goes on to point out that on the third day the Torah says, "it was good" twice, because then "the work of the waters," begun on the second day, was completed. In other words, the division effected on the second day was a less than desirable phenomenon, but only because it was not yet complete; on the third day, this divisiveness itself is deemed "good."[8]

Our sages tell us that G‑d's six days of creation correspond to the six millennia of human endeavor that follow.[9] Therein lies the significance of the *Midrash*'s words: in the third millennium of the world's existence, the element that resolves the conflicts created by diversity was introduced into our lives. This is the Torah, revealed to us at Sinai in the year 2448 from creation.

The Torah "was given to make peace in the world"[10]: peace between the conflicting drives within the heart of man, peace between individuals, peace between peoples, and peace between the creation and its Creator.

The *Midrash* expresses the peacemaking quality of Torah with the following metaphor:

Once there was a king who decreed: "The people of Rome are forbidden to descend to Syria, and the people of Syria are forbidden to ascend to Rome." Likewise, when G‑d created the world He decreed and said: "The heavens are G‑d's, and the earth is given to man."[11] But when He wished to give the Torah to Israel, He rescinded His original decree, and declared: "The lower realms may ascend to the higher realms, and the higher realms may descend to the lower realms."[12]

The schism and decree[13] to separate the heavenly from the earthly, effected by G‑d's "division of the waters" on the second day of creation, was thus alleviated on the third "day" of history with the revelation at Sinai. No longer were the material and the spiritual two irreconcilable realms. On that day, "G‑d descended upon Mount Sinai,"[14] "And to Moses He said, 'Come up to G‑d.'"[15] G‑d reached down to impart of His holiness to the world, and man was empowered to achieve a closeness to G–d.

But the Torah does not come to blur the distinction between the holy and the mundane. Nor does it endeavor to create a uniform world society. This would hardly qualify as a state of "peace" any more than a single-hued painting or a symphony composed entirely of identical notes could be said to be a "harmonious" creation.

The Torah makes peace in the world by defining the differing roles (man and woman; Jew and non-Jew; Israelite, Levite and *Kohen*; scholar and layman) to comprise the overall mission of humanity.

This is why the Torah is associated with the number three: a single entity or collection of identical entities can spell unanimity but not peace. If "one" represents singularity and "two" connotes divisiveness, then "three" expresses the concept of peace: the existence of two different or even polar entities, but with the addition of a third, unifying element that embraces and pervades them both, containing their differences as diverse but harmonious components of a greater whole.

The "third day" does not undo the divisions of the second. Rather, it introduces a "third" all-transcendent element that they all apply their own unique qualities to serve. And it is this introduction of harmony to diversity that "completes" it and renders it "good."

Back to Korach

In light of this, Korach felt, how can we speak of "higher" and "lower" roles in G–d's world? How can one say that the High Priest is loftier than the common laborer? True, the *Kohen Gadol*'s life is wholly devoted to spiritual pursuits while the "ordinary" Israelite must contend with the mundanity of the marketplace. But "within them is G–d"—they serve the divine purpose no less in the fulfillment of their role than does the *Kohen Gadol* in the fulfillment of his.

Korach was not opposed to division of the community by vocation, nor to the distinction between spiritual and material. On the contrary, he himself yearned for the spiritual path of the High Priesthood, to serve the Almighty utterly disinvolved from worldly affairs. What he did contest was the way in which Moses defined the division of roles within the people.

"Why do you raise yourselves over the congregation of G–d?" he argued. Why this "ladder" of spirituality on which the Moseses and Aarons of the generation occupy a *higher* rung than the farmer who works his land or the merchant engrossed in his accounts? Why is the "ordinary" Jew told to see Aaron as the one who represents him in the Sanctuary and who facilitates his relationship with G–d? Is G–d closer to heaven than to earth? Is serving Him by transcending the material a more important part of humanity's mission than utilizing the material existence to fulfill His will? Give me the High Priesthood, said Korach, and I will eliminate the connotations of "leadership" and "superiority" that Moses and Aaron have given it. To me, the most spiritual and the most material-bound of lifestyles, and all gradations between, are all distinct but parallel paths in our endeavor to serve the Almighty.

Korach's vision seems the paragon of harmony: diverse elements unified by a common goal. And yet, in neglecting to incorporate a crucial aspect of the Torah's conception of peace, it became the source of all divisiveness and discord.

Korach's "separate but equal" world may unite its various components in that they all serve the same overall goal, but it fails to provide for any connection between them. The paths may converge at the destination, but they are separated by walls which isolate and divide them. And without a give-and-take relationship between them, without any sense of where they stand vis-a-vis each other, their separateness will inevitably disintegrate into factionalism and conflict.

If we refer back to the *Midrash*'s parable of the Romans and the Syrians, we can see where Korach's vision departs from the Torah's definition of peace. The distinction between the two realms (the material and the spiritual) is preserved, but there is movement and interrelation between them. And their relationship is defined in terms of "higher" and "lower": the heavenly *descends* to earth and the earthly *ascends* to heaven.

As seen by Torah, the gradations of spirituality among the various segments of the people *do* take the form of a "ladder"—a ladder on which the material-bound individual looks up to his more spiritual brother, and the more spiritual reaches down to provide direction and inspiration to the material-bound. The farmer gives of his produce to the *Kohen*; he regards this gift as the holiest part of his yield, as it represents the spiritual focus of all his endeavors. The businessman looks to the scholar as the ideal; he feels trapped and stifled by the demands of his vocation and lives for the daily few minutes which he manages to devote to study.

And the spiritual leader descends to uplift his community. G‑d defines Aaron's role as one who "raises the lamps"[16]: in addition to (and because of) his "personal" spiritual service of the Almighty, Aaron is the flame which ignites the "soul of man—a lamp of G‑d"[17] calling forth its luminary potential.[18]

All this is *not* because those who fill the more spiritual roles are more important to the divine purpose than those who serve it through their involvement with the material. On the contrary, G‑d's purpose in creation, say our sages, is that "He desired a dwelling in the lowly realms"—that the lower realm of the material be transformed into an environment that is hospitable and receptive to His being.[19] In carrying this out, those on the "lowest rung" play the most central and crucial role. But their specialty lies precisely in that they deal with the lowest elements of creation (that is, those which least express the reality of G–d in any manifest way) and direct them towards the higher purpose of serving their Creator.

The moment the material-bound individual begins to feel comfortable in his environment, the moment he ceases his striving to escape the material, no longer can he truly sublimate it—he is now part of it. Only by seeing himself on the bottom looking up, only when his involvement with the mundane is forced by the call of duty as his soul yearns for a more spiritual existence, is he in the position to truly elevate his environment.

Interestingly enough, although Korach disavowed this "vertical" connection between matter and spirit, he himself is a prime example of the aspirations it is meant to evoke. Korach's desire for the High Priesthood, his yearning upward for a rung on the ladder more spiritual than his own, was a positive ambition[20]—and the ultimate refutation of his own divisive "peace."[21]

---

(1) Numbers 17:5. (2) Talmud, Sanhedrin 110a. (3) Numbers 16:2. (4) Midrash Rabba, Bamidbar 21:2. (5) Numbers 16:3. (6) "Is it not enough for you that the G–d of Israel has distinguished you from the community of Israel to bring you near to Himself, to do the service of G–d's Sanctuary and to stand before the community to minister to them... that you also desire the priesthood?!"—ibid., 5-10. (7) Genesis 1:6-7. (8) Midrash Rabba, Bereishit 4:8. (9) Nachmanides, Genesis 2:3; Thus, just as the six days of creation culminate in a seventh day of divine withdrawal and rest, 6,000 years of human achievement result in the "day of eternal Shabbat and

tranquility"—the era of Moshiach. *(10)* Talmud, Gittin *59b;* Mishneh Torah, Laws of Chanukah *4:14. (11)* Psalms *115:16. (12)* Midrash Tanchuma, Vayeira *15. (13) The Hebrew word used by the* Midrash, *g'zeirah, means both "decree" and "cut." (14)* Exodus *19:20. (15)* Exodus *24:1. (15)* Numbers *8:2. (17)* Proverbs *20:27. (18) See* Absolute Relativity *on pg. 49. (19)* Midrash Tanchuma, Naso *16. "This is what man is all about," writes Rabbi Schneur Zalman of Liadi in his* Tanya, *"this is the purpose of his creation and the creation of all worlds higher and lower—that G–d should have a dwelling place in this lowly world"* (Tanya, *ch. 33. See the essays,* Wood Submerged in Stone *on pg. 88,* Essence and Expression *on pg. 196,* Debating Truths *on pgs. 264-283, and* To Be or To Be Not *on pg. 326 in this book). (20) This explains why an entire section of Torah* (Numbers *16-18) carries the name "Korach"—the name of an unrepentant sinner. For we are to derive the positive aspect of Korach's deed—his upward yearning for an existence more spiritual than his own—and apply it to our lives (see* Staying Alive *on pg. 217). (21) Based on several talks by the Rebbe, delivered on the Shabbat on which the Torah section of* Korach *is read, in the years 5718, 5724, and 5727 (1958, 1964 and 1967).*

THE LOVING PRECEDENT

> Whoever possesses the following three traits is of the disciples of our father Abraham; and whoever possesses the opposite three traits is of the disciples of the wicked Bilaam.
>
> Ethics of the Fathers 5:19

Bilaam's identity as the evil counterpart to Abraham is a reoccurring theme in the Torah. On the verse, "And Bilaam rose in the morning, and saddled his ass, and went with the princes of Moab,"[1] describing the beginning of Bilaam's journey to curse the Jewish people, Rashi comments:

From here we see how hatred causes a person to break from convention. Bilaam had many servants at his disposal; yet, in his eagerness to go curse Israel, he saddled his ass himself. Said the Almighty: "Evil one! Their father, Abraham, has already preempted you, when, to fulfill My will, he 'rose[2] early in the morning and saddled his donkey.'"

This reflects King Solomon's observation, "One corresponding to the other, G–d created."³ In order to provide man with the "freedom of choice" that is essential to his mission in life, G–d created two mirror realities: every positive element has its negative counterpart. Were there to exist a positive force or phenomenon that cannot be put to corrupt use, then man's potential for evil would not present the equal challenge that makes for the choice factor in life.

Appearance and Substance

But this "equality" between good and evil exists only on the most superficial plane of reality. "The potter," says the *Midrash*, "does not test flawed vessels, because to tap them even once is to break them; but he does test good vessels, because no matter how many times he taps them they do not break."⁴ In his most elementary perception of his world, man will be challenged to choose between two equally potent realities; but if he learns to look beyond the surface of things— if he gives but the slightest of "taps" to the challenges of life—he will see that only the good is real and substantial, while evil's formability lies only in its appearance.

For good is the objective of the created existence, while evil exists merely to provide the challenge that imbues our positive deeds with meaning and significance. Thus, when viewed in terms of their inherent purpose and function, good is an existence in its own right, while evil is nothing more than a facilitator for good.

Hence, there cannot be anything "original" to evil. All it is is a shallow refraction of the good in the world. If Bilaam was able to transcend the norm with the intensity of his hate, this was only because, centuries earlier, Abraham had done the same out of love for his Creator.⁵

(1) Numbers *22:21*. *(2)* Genesis *22:3*. *(3)* Ecclesiastes *7:14*. *(4)* Midrash Rabbah, Bereishit *32:3*. *(5) Based on an address by the Rebbe*, Tammuz *12, 5742 (July 3, 1982)*.

WITH A GRAIN OF SALT

> Judah the son of Teima would say: Be bold as a leopard, light as an eagle, swift as a deer and mighty as a lion to do the will of your Father in Heaven. He would also say: The brazen—to purgatory; the bashful—to paradise.
>
> Ethics of the Fathers 5:20

Use the shamelessness of the leopard to do what is right regardless of what others may think or say, but never acquire its audacity as a personal trait. Every negative thing has its positive use, but exercise great caution and reserve in applying this rule. The same Rabbi Judah who exhorts us to "be bold as a leopard" denounces him who, in acting brazenly, becomes brazen.[1]

(1) Based on an address by the Rebbe, Av 29, 5741 (August 29, 1981).

FOR REAL

> May it be Your will, L–rd our G–d and G–d of our fathers, that the Holy Temple be rebuilt speedily in our days....
>
> Ethics of the Fathers 5:20

The *Mishnah* is purely an *halachic*, or legal, work, consisting of sixty-three tractates of legal material, arranged by topic in six "orders." Its concise, almost cryptic style is designed to compact as many rulings and guidelines in as few words as possible;[1] for the reasonings and deliberations behind its laws one must look to the *Gemara*, the lengthy exposition on the *Mishnah*. Also the rare *mishnah* that seems to digress with a philosophical insight or some background information, will always, upon closer examination, prove to be a statement of law and a practical instruction on daily living.

The *Ethics of the Fathers* differs from the other 62 tractates of the *Mishnah*, in that it deals not with Torah law per se but with the area defined as that which is "within the line of the law."[2] Yet the *Ethics* is no exception to the "no frills" approach of the *Mishnah*. Though many of its sayings apply to the interior world of the human heart and mind—addressing issues of outlook, emotion and character—its every word is a *halacha*, a directive.

This is no less true of the above-quoted passage. At first glance, it appears to be a prayerful appeal to the Almighty to send Moshiach. One wonders what it is doing in the middle of the twentieth *mishnah* of the fifth chapter of the *Ethics*, following the injunction to "be bold as a leopard, light as an eagle, swift as a deer and mighty as a lion to do the will of your Father in Heaven." But Rabbi Judah ben Teima is instructing us on a truth that lies at the heart of the Jew's belief in Moshiach and the Redemption.

To believe in Moshiach is not merely to believe that he will someday come. It is to *expect* him on a daily, hourly and momentary basis. It means that no matter what we are discussing, the subject turns to Moshiach at the slightest provocation.

It means that while discussing the need to be "fleet-footed" in fulfilling G–d's will, one is struck with an immense yearning to instantaneously be able to fulfill all of the *mitzvot*, so many of which are implementable only when the Jewish people are settled in the Holy Land and the Holy Temple stands in Jerusalem. It means that in the midst of studying a chapter of *halacha*, a spontaneous plea erupts from the depths of one's heart: "May it be Your will that the Holy Temple be rebuilt speedily in our days."

Foundations

To better understand why the constant anticipation of its immediate realization is inseparable from the Jew's very concept of Redemption, we must first examine the centrality of Moshiach and the Redemption to Judaism itself.

In his introduction to the eleventh chapter of the talmudic tractate *Sanhedrin*, Maimonides enumerates the thirteen basic principles of the Jewish faith. The first four principles deal with the belief in G‑d: that G‑d is the Original Cause upon which every creation is utterly dependent for its existence; that He is absolutely one and singular; that He is non-corporeal and timeless. The fifth principle establishes man's duty to serve Him and fulfill the purpose for which he was created. Principles six to eleven establish that G‑d relates to humanity: that He communicates His will to man; that every word of the Torah was transmitted by G‑d to Moses; that G‑d observes and is concerned with the behavior of man; that He punishes the wicked and rewards the righteous.

The final two principles deal with the era of Moshiach: the belief that there will arise a leader who will bring the entire world to recognize and serve the Creator, ushering in an era of universal peace and divine perfection.[3]

What does it mean when we say that something is a "basic principle" in Judaism? A simple definition would be that in order to qualify as a "believing Jew" one must accept the truth of these thirteen precepts. But the Torah clearly makes no such distinctions. As Maimonides himself writes in his eighth principle: "This entire Torah, given to us by Moses, is from the mouth of the Almighty—namely, that it was communicated to him by G‑d.... In this, there is no difference between the verses, 'The sons of Ham were Kush and Mitzrayim,' 'The name of his wife was Meheitavel' and 'Timna was a concubine,' and the verses, 'I Am the L‑rd your G‑d' and 'Hear O Israel, (the L‑rd is our G‑d, the L‑rd is One)': all are from the mouth of the Almighty, all is the Torah of G‑d, perfect, pure, holy and true.... Our sages have said: Anyone who believes that the entire Torah is from the mouth of the Almighty except for a single verse, is a heretic...."

So the "basic principles" are more than a required set of beliefs—that would apply to each and every word in the Torah. Rather, these are thirteen principles upon which everything else rests. The Hebrew word Maimonides uses[4] is *yesodot*, "foundations": different parts of an edifice could conceivably exist independently of each other, but without the foundation, the entire building would collapse. So, too, each of these thirteen principles is a "foundation" to the entire Torah.

In other words, while every word in the Torah is equally important to the believer as a person, these principles are crucial to the faith itself. A person who does not accept that "Do not steal" is a divine commandment is no less a heretic than one who denies the existence of G–d; but belief in the rest of the Torah is not dependent upon the fact that G–d said not to steal. On the other hand, things like the existence of G–d, His absolute and exclusive power, His involvement in human affairs, and His communication of the Torah to man, obviously prerequire the whole of Judaism. Without any one of these "foundations" the rest is virtually meaningless.

One difficulty, however, remains with this explanation: Why is the belief in Moshiach included among the foundations of the Jewish faith? Obviously, the concept of Moshiach is an important part of Judaism. The Torah speaks of it (in Deuteronomy 30 and Numbers 24, among others); the prophets are full of it. But could one not conceivably believe in the rest of the Torah without accepting its vision of a future perfect world?

Not in Heaven

The Torah details a most exacting and demanding code of behavior, governing every hour of the day, every phase of life, and every aspect of the human experience. It takes a lifetime of committed labor, tremendous self-discipline, and every iota of man's intellectual, emotional and spiritual prowess to bring one's life into utter conformity with the Torah's edicts and ideals.

Hence, there are two possible ways in which to view the Torah's vision of life.

One may conceivably argue that the level of perfection expected by Torah is beyond feasible reach for a majority of people. From this perspective, Torah is an ideal to strive towards, a vision of absolute goodness designed to serve as a point of reference for imperfect man. A person ought to seek this ideal—says this view—although he will probably never attain it, for he will much improve himself in the process.

The second view takes the Torah at its word: each and every individual is capable of, and expected to attain, the perfectly righteous and harmonious life it mandates. Torah is not an abstract ideal, but a practical and implementable blueprint for life.

The Torah itself leaves no room for doubt on its view of the matter: "For the *mitzvah* which I command you this day," it states, "it is not beyond you nor is it remote from you. It is not in heaven… nor is it across the sea…. Rather, it is something that is very close to you, in your mouth, in your heart, that you may do it."[5]

Underlying Perspectives

These two views reflect two different ways of looking at the essence of G‑d's creation. If man is inherently or even partially evil, then obviously he can go either way. There is no reason to assume that he will, or even can, attain a state of perfect righteousness. A world community that is utterly committed to goodness, in which every single individual acts in concert with the purpose for which he was created, can only be the dream of a chronic optimist, or of one who is hopelessly out of touch with "reality."

Yet if one believes that the world is intrinsically good; that G–d has imbued His every creation with the potential to reflect His absolute goodness and perfection; then, one's concept of reality is completely different. Then, our currently harsh reality is the anomalous state, while the reality of Moshiach is the most natural thing in the world.

So, where a person stands on Moshiach expresses his attitude vis-a-vis the entire Torah. Is Torah's formula for life a pipe dream, or is it a description of the true nature of creation? If the Torah is nothing more than a theoretical utopia, then one does not expect a world free of greed, jealousy and hatred any time in the near future. But if the Torah mirrors the essence of man, then one not only believes in a "future" Moshiach, but understands that the world is capable of instantaneously responding to his call.

This explains why belief in Moshiach entails not only the conviction that he will "eventually" arrive, but the anticipation of his imminent coming. In the words of Maimonides: "The Twelfth Principle concerns the era of Moshiach: to believe and to validate his coming; not to think that it is something of the future—even if he tarries, one should await him...." And in his *Mishneh Torah*, Maimonides states: "One who does not believe in him, or *one who does not anticipate his coming*, not only denies the prophets, he denies the Torah itself."[6]

When Moshiach is that very realistic possibility, for another moment to go by without the Redemption taking place is far, far more "unrealistic" (that is, less in keeping with the true nature of things) than the prospect of its immediate realization.

The Nature and Definition of Truth

Of course, man has been granted freedom of choice. But the choice between good and evil is not a choice of what to be—he cannot change his quintessential self—but the choice of how to act. Man can choose to express his true essence in his behavior, or choose to suppress it.

Ultimately, the truth, by nature and definition, always comes to light.[7] So, while man can choose how to act in any given moment, the very nature of humanity, and of G–d's creation as a whole, mandates that we not only can, but *will* attain the perfection of the era of Moshiach.

Moshiach means that the true nature of creation will ultimately come to light; that "evil" is but the shallow distortion of this truth and has no enduring reality; that man will free himself of hatred and ignorance; and that every human being will fulfill his divinely ordained role as outlined in the Torah, transforming the world into a place suffused with the wisdom, goodness and perfection of its Creator.

Moshiach means that the Torah is for real.[8]

---

(1) See footnote 5 to introduction to this book. Indeed, the very act of committing these laws to writing, in any form, was an unprecedented departure from tradition, which mandated that they be transmitted orally from master to disciple. (To this day, the Mishnah, Gemara *and the immense sea of rabbinic commentary and codification to follow is referred to as the "Oral Torah," as opposed to the "Written Torah" which Moses put to writing by Divine dictation. See* Written and Relayed *on pg. 266, and footnote 29, ibid.). (2) See introduction to this book and the essays* On the Essence of the Ethics *on pg. 97, and* Inside Work *on pg. 256. (3) Principle #12 concerns the belief in the immediate coming of Moshiach, and Principle #13 the belief in the resurrection of the dead in the Messianic Era. This essay deals with the centrality of the twelfth principle to the Jewish faith. For a discussion of the thirteenth principle, see* The Resurrection of the Dead *on*

pg. 207. (4) In his Mishneh Torah, *Maimonides calls the section that deals with these principles* Hilchot Yesodei HaTorah, *"Laws concerning the Torah's Foundations." Maimonides wrote his commentary on the* Mishnah *in Arabic, and authorized and approved its translation into the Hebrew by Rabbi Shmuel Ibn Tibbon. The Hebrew version also employs the word* yesod *in its discussion of the Thirteen Foundations. (5)* Deuteronomy *30:11-14. (6)* Mishneh Torah, Laws of Kings *11:1. (7) See* Absolute Relativity *on pg. 49. (8) Based on the talks of the Rebbe, on* Cheshvan 7, 5746 *(October 22, 1985), and on numerous other occasions. (Also see* Likkutei Sichot, *Vol. XVIII, pg. 280, footnote 63.)*

THE DISAPPEARING GROOM

[Age] eighteen, for marriage.

Ethics of the Fathers 5:22

The first marriage to be recounted in detail by the Torah is the marriage of Isaac and Rebeccah (Genesis 24). As such, we expect it to yield insights into the essence of the marriage relationship.

A most curious aspect of the Isaac-Rebeccah relationship is that immediately prior to their marriage, Isaac literally disappears for a couple of years.

A summation of Isaac's life leaves us with an unaccountable gap of over two years. The Torah tells us that Isaac was sixty years old when his twin sons, Esau and Jacob, were born.[1] However, according to the *Midrash*, the twins' grandfather, Abraham, passed away on the day that they reached the age of thirteen.[2] Since Abraham lived for 175 years,[3] and Isaac was born when Abraham was 100 years old,[4] Esau and Jacob must have been born at least sixty-two years after Isaac's birth. In other words, when Isaac turned sixty, more than sixty-two years had already elapsed from the time of his birth. Somehow, he had "lost" two to three years of his life.

One of the explanations offered by our sages is that before his marriage to Rebeccah, Isaac spent three years in the Garden of Eden. During this time he led an entirely spiritual existence, so that these years are not counted as part of his physical life.[5]

The implications are clear: a prerequisite to the marriage relationship is that one must first devote a certain period of time exclusively to spiritual and G–dly pursuits, with minimal involvement in the material aspects of life.

The Impossible Edifice

Marriage itself seems to be the very opposite of this: a time of increased enmeshment in the material. It is a time when a person begins to engage the most physical of human drives; it is also a time when he is forced to begin to involve himself, in earnest, in the earning of a living, often at the expense of higher and more idealistic pursuits.

In fact, our sages have referred to marriage as a second birth. First, the soul enters into the body and assumes a physical existence; then, at a later point in life, it further "descends" into the physical state by marrying. Nevertheless (indeed, because of this) marriage is the framework within which the most divine of human potentials is realized.

The traditional blessing given to the bride and groom is that they merit "to build an eternal edifice."[6] For out of the marriage comes the creation of life—life with the potential to produce yet another generation of life, which in turn can yield another, *ad infinitum*. The power of reproduction presents us with a logical impossibility: how can a finite entity (man) contain within itself an infinite potential? Indeed, our sages have said: "There are three partners to the creation of man: G–d, his father, and his mother."[7] G–d, the only truly infinite being, has done the impossible: He has imbued man and woman with an inherently infinite quality. In marriage, two finite and temporal creatures establish an eternal edifice.

It is therefore no accident that the quality with which man most emulates his Creator is realized only through a "descent" into the material. For so it is with G–d Himself: the infinite nature of His power is most potently expressed with His creation of the physical universe.

A truly infinite being is not constrained by any definitions and parameters: He is to be found anywhere and everywhere, even in the most confining and corporeal of environments. G–d's creation of sublime and abstract worlds cannot convey the infinite scope of His power in the same way that His creation of—and constant involvement with—our "lowly" and finite existence can. The same is true of the power of creation invested in the human being. Because of its divinely infinite nature, it can—and does—find realization in the most physical area of human life.

Spiritual Preface

Man has been granted freedom of choice. So when a man and woman join their lives, it is left to them to do what they will with the divine gift of infinity granted their union. They can choose to squander it in a relationship devoid of meaningful content—a relationship which never rises above its material nature, and which only further enmeshes them in their corporeal selves. Or, they can endeavor to construct an edifice that is eternal in more than the most basic, biological sense. They can endeavor to build a selfless and giving relationship, and a home and family committed to the timeless values set forth by the Creator of life.

This is the lesson in Isaac's disappearance from physical life prior to his marriage. To ensure that one's "descent" into the physical world of marriage yields the proper results, it must be preceded by a period of spiritual preparation. Although man's mission in life is the positive development of the physical world, one must enter the arena of the material well equipped with the spiritual vision and fortitude to carry it out.[8]

---

(1) Genesis 25:26. (2) See Midrash Rabba, Bereishit, 63:10 and 63:12. (3) Genesis 25:7. (4) Ibid., 21:5 (5) Asarah Ma'amarot. (6) From the "Seven Blessings" recited under the marriage canopy. (7) Talmud, Kiddushin 30b. (8) Based on the Rebbe's talks on Cheshvan 29, 5714 (November 7, 1953) and on numerous other occasions. See also following essay, The Challenge of the Twenties.

THE CHALLENGE OF THE TWENTIES

> Five years is the age for the study of Scripture. Ten, for the study of *Mishnah*; thirteen, for the obligation to observe the *mitzvot*; fifteen, for the study of *Gemara*; eighteen, for marriage; twenty, to pursue (a livelihood).
>
> Ethics of the Fathers 5:22

In other words, for the first twenty years of life, a person focuses almost exclusively on his individual growth: the acquisition of knowledge and wisdom and his moral and spiritual development. The age of twenty marks the point at which he ventures out to the world and begins to concern himself with the material involvements of life.

This is why the Torah considers the age of twenty such an important milestone in a person's life. In commanding Moses to take a census of the Jewish people, the Almighty directs: "Count the heads of all the congregation of the children of Israel.... From the age of twenty and upward, all who are fit to serve in the army of Israel, you shall count them."[1]

One who engages only in the spiritual enrichment of his own self cannot count himself as a member of the "army of Israel." While a period of intense self-development is crucial to a person's fulfillment of his mission in life, and while a person must continue to set aside inviolable "islands in time" devoted to the nurture and growth of his spiritual self, these must never be seen as an end in itself. The purpose of the "pre-twenty" times and aspects of a person's life is for the sake of the "pursuit" that must follow: that he apply his personal attainments to develop and sanctify the material world "out there."[2]

Enough!

A similar sentiment is expressed by the Torah in the opening chapter of Deuteronomy. Here, Moses reminds the Jewish people, "The L–rd our G–d spoke to us at Horeb, saying: 'Enough have you dwelt at this mountain! Turn away and travel on....'"[3]

The mountain in question is Mount Sinai, scene of the most monumental event in human history: G–d's communication of His wisdom and will to man.

But the enlightenment and perfection of one's own mind and character is a prerequisite to life, not its aim and end. One must view his own attainments as the tools by which to enlighten his fellows and perfect his environment.

No sooner had the people of Israel experienced and absorbed the greatest divine revelation of all times, when they were virtually driven away from the mountain. "Enough!" they were told, enough of your basking in your newly gained insight and spirituality. Turn away, travel on, there is a world out that has much to receive from you.[4]

---

(1) Numbers 1:2-3. (2) Cf. *Rabban Gamliel*, Ethics of the Fathers *2:2: "Beautiful is the study of Torah together with the ways of the world."* For

though Talmud *speaks of the individual for whom the study of Torah is his "sole occupation," it concludes that a wholly spiritual life is appropriate only for a select minority. To quote: Our sages learned: It is written, "And you shall gather your grain"* (Deuteronomy *11:14). What does this come to teach us? But since it says, "This book of Torah shall not cease from your mouth (and you shall study it day and night)"*(Joshua *1:8), I would have thought that one must take these words literally; comes the verse to teach us, "you shall gather your grain"—conduct yourself also in the ways of the world. These are the words of Rabbi Ishmael. Rabbi Shimon bar Yochai said: If a person plows in the plowing season, sows in the sowing season, reaps in the reaping season, threshes in the threshing season and winnows when there is wind—what shall become of the Torah? But when Israel does the will of the Almighty, their work is done by others, as it is written, "And strangers will stand and graze your sheep...."* (Isaiah *61:5). Said Abaye: Many did as Rabbi Ishmael, and succeeded; as Rabbi Shimon, and did not succeed* (Talmud, Shabbat *35b). (3)* Deuteronomy *1:6. (4) Based on an address by the Rebbe,* Iyar *29, 5722 (June 2, 1962) and on a letter of the Rebbe's from* Shevat *1, 5718 (January 22, 1958).*

TORAH AND STATE

> Rabbi Meir would say: Whoever studies Torah for Torah's sake alone merits many things.... From him, people enjoy counsel and wisdom, understanding and power.... The Torah grants him sovereignty, dominion and jurisprudence.
>
> Ethics of the Fathers 6:1

Much debate and polemic have been expended on the issue of "the separation of powers": how much power can "safely" be vested in a single individual or institution? In particular, much has been said, written and litigated on the relationship between religion and state. Should religious authorities be allowed to govern or judge, or, for that matter, be allowed any venue of political influence at all?

To the Jew who regards the Torah as G–d's blueprint for creation, Torah is the ultimate authority in all areas of life. Yet should the role of Torah scholar be coupled with that of political ruler? Should those qualified to teach the Torah and interpret its laws also be the ones to formulate traffic regulations, levy taxes, punish criminals and manage the economy?

Decline of the Generations, and a Look to the Future

The first chapter of the *Ethics* summarizes the "chain of tradition," the succession of leaders in whose hands lay the supreme authority for interpreting Torah and transmitting it to the next generation: "Moses received the Torah... at Sinai and transmitted it to Joshua, Joshua gave it over to the Elders, the Elders to the Prophets, and the Prophets... to the Men of the Great Assembly.... Shimon the Righteous was from the surviving members of the Great Assembly.... Antignos of Socho received the tradition from Shimon the Righteous.... Yossei the son of Yoezer of Tzreidah and Yose the son of Yochanan of Jerusalem received the tradition from them.... Joshua the son of Perachia and Nitai the Arbelite received [the tradition] from them...."

An examination of the roles of these Torah leaders reveals a progressive fragmentation of authority. Moses, aside from his role as teacher of Torah, was also king, general, judge and provider to the Jewish people: he reigned over them (Deuteronomy 33:5); led them in battle (Deuteronomy 3); mediated their petty disputes (Exodus 18); and provided them with food, water and shelter during their forty-year sojourn in the Sinai desert (Exodus 15-16, Numbers 11:11-13 and 20:11).[1] Joshua, who was the next link in the chain of Torah's transmission, was likewise both teacher and king, both spiritual master and military commander-in-chief. The same was true of the "Judges" who governed Israel following Joshua, and of King David.

But, in later generations, we find a division of roles to be the norm: the prophet as the leading moral authority and the king as manager of the nation's material affairs. Furthermore, following the era of the Great Assembly (4th century B.C.E.) we find a "separation of powers" existing within the Torah leadership itself: each generation had a pair of spiritual authorities—the *Nassi* and the *Av Bet-Din*.

Which is the Torah's ideal? The entire history of humanity is a prelude to the era of Moshiach, the result of close to six millennia of man's developing and bringing to light the inherent goodness and perfection of his world. The world of Moshiach is a world free of hatred, jealousy and suffering, a world suffused with wisdom, a world in harmony with itself and its Creator. And what model of leadership does the Torah envision for this perfect world? Moshiach, the world leader who will herald and preside over this climactic era, is described as both teacher and king, a paragon of spiritual and material leadership in one.

So the example of Moses represents the Torah's concept of the perfect leader. For Moses embodied the ultimate criteria for leadership: an utter self-effacement and a complete absence of self-interest. As the Torah attests: "And the man, Moses, was the most humble man on the face of the earth."[2] In such a man, absolute authority only ensures the optimum integration and harmony between all areas of communal life. For it is not power that corrupts, but the ego of the powerful. Only in lesser generations, whose leaders' selflessness is not on the level exemplified by Moses, is it necessary for authority to be fragmented and shared.

But the halving of life into "spiritual" and "material" spheres, its compartmentalization into "moral" and "political" domains, is an artificial one. Life, in its entirety, is a single endeavor: the development of the perfect world that G–d envisioned at creation and outlined in the Torah. The many "areas" of life are but the many facets to its singular essence.[3]

---

(1) See Talmud, Taanit *9a. (2)* Numbers *12:3. (3) Based on an address by the Rebbe,* Iyar *29, 5749 (June 3, 1989).*

THE SERVING FREE

> There is no free individual, except for he who occupies himself with the study of Torah.
>
> Ethics of the Fathers 6:2

Why the roundabout, "negative" wording of the *mishnah*? Why not simply say, "True freedom is attained through Torah"?

Man is a finite being, and everything he possesses and is capable of achieving is likewise finite in scope and extent. It would therefore follow that there is no such thing as a free human being. Not only do the proud, the envious, the ignorant and the greedy live in their own prison, but even the most emotionally stable and content individual, blessed with the most plentiful resources and leading the most uninhibited of lives, is still subservient to his own inherent limitations.

Thus, our *mishnah* opens with the statement, "There is no free individual." But one who occupies himself with Torah, subordinating his mind and self to the wisdom and will of the Almighty, transcends this most basic nature of every created thing.

Torah defies the unbridgeable gap between the finite and the infinite. It is the wisdom and will of G‑d, articulated in terms that the human being can comprehend, relate to and implement in his life. One who submits to the servitude of a life devoted to Torah experiences the freedom that eludes the most "independent" of men.[1]

---

(1) Based on an address by the Rebbe, Iyar 29, 5719 (June 6, 1959).

A BUSINESS ATTITUDE

...he who occupies himself (*osek*)
with the study of Torah.

Ethics of the Fathers 6:2

The verb most often used by our sages to describe our involvement with Torah is not *study*, *learn*, *practice*, *observe* or the like, but *osek* ("occupy oneself")—a word usually associated with the act of doing business. Indeed, a life devoted to the study of Torah and implementation of its ideals much resembles a businessman's occupation with his enterprise.

Consider this attitude: "I know that a crucial need exists for my product, and that my proposition constitutes the best value. I'll be more than happy to deal with anyone who feels likewise and manages to get ahold of me."

Sounds like a nice guy, but not much of a businessman.

Concern for one's fellow man is usually seen as something to be enlisted or, at the very least, appreciated. If someone needs and wants to be helped, lend a hand. Otherwise, what can be done?

But Torah insists that you relate to all your positive endeavors as a business. Your knowledge, your values, your talents—do not line your coffers with them (what businessman keeps his capital in a savings account?) or offer them only to those who seek them from you or at least recognize their worth. Instead, as any self-respecting businessman would, do everything within your power to convince your fellow that he stands to benefit from what you have to offer.

Mobile Man

Another area in which business mirrors life is the importance of mobility.

To succeed in business, one must be on the move. Thus, when Moses blessed the Jewish people before his passing, Zebulun, a tribe of merchants, was given seaports in the land of Israel and blessed with the gift of mobility[1]—a property as vital to the merchant of 3,000 years ago as it is to the businessman of today.

Stagnation is anathema to business. Despite the tremendous advances in communication technologies, the 20th-century businessman still commutes, traveling to a place situated and equipped for business's specific needs. From the office, he further ventures out to pursue business opportunities wherever they may present themselves.

In philosophy and temperament, the businessman must also be mobile and forward-looking. A person successful in business is one who has learned to continuously progress and develop, to constantly find new and innovative ways to optimally apply his talents and resources.

This is why commerce is a solely human endeavor. Of all G–d's creatures, man alone has been blessed with the capacity for progress. Man alone strives upwards, forever seeking to improve upon his inborn traits, forever seeking to perfect himself and his world.

One who "occupies himself" with Torah, is one who applies this mobility to his moral and spiritual endeavors. To be *osek* with Torah is to commit oneself to the business of life.[2]

---

(1) "Rejoice, Zebulun, in your excursions...."—Deuteronomy 33:18. (2) Based on the Rebbe's talks on Shavuot *5718 (May 26, 1958), on* Tishrei 7, *5751 (September 26, 1990) to a group of business leaders, and on other occasions.*

FERTILE WISDOM

> ...If David, king of Israel, who learned nothing from Achitofel except for two things alone, nevertheless referred to him as his master, guide, and intimate,[1] it certainly goes without saying that one who learns from his fellow a single chapter, a law, a verse, a saying, or even a single letter [of Torah], is obligated to revere him.
>
> Ethics of the Fathers 6:3

The Talmud compares the teachings of Torah to seedlings: Just as a seedling is fruitful and multiplies, so, too, the words of Torah are fruitful and multiply.[2] Once implanted in the mind of its student, a single concept of Torah germinates, develops and proliferates, yielding insight upon insight as its possessor goes through life. In the words of the *Zohar*, "there is not a word or a tiny letter in the Torah upon which do not hang many secrets of divine wisdom."[3]

The phrase, "fruitful and multiply," is a reference to G–d's blessing to the first man and woman, "Be fruitful and multiply, fill the earth, and conquer it."[4] Indeed, the conception and development of knowledge in the mind of the student parallels the conception and development of a life in the womb of the mother.

Our sages tell us, "There are three partners in the creation of man: G–d, his father, and his mother."[5] The capacity to procreate is, in essence, of a distinctly divine nature. All our other faculties—sight, hearing, etc.—are finite in scope; not so when it comes to our regenerative powers. Children multiply into grandchildren and great-grandchildren *ad infinitum*: there is no inherent limit as to how many generations can issue from a single union between man and woman. Thus, the express input of the "Third Partner"—only the Creator Himself can imbue two finite creatures with infinite potential.

The same is true regarding the "regenerative power" contained in a teaching: when G–d is a partner to their endeavor, the teacher-student relationship yields an infinite progeny. But unlike physical procreation, where the Almighty unequivocally bestows the gift of infinity to every conception, here the "Third Partner" participates by invitation only. If the teaching and pursuit of wisdom are towards positive and G–dly ends, then the seed implanted by the teacher is "fruitful and multiplied" in the mind of his student. But if they are nothing more than an exercise in self-enhancement, then the knowledge gained does not transcend the intrinsic finiteness of its imparter and its conceiver.

Sterile Wisdom

Therein lies the answer to the oft-asked question: Can one gain positive knowledge from a bad person? The answer is yes, but with a significant difference. Assuming that one is able to separate the good from the bad, one can learn from a wicked teacher;[6] what one will receive, however, is sterile wisdom, ideas that lack the regenerative quality to "be fruitful and multiply" and extend to infinite applications.

This explains the otherwise difficult wording in the *mishnah* quoted at the opening of this essay. Why is it that, "it certainly goes without saying that one who learns from his fellow ... even a single letter of Torah, is obligated to revere him" from David's reverence of Achitofel? By the *mishnah*'s own attestation, David actually learned "two things" from Achitofel. Also, why the seemingly redundant terminology, "he learned nothing from Achitofel except for two things alone"?

But this is "Achitofel the Wicked," the profferer of evil counsel to Absalom in his rebellion against David.[7] So, if on two occasions, King David learned something from Achitofel, these remained "nothing except for two things alone"—lessons consisting only of their actual message and import.

Nevertheless, David revered him as his teacher. How much more so, derives the *mishnah*, must a person revere one from whom he learns even a single point of wisdom—a single point in which G–d has a part, a single point that will continue to grow and diversify within him to address the myriad challenges to confront him as he grows through life.[8]

---

(1) See Psalms *59:14. (2)* Talmud, Chagigah *3b, based on* Ecclesiastes *12:11. (3)* Zohar, part III, *79b. (4)* Genesis *1:28. (5)* Talmud, Kiddushin *30b. (6) See* Talmud, Chagigah *15b: "Rabbi Meir (whose teacher was the apostate Elisha ben Avuyah) found a pomegranate, ate the inside and threw away the husk." (7)* II Samuel, *end of chapter 16; see* Talmud, Sanhedrin *106b. (8) Based on an address by the Rebbe,* Iyar *29, 5739 (May 26, 1979).*

MANNA EATERS

> Such is the way of Torah: Bread with salt you shall eat, water in small measure you shall drink, and upon the ground you shall sleep; live a life of deprivation and toil in Torah.
>
> Ethics of the Fathers 6:4

Contrast the above *mishnah* with Rabbi Jonathan's promise in the ninth *mishnah* of the fourth chapter of the *Ethics*: "Whoever fulfills the Torah in poverty, will ultimately fulfill it in wealth."

Is poverty the ideal, the way of life most conducive to the acquisition of Torah? Or is wealth the more desirable state, the reward for observing Torah *despite* one's poverty?

The Perfect Food

The *Midrash*[1] states that, "The Torah was given only to the eaters of the manna."

The generation of Jews who physically stood at Sinai to receive the Torah from G‑d derived their nourishment not from the conventional "bread from the earth,"[2] but from the more refined "bread from heaven"[3] with which the Almighty sustained them. But the Torah has been given to all generations of Jews. So how does one, today, become a "manna eater"?

After forty years of eating manna, as the people of Israel were poised to enter the Holy Land and assume the natural labors of plowing, sowing and harvesting for their bread, Moses spoke to them of the significance of the heavenly bread that had sustained them in their wanderings in the desert. "He afflicted you," Moses said, "He made you go hungry, and He fed the manna which neither you nor your ancestors had ever experienced. This was to teach you that man does not live by bread alone, but by the utterance of G–d's mouth does man live."[4]

For forty years, manna had freed them from all material concerns. It was the perfect food, providing its consumer with his precise daily nutritional needs—no more, no less. Nevertheless—indeed, for this very reason—Moses calls it bread of affliction and poverty. For the generation that lived on the manna experienced, on a daily basis, man's utter dependence on G–d as the sustainer of life. The manna taught them that man achieves nothing on his own: no matter how much a person labored to gather the manna, his efforts never yielded more than his exact requirements for a single day.

The challenge for us is that we, too, should be "eaters of the manna." That even as we eat ordinary bread, earned by the sweat of our brow, we recognize that it is G–d who creates the bread and imbues it with the ability to sustain life. That we recognize that it is the "utterance of G–d's mouth" within the bread—that is to say, the divine speech by which G–d created, and continues to create, all of existence—that nourishes us.[5]

Hence, in the opening section of the *Grace after Meals*, we acknowledge G–d as "He who in His goodness provides sustenance for the entire world." In fact, this is the very blessing composed by Moses in gratitude for the "bread from heaven" that rained down on his generation in the desert! We thank G–d for our bread, which our cunning and toil have "earned us," with the very same words with which our ancestors thanked Him for the manna. In other words, we strive to experience the same degree of dependency on G–d for our daily sustenance that the manna inspired in Moses's generation, to which man's intrinsic "poverty" was so obviously demonstrated.

The Way of Torah

This explains the seemingly contradictory *mishnahs* quoted above. Wealth, in itself, is not a liability to the acquisition of Torah—it can even be an asset. What is crucial, however, is an attitude and mindset of poverty—the poverty of the manna-eater who appreciates that he, on his own, has nothing save what he is granted from Above. "This—and only this—is the way of Torah," of gaining insight into the wisdom and will of G–d.[6]

---

(1) Mechilta, Beshalach. *(2) From the benediction on bread,* Hamotzi. *(3)* Exodus *16:4. (4)* Deuteronomy *8:3. (5) See* A Thing of Silence *on pg. 85, and* On the Essence of Eat *on pg. 149. (6) Based on an address by the Rebbe,* Tevet *26, 5751 (January 12, 1991).*

TO BE OR TO BE NOT

Gold and Tachash Skins

> All that G–d created in His world, He did not create but for His glory.
>
> Ethics of the Fathers 6:11

"I was created to serve my Creator."¹ With these words, the Talmud sums up the purpose of life. But there is also another version of this talmudic passage, which reads, "I was not created, but to serve my Creator."² A similar "double negative" is employed by our *mishnah*: "All that G–d created in His world, He did not create but for His glory."

The difference is significant. The statement, "I was created to serve my Creator," recognizes man as an existence in his own right ("I was created"), though one whose ultimate *raison d'etre* is defined by a reality greater than himself. The second version, however, attributes no legitimacy whatsoever to man as an entity distinct from his role: "I was not created, but to serve my Creator"—therein, and only therein, lies the fact of my being.

One of Torah's basic rules is that "These and these are both the words of the living G–d."³ When the Torah mentions two opinions or interpretations it is because both are valid and relevant. Differing versions and manners of articulation of the same statement also complement one another, each providing another perspective to the concept they express.

The same applies to these two descriptions of man's identity and purpose: both are integral to our lives. There is an aspect to our mission in life that involves the total abnegation of self. But our service of the Creator also includes an element that allows for—indeed demands—the retaining of an individual identity, an "I" that serves as opposed to an egoless service.

Object and Objective

> G–d makes the spiritual physical; the Jew makes the physical spiritual.
>
> Rabbi Israel Baal Shem Tov

The universe originated as a concept in the "mind" of G–d.

In the beginning, there arose within Him a vision of a home in a foreign land. He envisioned a world inhospitable to His presence—a world that conceals[4] His absolute truth, a world in which chance and caprice obscure the purpose He invests in its every entity and event. He envisioned a being, man, who would develop this alien environment to house and serve Him: a being with the capacity to transcend the concealment—to recognize the divine essence of every created thing, to transform the material world into an abode for the manifest presence of its Creator.

In the words of our sages, "G–d desired a dwelling in the lowly realms."[5]

The birth of this concept was itself an act of creation: G–d's creation of the "why" of the universe, of its purpose and utility. It is out of this "spiritual" reality that G–d proceeded[6] to create the physical universe—to embody His concept of reality in the myriads of entities and phenomena that make up our universe.

The task of man, G–d's "partner in creation," is to reverse the process. Confronted with a concrete and corporeal world, he seeks its soul—its inner essence. He seeks to uncover its significance, to realize its quintessential utility. He labors to transform the raw material of physicality into a home for G–d, to re-create from it the primordial divine concept of creation. Rabbi Israel Baal Shem Tov put it this way: G–d makes what is spiritual into a physical world, while we transform this physical world into a spiritual reality.

So the very act of serving G–d is an act of negation. The making of a "home for G–d" means divesting the world of its physical "somethingness." It means redefining reality in terms of its divine essence and function rather than its physical husk.

The same applies to man himself. Man, too, is part of creation. He is thus both the developer and the developed object: his mind, his heart, his energies and talents—of these, too, his goal is to remake substance into spirit, to shift the focus from object to objective. To supplant his physical identity with his role as a servant of the Almighty—"I was not created, but to serve my Creator."

From Concept to Blueprint

A person desires a home. Initially,[7] its dimensions and qualities are undefined: it is its quintessential homeness that he conceives of and desires. Then, the image of his home begins to form in his mind's eye. Putting pen to paper, he sketches its floor plan, its furnishings, the landscaping of its grounds; he notes the type and color of its materials, the architectural details of its façade, the precise design of its fixtures. But the blueprint contains nothing "new." Everything in it, down to the squiggle on the base of its door handles, is an outgrowth of his original concept of "home."

Blueprint in hand, the aspiring homeowner will now procure the necessary materials. He will entrust the blueprint and materials to a contractor, whose job is to transform unhomey things such as logs and stones into the inviting sanctum he has envisioned.

The Torah is G–d's "blueprint" of home, His detailed description of what He wants His "contractor" (man) to create out of the materials He provides (the physical creation).

Each of the divine commandments (*mitzvot*) of the Torah instructs us to take a specific object or resource and fashion it into an instrument of the divine will: a pair of *tefillin*, a *sukkah*, a prayer book, a check made out for charity. Each time we do a *mitzvah*, we forge another element of an "inhospitable" world into something that is receptive to and expressive of the divine truth. With each such act, we make the Almighty that much less "inhibited" by the concealments and distortions of the physical universe, and that much more "at home" in His creation.

The Resources

Our development of the resources of creation as a divine "dwelling" falls under two general categories:

a) Elements that are themselves made into "articles of holiness." These include the parchment and ink that are formed into a Torah scroll, the citron and palm branch (*etrog* and *lulav*) taken on Sukkot and the annual 26 hours of time that are sanctified as Yom Kippur. Their very substance has been sanctified and elevated as objects of G–d's will.

b) Elements that retain their material nature while supporting and enabling our service of the Almighty. For example: food is consumed and converted into energy, which, in turn, fuels the mind's toil in study, the heart's fervor in prayer and the body's efforts on behalf of a fellow in need.

Concerning the "holy" areas of a person's life, it can truly be said that the recognition that "I was not created, but to serve my Creator" has been effected. What is a Torah scroll, a pair of *tefillin*, a *lulav* and *etrog*? The very appearance and design of these objects now attest to their true function and essence. The fact that they exist solely to serve G–d becomes readily perceived, completely divesting them of any other function and identity.

The same is true of a person who is engaged in the performance of a *mitzvah*. The hand that distributes charity, the mind that studies G–d's Torah, the heart and lips that pray—these are all actively and demonstratively realizing their quintessential function: to serve their Creator.

But G–d wanted more. He wanted "a dwelling in the lowly realms."

What is a "dwelling in a lowly realm"? The basic meaning of these words is that what was previously "lowly" and unconducive to G–dliness has now been remade as a "dwelling" for the Almighty. But their deeper significance is that the "lowly realm" of the material *as it is*, in all its ordinariness and mundanity, is made to house the Divine Presence.

This is where the second category comes in. Though these elements actively serve the divine will, they remain ordinary food and drink, clothes, structures, etc. The same is true on the individual level. For the person who lives to serve his Creator, the pursuits of material life—earning a living, eating, sleeping, recreating—exist only to support this end; nevertheless, they remain "lowly" and material pursuits. First perceived is our existence and our needs ("I was Created") and only then their utility ("to serve my Creator").

But it is in this domain of our lives, where our physical self remains a reality distinct from its exalted purpose, that the ultimate "dwelling in the lowly" is constructed.[8]

Blueprint To Model

> G–d spoke to Moses, saying: Speak to the children of Israel that they bring Me an offering.... Gold, silver and copper. Blue, purple and scarlet-dyed wool, fine linen and goat's hair. Rams' skins dyed red, tachash skins and acacia wood. Oil... spices... shoham gems... gems for setting.... And they shall make for Me a Sanctuary, and I shall dwell within them.
>
> Exodus 25:1-8

> The verse does not say, "Make for Me a Sanctuary, and I shall dwell within it," but "within them"—within each and every one of them.
>
> Shaloh, Portal of Letters, lamed

A significant part of the Book of Exodus[9] is devoted to the construction of the *Mishkan*, the portable Sanctuary built by the Jewish people in the Sinai desert. The *Mishkan* was more than an interim house of worship for a wandering nation; it was the original model and prototype for our development of the material world into a "dwelling for G–d."

The division of our lives into two domains parallels a similar distinction within the components of the Sanctuary. Here, too, are substances that possess the existent identity of "I was created," as well as an element of the totally self-negating "I was not... but."

Our sages stated: "The world was not considered worthy to make use of gold. So why was it created? For the *Mishkan*."[10] Gold exists also outside of the Sanctuary, and the Torah sanctions its use to beautify one's personal life; but the recognition—that its true, ultimate function is to house the Divine Presence—drives home the lesson that also our "personal" gold is enlisted, directly or indirectly, to serve this end.

But another of the fifteen materials to comprise the *Mishkan* provides the model for the even more "selfless" dimension of our lives. The outer covering of the Sanctuary's roof was made of the hide of a *tachash*, an animal that "existed only in the days of Moses...it was provided to Moses, who used it for the *Mishkan*; then it disappeared."[11] Here we have the prototype for the "I was not created...but" identity: a being utterly devoid of a "self" that is distinct from the end it serves.

And so it is in the "dwelling" that is "within each and every individual." Each and every one of us is empowered to "make spiritual the physical"—to sanctify certain aspects of life so that they are utterly and exclusively identified with their divine purpose and essence.[12]

---

(1) Talmud, Kiddushin, *82b. (2) As per the* Melechet Shlomo's *version of the above talmudic passage. (3)* Talmud, Eruvin, *13b. (4)* Olam, *the Hebrew word for "world," means "concealment." (5)* Midrash Tanchuma, Naso *16;* see Tanya, *ch. 36. (6) Time is itself a physical creation of G–d's, evolved by Him from a "prior" conceptual-spiritual state. So when we say that G–d "first" created the spiritual essence of the world and "then" "proceeded" to embody it in a material existence, we are not referring to a sequential progression in terms of physical time but to a hierarchy of primary and secondary realities (see footnote 14 on pg. 282). (7) In our metaphor, the various stages to the development of a home (concept, blueprint, model and actual home) follow one another in physical time. When applied to G–d's creation, these are to be seen as levels of reality rather than an evolution over*

time (see footnote 6). (8) This is the meaning of the maxim, "All your deeds shall be for the sake of Heaven" (Ethics of the Fathers *2:12): There are elements of your life which remain "your deeds," part of your individual life, while serving your life's endeavor—to serve the Almighty. (9) Twelve of its forty chapters. (10)* Midrash Rabba, Bereishit, *16:2. (11)* Talmud, *Shabbat 28b. (12) Based on an address by the Rebbe,* Simchat Torah *5752 (October 1, 1991). See the latter part of* Debating Truths *on pgs. 273-281.*

MULTIPLICITY

Rabbi Chananiah the son of Akashiah would say: G–d desired to refine the people of Israel; therefore, He gave them Torah and *mitzvot* in abundance.

Talmud, Makot 3:16[1]

The purpose of creation, say our sages, is to "make a dwelling for G–d in the lowly realm" of our physical world.[2] To this end, the Almighty invested His wisdom within the teachings of the Torah and formulated the *mitzvot* to express His will. When man employs his physical mind to study and understand Torah, and when he uses the elements of his physical environment to observe the *mitzvot*, he fashions of these "lowly" substances an abode to house the manifest presence of his Creator.

But why so many *mitzvot*? Why so many dimensions to Torah? We have positive and negative commandments. The *mitzvot* also include logical laws, logic-defying laws, and everything in between. We have intellectual *mitzvot*, emotional *mitzvot*, agricultural *mitzvot*, business *mitzvot*, *mitzvot* dealing with food, dress, housing and family life. The

Torah includes every medium of teaching known to man: stories, legal codes, numerological calculations, history, philosophy, ethics, poetry, metaphorical and mystical works.

G–d is the ultimate singularity. Would it not have been more appropriate for Him to express His wisdom in a single venue? To have man fulfill His will with a single mode of action?

This is the question that Rabbi Chanania addresses in the above quoted *mishnah*: Why an abundance of *mitzvot*? The answer: G–d desired to refine the people of Israel. G–d desired "a dwelling below," and the "below" is diverse and multifaceted.

So if the "below" is to truly become a dwelling, then the Divine Presence must permeate its every aspect. If the human mind is to house the divine wisdom, then every genre of thinking must be employed. If the physical life of man is to become a vehicle for the fulfillment of the divine will, then every facet of life is to be involved. The refinement of man, down to his every element and component, is crucial to the realization of G–d's purpose in creation.[3]

---

(1) This mishnah is studied at the conclusion of each weekly lesson of the Ethics. (2) Midrash Tanchuma, Naso, 16; see Tanya, ch. 36. (3) Based on an address by the Rebbe, Iyar 13, 5724 (April 25, 1964).

GENERAL INDEX

Prologue	The Third Link 34
Chapter 1:1	G-d, Jew and Torah: The Dynamics of a Relationship
	Is there such a thing as a "non-religious" Jew? Can one still be Jewish without observing the edicts of Torah in his daily life?
1:1	Five Steps to Sinai 42
	Five stages in the history of the Torah's transmission through the generations, as they correspond to five steps in each individual's approach to Torah
1:1	Barrier and Gateway 46
	Much of what we know as "Judaism" is rabbinic in origin. But haven't the rabbis, by broadening and extending the Torah, also made it more demanding and difficult to observe? Does this not make the Torah less accessible to Jews who have drifted away from a Torah-observant life?
1:2	Absolute Relativity 49
	The human being, and everything human, is inherently finite and subjective. Does this mean that nothing we achieve or experience can ever be truly significant? On the ultimate definition of "truth"
1:3	Love and Fear: A Four-Runged Ladder 58
	Deed or feeling–which is more important? Is something missing from a mitzvah *if it's performed mechanically? Defining "love," "fear" and the four different levels of self they generate*
1:6	Minding the Child: The Soul of a Metaphor 66
	What is the function of a rebbe, rabbi, spiritual leader or—for that matter—a Moses? What role do they play in the Jew's relationship with G-d?
1:6	Double Standard 71
	What does it mean to "judge every man to the side of merit," as opposed to simply not judging him guilty? What positive implications are there to a person's shortcomings and misdeeds?
1:7	Evil Friend, Holy Foe 75
	Our sages have said: "One who wrestles with a filthy person, becomes soiled himself." Does this mean that one

	should have nothing to do with an evil individual? Can one seek to influence others without being influenced in turn?
1:12	Ulterior Motive ....77 *"Love your fellow creatures and draw them close to Torah." What kind of "love" is this, if you are unwilling to accept your fellow as he is?*
1:14	Super Physics ....81 *Should a person strive to break free of his nature and its limitations? Or is it preferable to work within the parameters of his natural self, to make the most of what he is?*
1:14	11:59:59 ....83 *"The world is a banquet," say our sages, "grab and eat, grab and drink...."*
1:17	A Thing of Silence ....85 *"I have found nothing better for the body than silence." Is this a figure of speech or is it literally true? The significance of the metaphor of speech as a description of G-d's creation of the world*
1:17	Wood Submerged in Stone: Joseph, Judah and the Servant King ....88 *What should a person strive for in life—personal growth, or the abnegation of self in commitment to a higher ideal? The deeper significance of the two "sanctuaries"—the organic* Mishkan *and the inorganic* Beit HaMikdash*— and of the "Joseph" and "Judah" elements within the Jewish people*
Chapter 2:1	On the Essence of the *Ethics* ....97 *To the Jew, the dos and don'ts of life are dictated by the divine revelation at Sinai, not by what one is comfortable with or what goes down well in the prevailing moral climate. So how can the author of the* Mishnah *say that "the right path for man to choose" is "whatever is harmonious for the one who does it, and harmonious for mankind"?!*
2:1	On the Essence of the *Mitzvah*: Commanding, Connection and Refining Deed ....104 *Two dimensions of the divine commandments of the Torah: a singular link between man and G-d, and a diverse, multifaceted tool to perfect the human character*

General Index   337

2:4	The Long But Short of It 111	
	When the direct approach is a bottomless pit and the roundabout route is the surest way to town: An examination of Rabban Gamliel's adage, "Make that His will should be your will," in light of the Chabad philosophy of Rabbi Schneur Zalman of Liadi	
2:4	The Mirror 116	
	"Do not judge your fellow until you have stood in his place." Indeed, can a person ever truly stand in his fellow's place? But perhaps he can look at his fellow and begin to understand where he himself stands.	
2:9-10	A Fearful Sight 121	
	The difference between fearing sin and fearing its consequences	
2:10	Existence as Birth 124	
	On the doctrine of "Perpetual Creation" and its implications	
2:10	The Third Party: On the Essence of Ownership 126	
	The ethics of crime: If everything is ordained from Above, is the victim's anger toward the criminal justified? Is there any reason for the criminal to feel remorse toward the victim?	
2:12	Property Rights 133	
	Torah as inheritance, purchase and gift	
Chapter 3:1	Three Times Three 137	
	What should man contemplate—the lowliness of the corporeal, the loftiness of the spirit, or G-d's purpose in creation? When the Mishnah *uses three sentences to make its point when it could have said it in one, it is expressing three variations on its message, addressed to three different types of individual.*	
3:1	Subjective Judge 143	
	When the most capable judge—indeed the only capable judge—is the defendant himself	
3:2	The Contemporary Cannibal 145	
	Even the most liberal-minded of men cannot but see his fellow with the I's eye: as a necessary, perhaps crucial, but	

	always secondary cog to the kingpin of self. Is there any way for man to transcend the moral and intellectual cannibalism of the ego?
3:3	On the Essence of Eat 149
	Eating is a most puzzling fact of life. Why does man derive life and sustenance from the animal, vegetable, and mineral worlds? How is it that the highest form of life is dependent upon the lower tiers of creation?
3:7	The Vacuum of Choice 152
	"Give Him what is His, for you, and whatever is yours, are His." Such is the Jewish attitude to charity: you are not "contributing" what is yours, but merely carrying out the purpose for which the wealth has been entrusted to you by the Almighty. But would this not seem to empty the act of charity of its moral significance?
3:11	The Human Element 154
	Man's *partnership* with G-d *means that he not only rejects evil and cultivates the good, preserving the cosmic* status quo *in G-d's world, but also redefines reality. Five dimensions to human creativity: physical objects, time, interpersonal relations,* mitzvot *and Torah study*
3:13	Your Vowing Daughter: Dealing with the Gray 162
	Somewhere between the good deed and the moral wrong is the permissible indulgence. How we are to regard these "neutral" pleasures? The Torah seems to convey mixed messages on the matter.
3:14	Expression, Connection and Union: The Threefold Identity of the Jew 164
	The Jew as human being, as Jew, and as knower of G-d: Three dimensions to his identity, and three stages in his national history, his individual development and his daily schedule
3:15	Knowledge and Choice 170
	G-d's all-encompassing and all-pervading knowledge, and the freedom of choice granted by Him to man—how to resolve the apparent contradiction between these two cornerstones of the Jewish faith? An analysis and integration of the different perspectives of Maimonides, the Raavad and other sages on the issue

Chapter 4:1	Bearing Witness 179	

A wiser person is also a more critical person. Or is it the other way around?

4:1 The Headless Investor 182

What does it mean to "eat of the toil of your hands"? Is the psalmist advocating that all businessmen, lawyers and teachers abandon their offices and classrooms for the carpenter's bench and the porter's cart?

4:10 Humility: Two Definitions 185

"Be humble before every man." Every man? A realistic look at those who are inferior to ourselves

4:13 Crime Repays 191

What happens when a hailstorm has its past pulled out from under its feet? The Jewish perspective on crime and punishment

4:16-17 Essence and Expression 196

What exactly is the "World to Come"? Couldn't G-d have included all the dynamics of His creation in a single "world"? On the essence of physicality and spirituality

4:19 The Humble Witness 205

One who celebrates his victory over his enemy has missed the point of his battle.

4:22 The Resurrection of the Dead 207

Why is it a fundamental principle of the Jewish faith that the body will be resurrected to physical life? An examination of the differing opinions of Maimonides and Nachmanides regarding the resurrection, the physical state, and the very definition of "perfection"

4:22 Staying Alive 217

The human soul is the scene of perpetual conflict between contrasting drives: the yearnings for immanence and transcendence, existence and dissolution, life and death—a conflict which may result in a rebounding cycle, a short circuit, or an upward spiral.

Chapter 5:1	Words and Names: On the Essence of Language 222	
	Language is G-d's tool of creation; and our ability to verbally identify the creatures, objects and phenomena of our universe is what most characterizes our worth as human beings.	
5:1	A Particular World 227	
	It is no coincidence that man enumerates the components of his world in sets of ten—ten is the basic number of creation. Indeed, G-d's creation of the world with "ten utterances" is what makes ours a numerous, diverse and particular existence.	
5:1	One and All 229	
	The "ten utterances" of creation, and the fact that "it could have been created with a single utterance," actually describe two existing dimensions to the created reality: a) the singular fact of its existence; and b) the individual qualities of its various elements. Four applications of these two dimensions of existence to the "miniature universe" that is man: our mind's perspective on G-d and reality; our utilization of the world's resources; prayer; and the study of Torah	
5:2	A History Lesson 236	
	Rejection and exploitation: two approaches to dealing with evil	
5:3	The Frontier of Self 238	
	Every generation and society has had its martyrs— individuals who gave their lives for their faith, for their homeland, and for virtually every cause under the sun. So is there anything unique about the Jew who sacrifices himself for the sake of the Almighty?	
5:5	No Good Reason 245	
	Family planning	
5:6	On the Essence of the Instrument:	
	The First Pair of Pliers 246	
	The Mishnah *lists fourteen things that were created "at twilight of Shabbat eve," including the manna, Moses' staff and the first pair of pliers. What is the deeper significance of the point in time that straddles the workweek and the holy day of Shabbat? And why these particular things? The week as a microcosm of history*	

General Index 341

5:10	Inside Work 256	

There are those who do what they must, and those who do what they will.

5:16	Reasonable Love 258	

Why do two people love each other? The Mishnah distinguishes between "a love that is dependent" on something and "a love that is not dependent" on anything. Is this the classic distinction between selfish and altruistic love? A closer examination of the Mishnah's words and the examples it cites shows that the root causes and facilitators of love are far more complex than that.

5:17	Debating Truths: On the Essence of the Machloket 264	

"Any dispute that is for the sake of Heaven is destined to endure." Why would we want a dispute, albeit one that is "for the sake of Heaven," to endure? Can two conflicting opinions both be "the words of the living G-d"? The two talmudic schools, the "House of Shammai" and the "House of Hillel," as the "potential" and "actual" perspectives on Torah and reality

5:17	Divisiveness, Diversity and Distinction 284	

We intuitively sense that "peace" is both a desirable and attainable state for humanity, despite the tremendous (and apparently inherent) disparities between us. But what exactly is peace? Is it the obliteration of the differences between men and nations? Is it the creation of a "separate but equal" society in which differences are preserved but without any distinctions of "superior" and "inferior"? Or is it neither of the above? The Jewish perspective on pluralism, equality and harmony

5:19	The Loving Precedent 293	

There is nothing original to evil, since it is but the negative mirror-image of good. On Bilaam's and Abraham's donkeys

5:20	With a Grain of Salt 296	

"Be bold as a leopard" to serve your creator; but in acting brazenly, do not become brazen.

5:20	For Real 297	

Where a person stands on Moshiach expresses his attitude vis-à-vis the entire Torah.

5:22	The Disappearing Groom 305	

In the first marriage recounted in detail by the Torah, why does the groom disappear for three years prior to the wedding? Marriage as both a time of increased enmeshment in the material and the most G-d-like human endeavor

5:22   The Challenge of the Twenties 309

A man may study and pray for eighty years and still not attain the age of twenty.

Chapter 6:1   Torah and State 312

Should religious authorities govern, or even have a say in the secular-political matters of the state?

6:2   The Serving Free 315

On the essence of freedom

6:2   A Business Attitude 317

Why Torah sees life as a business

6:3   Fertile Wisdom 320

Can one gain positive knowledge from a bad person? On the essence of reproduction, both biological and intellectual.

6:4   The Manna Eaters 323

Which is the greater virtue—wealth or poverty? An examination of two contradictory sayings in the Ethics of the Fathers

6:11   To Be or To Be Not: Gold and *Tachash* Skins 326

Implement or impediment? The Jewish perspective on ego and identity

Epilogue   Multiplicity 334

Why so many mitzvot? Why so many dimensions to Torah? G-d is the ultimate singularity. Would it not have been more appropriate for Him to express His wisdom in a single venue, and to have man fulfill His will with a single mode of action?

INDEX

Words and names followed by an asterisk (*) are explained in the glossary on page 361. The glossary offers a brief explanation of unfamiliar terms, concepts and personalities that are not explained in the essay itself or the accompanying footnotes.

Aaron
    49-57; 290
Abarbanel, Rabbi Don Isaac*
    240
Abraham
    xi; 158-159; 236-237; 238-244; 293
Abraham ben Dovid, Rabbi (the "Raavad")*
    171-172; 173; 177
Abstinence
    see: Pleasure and Asceticism
Accessory, The
    246-255; see also: Means and Ends
Achievement
    89-90; 154-161; 248-249
Achitofel
    322
Adam
    xxiii; 222-225
Ahavat Yisroel
    see: Fellow and Self
Akeidah, The
    see: The Binding of Isaac
Akiva, Rabbi
    88; 90; 127; 128; 164-169
Amnon and Tamar
    258-259; 260-262
Anger
    130
Animal Soul, The
    see: The Two Souls of Man: G-dly and Animal
Asceticism
    see: Pleasure and Asceticism
Ashi, Rav*
    viii

Astrology
  177; 178
Attitude Toward the Wicked
  71-74; 75-76; 77-80; 116-120; 205-206;
  see also: Fellow and Self, Judging Others
Avihu
  see: Nadav and Avihu
Baal Shem Tov, Rabbi Israel*
  viii; 116; 118; 124-125; 143; 205; 277; 327-328
*Barad**
  192-195
Beinoni, The*
  54; 138-140
Beit Hamikdash
  see: The Holy Temple
Benevolence
  viii-x; 51; 56
Besht, The
  see: Baal Shem Tov, Rabbi Israel
Beyond the Letter of the Law
  viii-xi; xiii; 97-103; 256-257
Bilaam
  293-294
Binding of Isaac, The
  238-244
Birth
  305
Brazenness
  see: Chutzpa
Brit Milah
  see: Circumcision
Business
  182; 317-319
Calendar, The Jewish
  xv; 156
"Candle of G-d"
  see: The Flame
Chabad Chassidism
  xi-xii; 111-114
Chaim ibn Attar, Rabbi*
  218

Chaim Vital, Rabbi*
    59
Cham*
    120
Channah and her Seven Sons
    239-240
Chanukah Lights
    271-273; 281
Charity
    152-153; 256
Chassid, The
    vii-xi; 97-103; 256-257;
    see also: Chassidism, Chabad-Chassidism, *P'nimiut*
Chassidism
    xi; see also: Chabad Chassidism
Chutzpa
    296
Circumcision
    159
Clothing
    167
Communal Responsibility
    see: Fellow and Self
Conflict
    205-206; 213; 217-220
    conflict and tranquility
        250
    conflict and divisiveness
        284-291
Consistency and Fluctuation
    49-57
Creation
    85-87; 174; 223; 227-228; 229-231; 245; 273-274; 286; 299; 327
    creation *ex nihilo*
        232
    G-d's perpetual creation of existence
        124-125
    the ten utterances of creation
        85-87; 222-225; 227-228; 229-235
    creation's mirroring of the Creator
        53-54; 144-145; 302

Creation (cont'd)
   purpose of creation
      91; 97; 149-150; 276-278; 327;
         see also: *Dira B'tachtonim*
   see also: Man's Partnership with G-d in Creation

Crime
   126-132

David, King
   94; 95; 180; 258-260; 262; 313; 322

Debate
   see: *Machloket*

Deed
      58-65; 100
   the paramountcy of deed
      59; 88-96
   deed as garment
      166
   see also: The *Mitzvot*, Physicality and the Material World

Depression
   see: Sorrow and Depression

Death
      210-213; 211
   death as divine kiss
      218-219

Diligence
   43

*Dira B'tachtonim**
   91; 196-204; 215; 232; 275-279; 290-291; 326-333; 334-335

Diversity
   see: Conflict, Pluralism, Singularity and Particularity

Divine Commandments, The
   see: The *Mitzvot*

Divine Kiss
   see: Death

Divine Knowledge
      170-178
   "higher knowledge" and "lower knowledge" of G-d
      176

Divine Names
  HaVaYaH*
    268; 281
  Elokim
    268
Divine Providence
  see: *Hashgacha Pratit*
DovBer of Lubavitch, Rabbi*
  203
DovBer, the Maggid of Mezeritch, Rabbi*
  151
Dwelling in the Lowly Realms, A
  see: *Dira B'tachtonim*
Eating
  149-151
Effort and Toil
  43; 58-65; 113-114; 135-136; 182-184
Ego and Selflessness
  87; 88-96; 145-147; 210; 226; 238-244; 253-254; 278-281; 309-311; 314; 326-333
  see also: The Two Souls of Man: G-dly and Animal
Eliezer, Rabbi
  160; 191; 272
Elisha ben Avuya
  322
Elitism and Equality
  284-291
Elokim
  see: Divine Names
Emotion and Feeling
  x; 58-65; 113; 256-257
Equality
  see: Elitism and Equality
Essence and Expression
  135; 196-203; 232-233; 314
Eternity
  306-307; 321; see also: Finiteness and Infinity
Etzem and Gilu
  see: Essence and Expression
Evil
  see: Good and Evil

Evil Inclination, The
  see: The Two Souls of Man: G-dly and Animal
Exodus, The
  271
Ezekiel
  94
Faith, The Jewish
  see: Judaism
Family Planning
  245
Farbrengen
  xv-xvii
Fear of Heaven
  58-65; 113; 121-123; 145-148
Fellow and Self
  71-74; 75-76; 77-80; 116-120; 145-148; 157-158; 185-190; 205-206; 309-310; 317-319
Finiteness and Infinity
  49; 81-82; 106-107; 136; 176; 214-215; 276-277; 306-307; 315-316; 321
Flame, The
  60; 63; 217
Food
  167; 323-324; see also: Eating
Freedom
  271; 324;
  see also: Transcendence and Sublimation
Freedom of Choice
    72; 131-132; 150; 152-153; 165; 198; 211; 224; 294; 300
  freedom of choice and divine knowledge
    170-178
Friday Evening at Twilight
  see: Twilight, Friday Evening
Friendship
  157; 259
Gemara*
  viii; 297; 303
Gideon
  93
Gilu; Goluim
  see: Essence and Expression
G-dly Soul, The
  see: Two Souls of Man: G-dly and Animal

Index   349

Gold
    331-332
Good and Evil
    207-209; 213; 236-237; 293-294; 302-303
Good Inclination, The
    see: The Two Souls of Man: G-dly and Animal
Grace After Meals
    325
Great Assembly, The*
    44; 313
*Halacha**
    viii-x; 264-271; 281; 297-298; see also: Torah
Hama'aseh Hu Ha'ikar
    see: Deed (the paramountcy of deed)
Harmony
    284-291
*Hashgacha Pratit**
    116-120; 129-130; 170-178; 205
*HaVaYaH**
    see: Divine Names
Hechsher Mitzvah
    see: The Accessory
Heller, Rabbi Yom Tov Lippman
    172-173
Hillel; House of Hillel
    264-283
Holiness
    155; 156; 162; 224; 232-234; 329-330
Holy Temple, The
    81; 92-93; 227; 297
Human Being, The
    49; 51-53; 62; 67-68; 149-151; 165; 167-168; 179-181; 217-221; 222-225; 242; 244; 246; 274-275; 278-280; 285; 318; see also: Man and his G-d, Man and his World, Man's Partnership with G-d in Creation, Torah (human involvement in development of Torah)
Human Condition, The
    see: The Human Being
Humility
    42; 185-190; 205-206; see also: Ego and Selflessness
Hunger
    151; 324
Hypocrisy
    83-84

Infinity
see: Finiteness and Infinity
Inherent Goodness of Man, The
73; 75-76; 80; 144; 165; 179-180; 260-262; 301-303
see also: The Two Souls of Man: G-dly and Animal
Inheritance
134-135
Innerness
see: *P'nimiut*
Integrity
126, 145, 147, 281
Intellect
see: Mind and Intellect
Isaac and Rebeccah
305-306; 307
Ishmael, Rabbi
311
Jacob
182-184
Japheth*
119-120
Jeroboam
94; 95
Jewish Identity
34-41; 78-80; 164-169; 232-233; 244;
see also: Man and his G-d
Jewish Faith, The
see: Judaism
Jonathan
258-260; 262
Joseph
93-95
Joshua
43; 93; 311
Judah
93-95
Judah HaNassi, Rabbi*
vii; viii; x; xxiii; 97; 101; 283
Judaism
34-48; 207; 298-304
Judges, The*
313

Judging Others
    71-74; 77-80; 116-120; 143-144; 179-181;
    see also: Fellow and Self
*Kehunah**
    286; 289
Knowing G-d
    see: Man and his G-d, Mind and Intellect,
    The Metaphor
Know Thyself
    see: Self Evaluation
*Kodoshim**
    154; 156; 245
Korach
    284-286; 288-291
Laban
    183
Language
    222-226
Laws of Nature, The
    see: Natural Law
Leadership
    66-70; 312-314
Liberty
    see: Freedom
Life
    208; 217-221; 272
Lifnim Mishurat HaDin
    see: Beyond the Letter of the Law
Love
    viii; xi; 58-65; 77-80; 113; 117; 258-263;
    see also: Emotion and Feeling
Lubavicher Rebbe, The
    see: Schneerson, Rabbi Menachem Mendel
Machloket *
    159-160; 264-282; 326-327
Maimonides*
    159; 170-174; 177; 197; 214; 260-261; 269-270; 299-300; 302
Male and Female
    see: Marriage
Man
    see: The Human Being, and the next four entries

Man and his G-d
    viii-xi; 34-41; 49-57; 58-65; 66-70; 106-107; 144; 230-231; 233-234; 317-319; 320-322; 326
  man's creation in G-d's image
    164-165; 179-181; 249-250
  see also: Man's Partnership with G-d in Creation, The *Mitzvot*, Prayer, Torah

Man and his World
  86-87; 124; 149-151; 222-226; 231-232; 246-247; 305-308; 309-311

Man's Partnership with G-d in Creation
  97; 154-161; 246-251; 265; 270-271; 328

Man and Woman
  see: Marriage

Manna
  323-325

Marriage
  50; 305-308

Martyrdom
  242

Material World, The
  see: Physicality and the Material World

Means and Ends
  38; 65; 77-80; 88-96; 196-204; 245-254; 258-263; 294; 296; 305-308; 309-311; 326; 329-330; 331-332;
  see also: Potential and Actuality

Meir, Rabbi
  312; 322

Mendel of Kotzk, Rabbi*
  226

Mesirat Nefesh
  see: Martyrdom, Self-Sacrifice

Metaphor, The
  86; 134

Metric System, The
  227

*Midrash Shmuel**
  95; 172-173; 229

Mind and Intellect
  66-70; 88-96; 100; 112-114; 159-161; 228; 233-235; 265-271; 300, 320-322; 334

Miracles
  see: The Supernatural, Natural Law

Mishnah, The*
   vii-viii; xii; 147; 281; 283; 297-298; 303-304
Mishkan, The
   see: The Tabernacle
Mishneh Torah
   see: Maimonides
Mitzvot, The
   36; 61; 91; 104-110; 154-161; 165; 180; 196-204; 252; 298; 329-330; 334-335;
   see also: Deed
Mobility
   318-319
Money
   see: Wealth and Poverty
Moses
   42; 49-57; 66; 275; 299; 313-314
Moshiach
   belief in Moshiach
      297-304
   era of Moshiach
      84; 90; 208-214; 246-255
   Moshiach as the soul of creation
      249
   Moshiach as teacher and king
      314
Nachmanides*
   209; 214-216; 250; 291
Nadav and Avihu*
   52; 57; 219-220
Names
   222-225
Natural Law
   191-193; 211; 247;
   see also: Physicality and the Material World
Noah
   119-120; 237
Objectivity and Subjectivity
   145-148; 243
Ohr Hachaim
   see: Rabbi Chaim ibn Attar
Oneness of G-d, The
   130-131; 153; 174; 299; 335

Oral Torah, The
　　see: The Torah (written and oral)
Orthodoxy
　　46-48; 79-80
Ownership
　　126-132; 153
Parenthood and Procreation
　　67-69; 244; 306-307; 320-321
Particularity
　　see: Singularity and Particularity
Partnership
　　see: Man's Partnership with G-d in Creation
Peace
　　284-288
Pharaoh
　　192-195
Physicality and the Material World
　　85-87; 141-142; 149-151; 163; 193-195; 198-199; 203; 207-216; 217-221; 273-281; 289-291; 305-308; 313-314; 327-328; 330
Pleasure and Asceticism
　　162-163; 200-201
Pliers, the First Pair
　　246-255
Pluralism
　　284-291; 334-335
P'nimiut*
　　x-xii; 36; 38; 40; 44-45; 54-57; 59; 81-82; 83-84; 89; 97-103; 107-108; 111-115; 135; 138; 159; 166-168; 202; 219-221; 227-228; 232-235; 256; 262-263; 334-335
Politics; Political Power
　　see: Religion and State
Potential and Actuality
　　73-74; 230; 272-283
Poverty
　　see: Wealth and Poverty
Prayer
　　54-57; 147; 220; 232
Priorities
　　83-84; 115; 139-140; 182-184; 245; 252-255; 256-257; 281-283; 290-291; 309-311
Procreation
　　see: Parenthood and Procreation

Prophecy
  44; 299
Punishment
  see: Reward and Punishment
Rabbinical Law
  46-48
Rashi*
  70; 122; 123; 131; 132; 184; 195; 216; 221; 248; 281; 282; 293
Ravina*
  xii
Reality
  81-82; 85-87; 124-125; 153; 211; 273; 276; 277; 278; 293-294; 301-302;
  see also: Physicality and the Material World
Reason
  see: Mind and Intellect
Rebbe, The
  see: Schneerson, Rabbi Menachem Mendel
Rebeccah
  see: Isaac and Rebeccah
Redemption, The
  see: Moshiach
Religion and State
  312-314
Repentance
  191-195
Resurrection of the Dead
  207-216; 303
Reward and Punishment
  x; 104; 191-195; 196-204; 208; 299
Schneersohn of Lubavitch, Rabbi Yosef Yitzchak*
  69; 74; 185; 234
Schneerson, Rabbi Menachem Mendel*
  vii; xi-xxi
Schneur Zalman of Liadi, Rabbi*
  xi; 54; 78; 108; 110; 112; 130; 138; 175; 203-204; 276; 292
Second Day of Creation
  286
Seder HaHishtalshelut*
  274; 327-328; see also: *Tzimtzum*
Self-Evaluation
  185
Self-Improvement; Self-Transformation
  54-56; 81-82; 89; 99-103; 107-108; 111-115; 186-187

Self-Sacrifice
   238-241
Self and Selflessness
   see: Ego and Selflessness, Self Sacrifice
Self-Transcendence
   see: Transcendence and Sublimation
Sensitivity
   see: Judging Others, Fellow and Self
Shammai; House of Shammai
   264-283
Shabbat
   248-251; 254-255; 291
Shem*
   120
Shema, Reading of
   271
Shimon bar Yochai, Rabbi
   311
Shmuel "The Small"
   205-206
Shmuel Uceda, Rabbi
   see: *Midrash Shmuel*
Sichot In English (organization)
   xvii
Sin
   see: Transgression
Sinai, Mount
   40; 41; 42; 45; 50; 92; 98; 100; 159; 160; 168; 212-213; 234; 265; 266; 268; 275; 287; 310; 313; 323; 331
Singularity and Particularity
   xvi; 227-228; 229-235; 334-335
Sleep
   272
Solomon, King
   94; 96; 122; 294
Sorrow and Depression
   188-189
Soul, The
   see: The Inherent Goodness of Man, The Jew, The Two Souls of Man: G-dly and Animal
Sparks of Holiness
   150-151

Specific Divine Providence
see: *Hashgacha Pratit*
Speech
85-87; 222
Spirituality
199-200; 207; 214-215; 274-279; 288-291; 306; 307-308; 309-310; 327-328
Stone
91-93
Subjectivity
see: Objectivity and Subjectivity
Sublimation
see: Transcendence and Sublimation
Superficiality
see: *P'nimiut*
Supernatural, The
81-82; 243; 247
Synopsis (publication)
xv-xviii
Tabernacle, The
92-93; 331-332
tabernacle at Shiloh
96
Tachash
332
Talmud, The ‡
viii; ix; 99-100; 256; 283; 303;
see also: *Gemara, Mishnah*, Torah (written and oral)
Tamar
see: Amnon and Tamar
Tanya*
54; 112; 130; 138; 276; 292
Tarfon, Rabbi
88; 90
Ten (the number)
227-228
Ten Utterances of Creation, The
see: Creation (the ten utterances of creation)
Theocracy
see: Religion and State

---

‡ Virtually every page in this book contains references to the Talmud; we list here only those pages in which the nature of the work is touched upon.

Three (the number)
  287-288
Time
  xv; 156-157; 172; 194-195; 282; 332; see also: The Week
Toil
  see: Effort and Toil
Tongs
  see: Pliers, The First Pair
Torah
  acquisition and possession of Torah
    42-45; 133-136; 148; 233-235; 323-325
  G-d's blueprint for creation
    97-98; 249; 281; 312-314; 328-329
  G-d's wisdom and will
    148; 159-161; 233-235; 264-265; 334-335
  human involvement in development of Torah
    46-48; 159-161; 264-281; 320-322
  instrument of harmony
    287-288
  integrity of Torah
    xii; 299-300; 326
  realizable goal
    112; 300-304
  the giving of the Torah at Sinai
    275; 287; 299; 310
  Torah as one's sole occupation
    311
  Torah's role in man's relationship with G-d
    34-41; 78-80; 166-168; 334-335
  written and oral
    266-267; 283; 303; 315-316
      see also: The *Mitzvot*, Mind and Intellect, *Machloket*
Transcendence and Sublimation
  81-82; 149-151; 155; 217-221; 236-237; 243-244;
    see also: Physicality and the Material World
Transgression
  36; 72-73; 80; 137; 191-195;
    see also: Attitude Toward the Wicked
Truth
  49-57; 261; 265; 294; 302-303
Twilight, Friday Evening
  246-255

Two Souls of Man: G-dly and Animal, The
  60-65; 151; 163; 187-190; 261
Tzaddik, The*
  54-56; 138-141
Tzimtzum*
  153; 175-178; see also: *Seder HaHishtalshelut*
Vaad Hanachot Hatmimim (organization)
  xvii-xviii
Value
  230; see also: Priorities
Wealth and Poverty
  323-325
Week, The (as microcosm of history)
  246-255
Week In Review (publication)
  xvii-xviii
Wicked, The
  see: Attitude Toward the Wicked
Will
  63-64; 97-103; 165-166; 199-200; 217-218; 243-244; 256-257;
  see also: Torah (G-d's wisdom and will)
Wisdom
  179-180; 222-224;
  see also: Torah (G-d's wisdom and will)
Written Torah, The
  see: Torah (written and oral)
Wood
  91-93
World To Come, The
  154-155; 196-204; 207-216
Zebulun, Tribe of
  318
Zohar*
  viii; 37; 50; 80; 86; 320
Zusya of Anipoli, Rabbi*
  179

GLOSSARY

Abarbanel, Rabbi Don Isaac
    1437-1508; Portugal, Spain and Venice; leader of Spanish Jewry and minister to the king of Spain, exiled in the expulsion of 1492; author of commentary on Torah

Abraham ben Dovid, Rabbi (the "Raavad")
    1120?-1198; Posquières, Provence; author of *Hasagot* (critical glosses) on Maimonides' *Mishneh Torah*

Ashi, Rav
    ?-427; Matta Mechassia, Babylonia; co-compiler of the *Gemara** portion of the Talmud

Baal Shem Tov, Rabbi Israel
    1698-1760; Mezhebozh, Polish Ukraine; founder of the chassidic movement

Barad
    "hail," the seventh of the Ten Plagues

Beinoni
    "intermediate" individual of the Tanya: perfect in behavior though imperfect in character

Chaim ibn Attar, Rabbi
    1696-1743; Morocco and Jerusalem; author of *Ohr Hachaim* commentary on Torah

Chaim Vital, Rabbi
    1542?-1690; Sefad; senior disciple of kabbalist Rabbi Isaac Luria, the "Ari"

Cham
    also Ham, the third son of Noah

Dira B'tachtonim
    "a dwelling in the lowly realms;" the concept that G-d desired to create a reality that is "lowly" and obscuring of His truth, in order that it be made into a "home" for Him—an environment that is hospitable to, subservient to, and expressive of His manifest presence

DovBer of Lubavitch, Rabbi
    1774-1827; Lubavitch, White Russia; son and successor of Chabad-Chassidism's founder, Rabbi Schneur Zalman of Liadi

DovBer, the Maggid of Mezeritch, Rabbi
    ?-1772; Mezeritch, Polish Ukraine; second leader of the chassidic movement

Gemara
    "learning;" commentary on the *Mishnah*, compiled in 5th century Babylonia by Rav Ashi and Ravina; together, the *Mishnah* and *Gemara* comprise the Talmud

Great Assembly, The
    Knesset Hagdolah. Council of 120 sages—including Ezra, Nehemia, Mordechai, Daniel, Shimon HaTzaddik and the prophets Chaggai, Zecharia and Malachi—who led the Jewish people in the Holy Land in their first generation of their return from Babylonian exile in the 4th century B.C.E.

Halacha
    Torah law

Hashgacha Pratit
    the concept that every event in the universe and every experience in a person's life, and their every aspect, is specifically determined by divine Providence

HaVaYaH
    the Tetragrammaton

Heller, Rabbi Yom Tov Lippman
    1579-1654; Prague and Vienna; author of *Tosafot Yom Tov* commentary on the *Mishnah*, and *Lechem Chamudot* commentary on *Mishneh Torah*

Japheth
    son of Noah

Judah HaNassi, Rabbi
    2nd century C.E.; compiler of the *Mishnah*

Judges
    shoftim—succession of Torah authorities and leaders who ruled Israel from the year 2533 from creation (1228 B.C.E., 17 years after the death of Joshua) to the anointing of Saul as king in 2882 (879 B.C.E.)

Kehunah
    "priesthood;" G-d's sanctification of Aaron and his descendants to serve Him in the Holy Temple as the emissaries of the people of Israel

Kodoshim
    animals or other objects consecrated to the service of G-d in the Holy Temple

Machloket
: "debate" or "dispute;" in Torah, a dispute between two or more Torah sages regarding the interpretation or application of a law or principle

Maimonides
: Rabbi Moses ben Maimon, the "Rambam," 1135-1204; Cordoba (Spain), Fez (Morocco) and Fostat (old Cairo, Egypt); codifier, philosopher, communal leader, and court physician to Sultan Salamin of Egypt; author of a *Commentary on the Mishnah*, the *Book of Mitzvot*, *Mishneh Torah*, the *Guide for the Perplexed* and many other works

Mendel of Kotzk, Rabbi
: 1787-1859; Kotzk, Austrian Galicia; chassidic rebbe, forebear of the Gur dynasty

Midrash Shmuel
: commentary on *Ethics of the Fathers* by Rabbi Shmuel Uceda; 1540-1600; Sefad

Mishnah, The
: first written summary of Torah law, compiled by Rabbi Judah HaNassi at the end of the 2nd century; The *Mishnah* forms the core of the Talmud.

Nachmanides
: Rabbi Moses ben Nachman, the "Ramban," 1194-1270; Spain and Jerusalem

Nadav and Avihu
: the two elder sons of Aaron

P'nimiut
: "innerness;" the endeavor to make one's deeds and attainments an integral part of one's being; the opposite of superficiality

Rashi
: Rabbi Shlomo Yitzchaki, 1040-1105; Worms, France (Germany); his works are widely accepted as the most basic commentaries on the *Tanach* (Bible) and Talmud

Ravina
: ?-421; Matta Mechassia, Babylonia; co-compiler of the *Gemara** portion of the Talmud

Schneersohn of Lubavitch, Rabbi Yosef Yitzchak
: 1880-1950; Lubavitch, Warsaw and New York; sixth rebbe and leader of Chabad-Lubavitch

Schneerson, Rabbi Menachem Mendel
> 1902-1994; Nikolayev and Dnieperptrosk (Ukraine), Leningrad, Berlin, Warsaw, Paris and New York; seventh rebbe of Chabad-Lubavitch

Schneur Zalman of Liadi, Rabbi
> 1745-1812, Liozna and Liadi, White Russia; founder of the Chabad branch of chassidism; author of *Tanya* and *Shulchan Aruch HaRav*

Seder HaHishtalshelut
> "order of evolution;" G-d's evolvement of successively more defined and material realities out of His initially abstract and spiritual concept of creation, down to our finite, physical universe

Shem
> son of Noah

Tanya
> basic work of Chabad-Chassidism; a twenty-year (1777-1797) labor by Rabbi Schneur Zalman of Liadi

Tzaddik
> perfectly righteous individual

Tzimtzum
> G-d's so-called "constriction" of His infinite reality to allow for our existence

Zohar
> basic work of Kabbalah; compiled by 2nd century mishnaic sage Rabbi Shimon bar Yochai

Zusya of Anipoli, Rabbi
> 1718?-1800; disciple of Rabbi DovBer of Mezeritch